The Healthy

PRESSURE
COOKER
COOKBOOK

The Healthy
PRESSURE
COOKER
COOKBOOK
Nourishing Meals Made Fast

Janet A. Zimmerman

FALL RIVER PRESS

New York

FALL RIVER PRESS

New York

An Imprint of Sterling Publishing Co., Inc.
1166 Avenue of the Americas
New York, NY 10036

ISBN 978-1-4351-6420-8

For information about custom editions, special sales, and premium and corporate purchases, please contact
Sterling Special Sales at 800-805-5489 or specialsales@sterlingpublishing.com.

Manufactured in China

2 4 6 8 10 9 7 5 3 1

www.sterlingpublishing.com

Cover design by Patrice Kaplan

Cover photography © Offset/Andrew Purcell

Interior photography:
iStockphoto: © A Namenko 12, © AlexPro9500 40, © Alleko 260, © Leslie Banks 93,
© Eddie Berman 2, © Johnny Chencomau 46, © Esseffe 276, © Gwylan Goddard 153, 251,
© Oksana Kiian 233, © Anna Kurzaeva 194, © Peng Li 24 (top), © Lisovskaya 86, © Luchezar 115,
© Rez-art 59, © Villorejo 160, © Nata Vkusidey 186, © Zkruger 108, ©amberto4ka 240
Shutterstock: © AlexPro9500 11, © Olha Afanasieva 208, © Nataliya Arzamasova 169,
© Beta7 122, © Alena Haurylik 6, © Bogdanhoda 70, © Cgissemann 201, © Dolly MJ 102,
© Dream79 78, © Gorillaimages 176, © Brent Hofacker 32, © MaraZe 137, © Tatiana Vorona 271,
© Tatyana Vyc 24 (bottom), © Westend61 144, © Wiktory 128, © Zaira Zarotti 226, © Zkruger 218
Stockfood: © PhotoCuisine/Roulier/Pardo 8

To my mother, who taught me how to cook; my sister, Eileen, with whom I shared an Easy Bake Oven; and Dave, my partner in cooking, teaching, and everything, who edits my prose, tests my recipes, cleans up my messes, and keeps me sane.

CONTENTS

INTRODUCTION

If you're under a certain age, you may never have seen a pressure cooker in action or have never been scared away by mutterings about "danger" and vague warnings of "possible explosions." And those warnings weren't unfounded. Early versions could and did explode. It didn't happen that often, but often enough to scare a generation of cooks away from the contraptions all together.

But these days, as pressed for time as we are, we all need work-arounds if we want to eat healthy, home-cooked meals. Most of us simply don't have time to spend all day babysitting dinner. Slow cookers seem promising at first glance. You put the ingredients into the slow cooker before heading out the door in the morning and dinner is ready when you get home. But slow cookers have their drawbacks. For one thing, the low temperature doesn't encourage the caramelization or browning that gives food deep and complex flavor. Further, most slow cookers don't allow you to first sauté vegetables or brown meat, so you have to dirty another pot to do that. And, perhaps most disappointing of all, no matter how many flavorful ingredients you load into the slow cooker in the morning, everything ends up tasting the same by the end of the day. Plus, of course, there's that little issue of having to wait eight hours for your meal to cook, meaning you have to be organized and plan ahead.

Luckily, pressure cookers have made a comeback and they offer a great solution. Today's pressure cookers are far safer and easier to use than those of previous generations, and they are a dream come true for those who are short on time, but want to cook healthy and delicious meals made of whole foods. They cook food quickly, which saves time, saves energy, and helps to preserve the nutrients in the ingredients. They allow you to brown and sauté foods right in the pot, which means less cleanup is needed. And they allow your food to develop rich flavor. Many foods, like stocks and broths, taste better when they are pressure cooked than when they are simmered on the stovetop for hours.

As it turns out, there's no actual magic involved in pressure cooking, just some basic science. A pressure cooker is a cooking pot with a lid that seals tightly to lock in the steam that builds up while the food and liquid inside heat up. As that steam builds, so does the pressure inside the pot. In this high-pressure environment, the boiling point of water is raised from around 212°F (at sea level) to as high as 250°F. This means that the food inside cooks faster. Another effect of this high pressure is that it forces liquid into the food, helping foods like tough meat and dense root vegetables become very tender very quickly. The high heat of the pressure cooker also promotes the Maillard reaction—caramelization and browning—that doesn't happen in other "wet" cooking environments. As a result, foods cooked in a pressure cooker can develop really deep, complex layers of flavor.

With a pressure cooker, you can cook risotto in less than 10 minutes with very little hands-on time, rather than the 30 minutes and constant stirring required for the traditional method. Tough meats become meltingly tender in less than half the cooking time required by traditional cooking methods. Root vegetables, dried beans, and other ingredients that normally require hours on the stove are done to perfection in minutes.

Whether your preferred diet is vegetarian, ketogenic, paleo, Mediterranean, or just "clean," your pressure cooker will quickly become one of the most valuable tools in your kitchen. No magic and no explosions, just a little bit of culinary science.

Hearty, Healthy Meals in a Flash

CHAPTER ONE

Today's home cooks face a quandary. We want to cook healthy foods—that is, more whole foods from scratch and fewer frozen dinners or convenience foods—but at the same time, we don't have endless hours to do so. Enter the pressure cooker. Today's pressure cookers, whether electric or stove top, are completely safe and easy to use. They make it possible to prepare healthy, tasty meals with real foods on the busiest of nights, giving new meaning to the term "fast food."

The notion that it's possible to cook under pressure has been around for several centuries, but until the early 1900s, pressure cooking was more theory than practice. The first commercial pressure cookers were designed for pressure canning and used by manufacturers, not home cooks. Smaller stove-top models designed for the home kitchen showed up a few decades later, but it wasn't until World War II ended that they became popular with home cooks for their ease of use and time-saving features. The earlier versions, however, weren't perfectly safe, and, with the rise of other time-saving cooking methods, they lost some of their popularity.

Eventually stove-top models became safer, with multiple safety features that kept the pressure under control. The 1990s saw the first electric models on the market. The first versions were simple, with mechanical timers and no programming. Before long, newer versions included digital controllers and added safety features— for instance, the unit would not turn on if the lid was not locked. Today's electric pressure cookers offer many more features, such as settings to brown or sauté foods, and some even double as slow cookers, rice cookers, and yogurt makers.

What Is Pressure Cooking?

In the simplest terms, pressure cookers work because the boiling point of liquid depends on the atmospheric pressure.

In a conventional pot, whether it's on the stove or in the oven, water-based cooking liquids will never reach temperatures above 212°F. Water boils at that temperature and turns to steam, and the steam dissipates—even if the pot has a lid. But in the sealed chamber of a pressure cooker, the water that turns to steam cannot escape, which increases the pressure in the pot. With the higher pressure, more energy is necessary for the water to boil, so the boiling temperature rises as the steam builds up. When the pressure reaches 10 psi (pounds per square inch), the boiling temperature is actually 237°F; at 15 psi it's 250°F.

Contrary to what many cooks believe (as I used to), the liquid inside a pressure cooker is not actually boiling. In most cases, that is the point of using one: You want hot, but not boiling, liquid for braising where boiling the meat would toughen it, or for making broth when boiling would cloud the liquid.

Because pressure cooking depends on liquid, only *wet* cooking methods are possible in a pressure cooker once the lid is on and the pot is under pressure. Steaming, boiling, and braising are such methods; roasting, baking, and frying are not. And, because the system is closed with virtually no evaporation, you will never be able to reduce a sauce in a pressure cooker. However, you can combine cooking under pressure with other cooking methods, before and after, for a wider variety of dishes. You can sear meat before you start your braising or brown it under the broiler afterward, and you can simmer a sauce after pressure cooking to reduce it to a gravy or a glaze.

> Because pressure cooking depends on liquid, only wet cooking methods—such as steaming, boiling, and braising—are possible in a pressure cooker.

Why Pressure Cook?

Chances are good that if you're reading this book, you already know why cooking under pressure makes sense. But if you're not sure that a pressure cooker (stove top or electric) is worth the investment, or if you received one as a wedding gift but need a little push to start using it, these benefits should be reason enough to get started.

PRESSURE COOKERS ARE SAFE. Many people still think pressure cookers are prone to exploding. While that may have been true years ago, today's models have layers of safety features that bring the danger level down to zero.

PRESSURE COOKERS ARE FAST. You can cook wholesome soups from scratch in 20 minutes, braise meat in 40, and make homemade broth in about an hour.

PRESSURE COOKERS SAVE ENERGY. Not only do they cook foods faster, but there's usually no need to turn on the oven or even another burner—and there's less cleanup. It's good for your budget and the environment.

YOU'LL CUT DOWN ON FAST FOOD, TAKEOUT, AND CONVENIENCE FOODS.
Faster cooking times mean you can cook real foods from scratch
in the time it takes for pizza delivery or to cook a frozen dinner.
Your food budget and overall health will both benefit.

PRESSURE-COOKED FOOD TASTES BETTER. The higher temperatures
in pressure cooking draw out more flavors than cooking the
same food conventionally. The better your food tastes, the more
incentive you have to cook. The more you cook, the better your
dishes will be.

YOU'LL GET MORE NUTRIENTS FROM YOUR FOOD. Steaming vegetables
for shorter periods means they retain more of the vitamins that
otherwise leach into cooking liquid that, most of the time, ends
up going down the drain.

Pots and Their Parts

Before you start cooking, it's crucial to familiarize yourself with your
pressure cooker. When you know the parts of your cooker and their
roles, your cooking will be easier, less stressful, and more success-
ful. The time to find the pressure release knob is *not* when you need
to release the pressure, for example. While every model is different,
stove-top pressure cookers share a core set of features and parts:

THE COOKING POT. Most models are marked with cup or quart
measurements on the inside or, at the very least, include markers
indicating half full and the maximum fill amount.

THE LID. Sometimes including the pressure gauge, the lid is often
marked with a dot or arrow to indicate the correct placement for
locking it into place on the pot. It may lock automatically when
in the correct position, or there may be a button you have to slide
into place to lock it.

THE GASKET. This seals the lid onto the pot and allows the pressure
to build. The gasket fits into a groove on the underside of the lid.

THE PRESSURE INDICATOR OR GAUGE. This indicates when the proper
pressure is reached. Some pots have a knob you can turn to select
"low" or "high" pressure; some have a pin or button that rises to

reveal the "low" or "high" pressure ring. The pressure indicator also works as a safety mechanism; if there is pressure inside the pot, the indicator will make it impossible to open the lid.

THE STEAM RELEASE VALVE. This releases steam quickly. In models with a low/high pressure knob, the knob also typically controls the release of steam.

THE STEAMER TRIVET OR BASKET. This feature is used inside the cooking pot to keep food off the bottom of the pot while being steamed.

ELECTRIC EASE?

Electric pressure cookers are relatively new to the market. If you're wondering whether to buy an electric model, here are a few things to consider. Your choice will depend on the features—or drawbacks—that matter most to you.

ADVANTAGES

Electric cookers have two big advantages over stove-top cookers:

> **NO MONITORING IS REQUIRED.** You don't have to stay nearby to monitor the cooker constantly. Just select the pressure, set the timer, and go do whatever you'd like to while it comes to pressure and cooks.

> **ELECTRIC PRESSURE COOKERS ARE VERY CONSISTENT.** The heat level is always the same, with no need for the adjustments a stove-top cooker requires. Some models also have automatic settings for some commonly cooked foods, and some double as rice cookers or slow cookers.

DISADVANTAGES

In my experience, the main disadvantage of electric pressure cookers is with the liner pot that holds the food. Many models have pots with a nonstick coating, which requires extra care and makes it difficult to see when you're browning food. Most, too, have pots that don't lock into place, so the pot spins when you're sautéing onions or browning meat. Additionally, many of the liner pots have convex bottoms, so oil pools around the edges rather than spreading out evenly.

The other disadvantage is a result of many electric cookers being programmed to switch automatically to a "warm" setting when cooking is complete, which can overcook your food. While not insurmountable, this drawback does mean you have to return to the cooker and turn it off.

ELECTRIC COOKERS

Note that while electric pressure cookers have the same features described for stove-top models, there are a few differences:

› The cooking pot is actually a separate insert that can be removed for cleaning.

› The lid may have a lining that comes apart for cleaning.

› While there is a separate pressure indicator, the display panel of some electric cookers will also indicate when the correct pressure has been attained.

› Electric cookers include a control panel with a menu to select the pressure level, as well as cooking functions such as "simmer" or "brown," and to set the cooking time. They also have a display that shows the cooking time and, sometimes, the mode selected.

› Obviously, an electric cooker will also have a cord, which is generally detachable. In some models, the only way to turn it off is by unplugging the cooker.

How to Use Your Pressure Cooker

If you're new to pressure cooking, you'll want to read the manual that came with your cooker. Unlike an instruction manual for putting together IKEA furniture, this one is your friend, provided to truly help you understand how your specific model works and how to make the most of it.

Okay, now that you've read the manual, let's go over the basics of cooking in a pressure cooker.

PREPARING YOUR INGREDIENTS

Some recipes require only a little chopping and measuring before adding the ingredients to the cooker and locking the lid. For others you'll want to develop more flavor by sautéing or searing some of those ingredients first.

HEALTHY EATING—HOLD THE DIETING

This book offers a collection of healthy recipes designed to be prepared with a pressure cooker. But what does "healthy" mean? With the countless diets out there, it's impossible to present recipes that conform to all of them. The recipes included in this book don't fit neatly into any one diet's prescripts; rather, they transcend "dieting." Taken as a whole, they are designed to support a lifestyle approach to balanced eating—consuming whole foods and grains, eating healthy fats in moderation, and avoiding processed or refined ingredients—delivering nutritious foods that are delicious as well. You won't find any "diet-food" ingredients like fat-free cheese or sugar substitutes.

You'll also find:

> **LOTS OF VEGETABLES AND FRUITS**. If there's one thing almost everyone agrees on, it's that we should eat more vegetables. I've tried to include plenty of vegetables in as many dishes as possible, except for dessert recipes.

> **A VARIETY OF ANIMAL- AND PLANT-BASED PROTEINS**. I've included a wide selection of recipes for all kinds of eaters; some dishes will appeal to vegetarians while others will satisfy the carnivores.

> **HEALTHY FATS IN MODERATION**. We all need fat in our diets—from both a health standpoint and a flavor standpoint. The trick is to get enough to satisfy without going overboard. You won't find nonfat yogurt or skim milk in the recipes; a little bit of the real thing is my motto.

> **MORE COOKING FROM SCRATCH**. One great thing about pressure cooking is that you can cook so many ingredients from scratch more quickly that you'll no longer rely on highly processed ingredients to save time.

Eating healthy doesn't have to mean counting every fat gram, carb, milligram of sodium, or calorie. While the recipes do include nutritional analyses, they are intended to be informative about the overall meal, especially if you're new to cooking healthier or to cooking in general.

Because the delicious flavors that come from browning foods with dry heat cannot develop in the steamy interior of a pressure cooker, you'll want to create them beforehand. It might seem like an unnecessary step, but it's not. A typical first step in savory pressure-cooker recipes is to heat some oil or butter in which you'll then sauté onions or garlic, sear meat, or both. The searing or sautéing step is almost always followed by deglazing the pan, which just means adding some liquid to dissolve and dislodge the browned bits from the pan's bottom. Not only do these bits have tons of flavor, but they can also cause scorching if left on the bottom of the pan for the remainder of the cooking time.

LOCK THE LID AND BUILD THE PRESSURE

Once you have all the ingredients in the cooker, lock the lid in place, and bring the cooker to the correct pressure. *All the recipes in this book use high pressure*, so if you're using other recipes, make sure to use the correct pressure level specified.

In most recipes, the slight difference in high pressure between stove-top and electric cookers will not affect cooking times. Low pressure is often suggested for large batches of foods that foam during cooking, such as beans or rice.

For most stove-top cookers, low pressure is 8 to 10 psi, and high pressure is 15 psi.

For most electric cookers, high pressure is 9 to 11 psi.

SET THE TIMER

If you're using a *stove-top cooker*, pay attention to when the cooker reaches the correct pressure specified for the recipe and then start the timer. The correct pressure is then maintained by regulating the heat under the cooker. As the cooker comes to pressure, turn the heat down to medium-low, or as low as necessary to keep the pressure at the correct level. Stoves and cookers vary, so you may need to experiment to find the best heat level for your stove.

If you're using an *electric model*, set the timer when you start the cooking process. Electric cookers maintain the correct pressure for you.

RELEASE THE PRESSURE

There are two ways to release pressure in a pressure cooker (which you know because you read the manual):

› The *quick release* can be achieved with electric cookers by switching the regulator to the "release" mode, which then releases the pressure all at once.

› This is the case, as well, for stove-top cookers. It's also possible to release their pressure quickly by moving the pot into the sink and running water over the lid. (I use that method because the release valve is not very well directed.)

› The *natural release* is achieved by taking the stove-top cooker off the burner or turning the electric cooker off and simply waiting.

IN PRAISE OF FAT SEPARATORS

Pressure cookers excel at turning tough cuts of meat, like pork, beef shoulder, or lamb shanks, into tender, flavorful meals. No matter how well trimmed of visible fat, though, these cuts (and even poultry thighs) will release fat as they cook. When the dish is finished, you'll need a way to remove that fat from your sauce. Not only does it add calories, but it also feels and tastes unpleasant. The quickest and easiest way to remove the fat is with a *fat separator*.

This tool looks like a measuring cup but with a spout that opens near the bottom of the cup. When you pour a sauce containing fat into the separator, the fat rises to the top. The fat separator allows you to pour the liquid from the bottom of the cup and leave the fat at the top behind. When using a fat separator, make sure to strain any solids out of the liquid before pouring it into the separator, as they can clog the spout and may trap some of the fat. Some fat separators come with a strainer that sits on top of the cup, which can be handy for sauces with small amounts of solids.

You'll put this tool to good use in recipes like Pot Roast with Root Vegetables (page 54), Onion-Thyme Smothered Chicken (page 82), and Duck Quarters with Apricots and Prunes (page 106).

> Depending on what you've cooked, how much is in the cooker, and whether your model is stove-top or electric, this can take anywhere from 12 to 25 minutes. Usually, if you let the pressure release naturally for 15 minutes, you're fine to release the rest with the valve.

In some recipes, I specify a natural release for a shorter period before finishing with the quick-release method.

FINISH THE DISH

In some cases, after releasing pressure and removing the lid, you'll need to let the dish rest, reduce a sauce by simmering for 2 to 10 minutes, or add more ingredients to finish the recipe.

The Dos and Don'ts of Pressure Cooking

As you become familiar with your pressure cooker and start using it more, here are a few "dos and don'ts" to keep in mind that will help ensure success in your new cooking venture.

DO

> **READ THE RECIPE ALL THE WAY THROUGH BEFORE YOU BEGIN, AND PREPARE THE INGREDIENTS AS SPECIFIED.** Cut foods to the sizes indicated, and measure the correct amount of liquid (do not try to "eyeball" it).

> **PAY ATTENTION TO THE COOKING TIME, ESPECIALLY IF IT IS LESS THAN 10 MINUTES.** If you cook your pot roast for 65 minutes instead of 60, your dinner will be fine. If you cook your eggs for 10 minutes instead of 5, you'll have rubber eggs.

> **RELEASE THE PRESSURE USING THE METHOD SPECIFIED IN THE RECIPE.** Letting the pressure release naturally when the recipe calls for a quick release will lead to overcooked food; doing the opposite is just as bad.

> **REMOVE THE LID CAREFULLY, ALWAYS OPENING THE COOKER AWAY FROM YOU.** Even after the pressure is released, there will be steam inside the pot, and the contents will be very hot, sometimes boiling.

> **FOLLOW THE INSTRUCTIONS FOR FINISHING THE DISH AFTER THE LID IS REMOVED.** Sometimes it's just a matter of adding a garnish, but in some cases, the stirring or simmering is crucial to the success of the dish. Some recipes will specify adding foods to the pot or actually cooking off pressure. The dish won't be complete without these steps.

DON'T

> **OVERFILL THE PRESSURE COOKER.** Without enough space above the food, the proper pressure won't be reached, and with foods that create a lot of foam, such as rice or beans, the foam may block the valves. Most pressure cookers are marked with at least two lines: one for the maximum volume (usually two-thirds of the total) and a second line for foods that foam up (usually about half of the volume).

> **COOK WITHOUT LIQUID. LIQUID CREATES THE STEAM, WHICH CREATES THE PRESSURE.** It also keeps the food in the cooker from scorching. Keep in mind, though, that it doesn't take much, and some of the liquid often comes from the food itself. When steaming food, refer to your manual for the proper amount of water to add.

> **SUBSTITUTE FAT-FREE OR LOW-FAT DAIRY PRODUCTS FOR WHOLE-MILK PRODUCTS.** Nonfat yogurt and sour cream contain additives that can wreak havoc on a pressure-cooked sauce.

> **TRY TO CAN FOODS OR PRESSURE FRY IN YOUR PRESSURE COOKER.** Yes, there are pressure canners, and yes, there are pressure fryers. Your cooker is neither.

> **FREAK OUT IF YOUR DISHES DON'T TURN OUT EXACTLY RIGHT THE FIRST TIME.** There's a learning curve to every new task, and pressure cooking is no exception. Except under extreme circumstances, your food will taste fine. Take notes, and learn from your experience.

ADAPTING A STOVE-TOP PRESSURE-COOKER RECIPE FOR AN ELECTRIC PRESSURE COOKER

In many cases, you won't have to alter anything about a stove-top pressure-cooker recipe to make it in an electric pressure cooker. Although high pressure on most electric models is actually lower than the high pressure achieved with a stove-top cooker, in my experience, the longer time needed to come up to pressure (during which the food is still cooking) and the longer time needed to release pressure (when natural release is used) make up for the lower pressure level.

Some pressure-cooker cookbooks and website authors recommend increasing cooking times by 14 to 20 percent when using an electric cooker, but I find this unnecessary at best and detrimental at worst. *I use the same cooking times with electric cookers as with stove-top cookers for almost all recipes that call for cooking times over 8 minutes.*

On the other hand, the longer time coming to pressure in an electric cooker can make a difference in recipes that call for only a very short cooking time—5 minutes or less. Especially with egg dishes, like the Crustless Quiche Cups with Bacon and Onions (page 234), you'll probably want to *reduce* the time under pressure for an electric cooker by a minute or two. With pasta dishes, like Chicken Noodle Soup (page 156), I find that cooking for 5 minutes under high pressure in a stove-top cooker can result in pasta or noodles that need another minute or two of simmering to be done perfectly, whereas 5 minutes under high pressure in an electric cooker produces noodles that are done completely.

STOVE-TOP PRESSURE COOKER

ELECTRIC PRESSURE COOKER

A Few Words on Pantry Staples and Equipment

To help you get the most from the recipes in this book, here are a few notes about what you should buy, or at least keep in mind, when it comes to basic ingredients and helpful supporting equipment.

STAPLES

These items belong in your "everyday" pantry, as you'll use them consistently. In some cases, I do recommend specific brands for best results. Keeping track of your pantry stock helps you avoid an unexpected trip to the grocery store, which would definitely negate the timesaving value of cooking with your pressure cooker.

SALT. The recipes in this book, with very few exceptions, were developed using Diamond Crystal brand kosher salt. I find kosher salt easier to use in cooking. It's easier to sprinkle evenly over food than fine salt, and because it's coarser and thus contains less sodium per unit of volume measurement, it's harder to over-salt a dish accidentally. Keeping a bowl on the counter makes it a breeze to measure or pinch for sprinkling. And, while it is not absolutely necessary to use this brand, be aware that if you use something different, you'll need to adjust the amounts called for in the recipes.

Kosher salt is much coarser than fine salt, so it doesn't pack as densely. Thus, per unit of volume measurement, it contains less sodium. A teaspoon of Diamond Crystal kosher salt weighs about half as much as a teaspoon of fine salt and about two-thirds as much as a teaspoon of most other brands of kosher salt, including Morton's. *If you use fine salt in the recipes in this book that call for kosher salt, use half the amount called for.*

STOCK. Chapter 9 includes recipes for Chicken Stock (page 262), Beef Stock (page 264), and Mushroom Stock (page 268). If you've never made your own stock, I recommend you try them. They're much more flavorful and nutritious than canned versions, and you can control the amount of salt used.

That said, you don't need homemade stock for most of the recipes in this book. When using a store-bought version, I generally specify low-sodium stocks or broths since regular versions can be very salty. If you don't make your own, choose whatever brands you like. In most cases the chicken broth is not the crucial element needed to add a definite chicken flavor. The exceptions to that rule are recipes that do need a real chicken flavor, such as Chicken and Dumplings (page 95) or Chicken Noodle Soup (page 156). In those cases, I recommend College Inn brand Rotisserie Chicken Bold Stock if you're not going to make your own. College Inn brand Tender Beef Bold Stock is my choice whenever I need beef stock and don't have homemade on hand; other brands tend to taste unpleasantly metallic. For commercial vegetable stock, I use Kitchen Basics Unsalted Vegetable Stock.

CANNED TOMATOES. While I don't include many canned ingredients in these recipes, I do rely heavily on canned tomatoes—primarily because they're consistent. They taste the same regardless of the season, and they're packed with a dependable amount of liquid. You'll find a wide variety of brands and styles available; use whatever you prefer. If you're concerned about BPA in the can lining, there are BPA-free brands available, just as there are organic brands.

WHEN TO PASS ON PRESSURE

Great as a pressure cooker is for an amazingly wide variety of foods and recipes, it's not ideal for everything.

Breads, pastries, and desserts like most cakes and pies that rely on the dry heat of an oven fail miserably in the steamy interior of a pressure cooker.

Foods that cook quickly and suffer from overcooking, like shrimp, scallops, and very delicate vegetables, are best cooked separately or added to pressure-cooked dishes after the pressure is released so they can be monitored more closely while cooking.

Tender steaks like rib eyes or New York strips are best cooked with dry-heat methods like pan searing or grilling.

And while you may find recipes in other pressure-cooker cookbooks that use whole chickens or game hens, I personally find the results unsatisfying; not only is there no crisp skin, but the breast meat is overcooked by the time the thighs are done.

EQUIPMENT

The recipes in this book, for the most part, use very common kitchen tools, but there are a few tools that are essential, or at least very helpful, to have on hand.

TONGS. Not only will you use these for flipping meat, you'll also need them for removing food (and in some cases custard cups) from the cooker. They also come in handy for flipping the pressure release valve on some cookers so you can keep your hands away from the steam.

COLLAPSIBLE STEAMER BASKET. Even if you have the steamer trivet that comes with your cooker, some recipes just work better with a removable basket that holds many smaller pieces of food, as with the Warm French Potato Salad (page 224).

LARGE SKILLET OR SAUTÉ PAN. All the recipes in this book that require searing or sautéing use the pressure cooker for that step—and it's perfectly possible to do so. However, especially with an electric cooker, it can be less than ideal. If you have a lot of meat to sear, you'll have to work in batches. It can also be difficult to turn chicken thighs or country ribs in a deep pot. If you don't get all the browned *fond* (browned bits on the pot's bottom) up when deglazing, you'll risk scorching. I almost always do my sautéing and searing prep work in a separate sauté pan. I then deglaze that pan and transfer the sauce and other ingredients to the pressure cooker. It means I have an extra pan to clean, but it saves me time and aggravation. Try cooking recipes both ways, and decide which way works better for you.

FAT SEPARATOR. See page 21.

CUSTARD CUPS OR SMALL RAMEKINS. See page 227.

Converting Your Favorite Recipes

If you're new to using a pressure cooker but are not a novice cook, you may be wondering whether you can convert your favorite recipes to pressure cooking. In many cases the answer is yes, but you may have to make some small adjustments. First of all, remember that as wonderful as a pressure cooker is, it does have limitations.

Primarily, it can only be used for wet cooking methods like steaming, boiling, and braising.

If you're converting slow-cooker recipes, you're in luck, because most types of dishes that work for a slow cooker also perform well in a pressure cooker.

If you're converting other recipes, it's best to weed out any that rely on dry cooking methods, like baking, roasting, or deep-frying.

Before embarking on conversions, though, use your pressure cooker with recipes developed for it, like those in this book, to get a feel for how your pressure cooker works and how the finished dishes turn out.

When you're ready to start converting your favorite recipes for the pressure cooker:

› Always choose a recipe that contains some liquid, either cooking liquid or water for steaming.

› Choose a recipe similar to something you've cooked in a pressure cooker; if you're familiar with how Hungarian goulash cooks in the pressure cooker, it will be easier to convert your favorite beef stew recipe.

› Concentrate on the main ingredient(s), and look up pressure-cooking times on a reliable chart (see page 277) to determine the cooking time for your recipe.

› Know whether your recipe contains ingredients that cook at vastly different rates. You need to decide if you can adjust for the differences by cutting the ingredients into different sizes or if you'll need to add them at different times.

› Brown meats or vegetables before locking on the lid, and keep in mind that if you brown food in the cooker, you may be limited by its size.

› Reduce the amounts of any liquids used because there's little to no evaporation from a pressure cooker. My starting point is to cut liquids by one-third.

› Take notes and learn from your successes and your mistakes.

Cleaning and Caring for Your Electric Pressure Cooker

The manual that comes with your electric pressure cooker is the key to taking care of it properly; make sure you read it thoroughly. In short, though, there are a few things to remember.

> › If the lid comes apart for cleaning, take it apart every time you use it to get it clean and dry.

> › Take care of the gasket; wash and dry it by hand, and make sure no tears, nicks, or hard spots develop.

> › The pot insert for some electric pressure cookers is nonstick, and like all nonstick cookware, it requires a little care and attention. Many pressure-cooker recipes start by browning meat or vegetables, then pouring a liquid into the pan to deglaze it with instructions to scrape the bottom of the cooker to release the browned bits. While it's necessary to get the brown fond off the bottom so it doesn't scorch, don't use a sharp metal utensil to do it; use a wooden paddle with a flattened edge.

PRESSURE COOKING AT HIGH ALTITUDE

If you remember your science lessons, you know that the higher the altitude, the lower the atmospheric pressure. One thing this means for the cook is that *the higher the altitude, the lower the boiling point of water* (and other liquids), and the faster it evaporates. With slight changes in altitude, the difference is negligible, but when you get high enough (above 2,000 feet), it can be significant. While the sealed interior of a pressure cooker helps make up for the lower atmospheric pressure, you'll still have to adjust cooking times if you live in the mountains. Most pressure cooker manufacturers recommend increasing cooking times by 5 percent for every 1,000 feet above 2,000 feet. For example, a dish that cooks under pressure for 20 minutes would cook for 21 minutes at 3,000 feet and 22 minutes at 4,000 feet. Some also recommend slightly increasing the amount of liquid. Check with your cooker's manufacturer for their specific recommendations.

This Book's Recipes

The recipes in this book are grouped by main ingredient, except in the last two chapters (Breakfast and Dessert, and Stocks and Sauces). Each recipe also includes the following helpful information:

DIETARY LABELS

Recipes are tagged with the following labels to help you easily choose meals according to specific guidelines you may be following:

> **GLUTEN FREE:** If you have a gluten allergy or sensitivity, always double-check the ingredients list to be sure there is nothing there that contains hidden triggers for you. Keep in mind that if a recipe is both gluten-free and Paleo, the gluten-free label will not appear, as Paleo is a gluten-free diet.

> **ONE POT**, which means the recipe can be made entirely in the pressure cooker and makes a complete meal on its own.

> **PALEO**, which means that the dish does not include any dairy, beans, legumes, grains, or refined or processed ingredients

> **PALEO FRIENDLY**, meaning, usually, that an easy substitution or omission will result in a paleo dish.

> **VEGAN**

> **VEGETARIAN**

KEY PRESSURE COOKING INFO

Each recipe starts with an "at a glance" section that quickly indicates the pressure level (high or low), time under pressure (with two separate times if an electric cooker requires a different time), and release method used. Note that the time under pressure is precisely that; it does not include any prep time, searing or sautéing time, or time finishing sauces. This information is also repeated in the body of the recipe.

The recipes were developed and tested using a 5-liter stove-top cooker and a 6-quart electric model; different sizes of pressure cookers may require different cooking times.

SERVINGS

Most recipes in this book make two servings. Except when noted, they can be doubled in a 5- to 6-quart pressure cooker. The recipes that make four or more servings generally cannot be scaled down, as they rely on a certain amount of food and liquid in the cooker to turn out well.

TIPS

Many recipes include helpful tips, which range from ways to prep ingredients more easily and ingredient substitutions to pairing suggestions and serving suggestions.

Meat

CHAPTER TWO

While the best cuts of meat for a pressure cooker
come from the shoulder or leg—think chuck
roast, pork shoulder, or lamb shanks—it's also
possible to cook leaner, tender cuts like pork
tenderloin or flatiron steak. A few recipes for
those popular cuts are included as well. Because
you don't get any browning of meats under
pressure, most of the recipes here start by
searing the meat. It might be tempting to skip
that step, but you'll sacrifice the flavor of the
final dish. You can often save time, however, with
stews or other recipes for which the meat is cut
up by browning only half of the meat or searing
it on only one or two sides. You'll get the great
flavors that come from browned meats and their
fond in about half the time.

Short Ribs *with* Porter *and* Onions

SERVES 2

PRESSURE: High
TIME UNDER PRESSURE: 40 minutes
RELEASE: Natural

PALEO FRIENDLY

½ teaspoon kosher salt, plus additional for seasoning

2 pounds bone-in short ribs

1 tablespoon olive oil, plus additional as needed

1½ cups sliced onion

¼ teaspoon dried thyme

1 cup porter or other dark beer, divided

⅓ cup low-sodium beef broth

½ teaspoon Dijon mustard

½ teaspoon packed brown sugar, plus additional as desired

This luscious dish pairs beef with onions and dark beer, always a delicious combination. Short ribs have gained in popularity over the past couple of years—with good reason. Using conventional cooking methods, they take hours to become fall-off-the-bone tender, but a pressure cooker cuts that time dramatically so you no longer have to wait for a long weekend to enjoy them.

1. Liberally salt the short ribs on all sides. In a stove-top pressure cooker set over medium heat, or an electric cooker set to "brown," heat the olive oil until it shimmers and flows like water. When the olive oil is hot, add the short ribs in a single layer without crowding the pan. Brown the meat on all sides, about 4 minutes per side, working in batches if necessary. Remove and set aside, leaving the cooker on medium heat, or "brown."

2. If the pan is dry, add another coat of oil. Add the onions. Sprinkle with ½ teaspoon of kosher salt and the thyme. Stir until the onion slices separate and just begin to soften. Add ½ cup of porter, and stir to deglaze the pan, scraping up all the browned bits from the bottom. Add the remaining ½ cup of porter and the beef broth. Return the short ribs to the pan, placing them in a single layer.

3. Lock the lid in place, and bring the pot to high pressure (15 psi for stove top or 9 to 11 psi for electric).

STOVE TOP: Maintain pressure for 40 minutes, adjusting the burner as necessary.
ELECTRIC: Cook at high pressure for 40 minutes. When the timer goes off, turn the cooker off. Do not let it switch to the "warm" setting.

4. After cooking, use the *natural method* to release pressure.

5. As the pressure releases, preheat the oven to its lowest setting—usually 170°F—or turn on the warming drawer if you have one. Unlock and remove the lid. Using tongs, carefully remove the ribs from the cooker. They'll be quite tender and will fall off the bones if you're not gentle. Place them on a sheet pan and put them in the oven or warming drawer while you finish the sauce. Strain the onions out of the sauce, and set them aside. Allow the fat to come to the surface of the cooker, skim or spoon off as much as possible, and discard. Stir in the mustard and brown sugar.

6. Over medium-high heat, or "brown" on an electric cooker, bring the sauce to a boil. Cook for 8 to 10 minutes, or until the sauce is the consistency of gravy, stirring frequently to prevent scorching. Add the onions back into the cooker and heat for 1 to 2 minutes. Taste and adjust the seasoning, adding more brown sugar to counteract the bitterness if the beer is highly hopped.

7. Pour the sauce over the warm short ribs, and serve with Tangy Garlic Mashed Potatoes (page 202).

TIP *Like with most of the braised dishes in this book, you can start this recipe one day and finish it the next if you're really pressed for time. At step 5, remove the ribs and onions from the sauce and refrigerate. Pour the sauce into a separate container and refrigerate it as well. The next day, you can easily peel any fat from the sauce. Then all that's left to do is combine the sauce with the meat and onions, and simmer the whole dish until warm. The sauce reduces as the meat and onions heat.*

PER SERVING: CALORIES: 910; FAT: 65G; SODIUM: 776MG; CARBOHYDRATES: 13G; FIBER: 2G; PROTEIN: 62G

Beef Barbacoa Tacos

SERVES 4

PRESSURE: High
TIME UNDER PRESSURE: 25 minutes
RELEASE: Natural

PALEO FRIENDLY

1½ teaspoons kosher salt, divided, plus additional for seasoning

1½ pounds chuck roast, sliced into 2-inch-thick slices about 3 inches wide

1 ounce dried ancho chiles (3 to 5 chiles), stemmed and seeded

1 tablespoon olive oil, plus additional as needed

1 cup sliced onion

4 garlic cloves, peeled and smashed

½ cup mild beer

½ cup low-sodium beef broth

2 or 3 chipotle chiles in adobo sauce

1½ teaspoons sugar

½ teaspoon dried oregano

½ teaspoon ground cumin

2 tablespoons cider vinegar

Corn tortillas, for serving

Avocado slices, for garnish

Red Table Salsa (page 272), for serving

If you've ever wanted to learn how to make this popular taco filling, here's your chance. The sauce is similar to what you may think of as red enchilada sauce, but the homemade version is in a different world from the canned sauce. It takes a little time to make but not as much as driving to your local Chipotle restaurant or taqueria would.

1. Using ½ teaspoon of kosher salt, season the chuck roast on all sides. Set it aside while you prepare the chiles.

2. Tear or cut the ancho chiles into wide strips. Fill a medium bowl with very hot tap water, and submerge the chile strips in the water. Rehydrate the chiles for about 15 minutes while you prepare the rest of the sauce ingredients.

3. In a stove-top pressure cooker set over medium heat, or an electric cooker set to "brown," heat the olive oil until it shimmers and flows like water. Add the beef, and sear the pieces on two sides. Remove the beef from the cooker.

4. If necessary, add a little more olive oil to the pan. Add the onion and garlic, and sprinkle with a pinch or two of kosher salt. Cook, stirring, for about 6 minutes, or until the onions and garlic are quite brown. Pour the beer and beef broth into the pan, and scrape the bottom of the cooker to release the browned bits. Bring to a boil and cook for about 4 minutes, or until the liquid is reduced by about half.

5. Transfer the liquid, with the onions and garlic, to a blender jar. Add the rehydrated ancho chiles from step 2 to the blender jar along with 1 cup of their soaking liquid. Add 1 teaspoon of kosher salt and the chipotles in adobo, sugar, oregano, cumin, and cider vinegar. Purée until very smooth.

Ancho chiles, which are dried poblano peppers, can be found in the international section of many mainstream supermarkets. Dried New Mexico chiles make a fine substitute.

6. Return the beef to the pressure cooker, and pour the puréed sauce over it.

7. Lock the lid in place, and bring the pot to high pressure (15 psi for stove top or 9 to 11 psi for electric).

STOVE TOP: Maintain pressure for 25 minutes, adjusting the burner as necessary.
ELECTRIC: Cook at high pressure for 25 minutes. When the timer goes off, turn the cooker off. Do not let it switch to the "warm" setting.

8. After cooking, use the ***natural method*** to release pressure.

9. Unlock and remove the lid. Remove the beef pieces from the sauce, and set aside. Let the sauce sit for a few minutes to allow the fat to come to the surface. Skim or spoon off as much fat as possible and discard. Alternatively, pour the sauce into a fat separator, allow the fat to rise to the surface, and pour the defatted sauce back into the cooker, leaving the fat in the separator. While the sauce sits, shred the meat, discarding any fat or gristle.

10. In the stove-top cooker over medium heat, or in the electric cooker set to "brown," simmer the sauce for about 5 minutes, or until it's the consistency of a thick tomato sauce.

11. Add the shredded beef.

12. On a microwave-safe plate, cover the corn tortillas you are serving with a damp paper towel and heat 30 seconds, until warmed through. Serve the beef in the warmed corn tortillas garnished with avocado and Red Table Salsa (page 272).

PER SERVING: CALORIES: 594; FAT: 29G; SODIUM: 1,214MG; CARBOHYDRATES: 22G; FIBER: 7G; PROTEIN: 60G

Goulash

SERVES 6

PRESSURE: High
TIME UNDER PRESSURE: 25 minutes
RELEASE: Natural

**GLUTEN FREE, ONE POT,
PALEO FRIENDLY**

2 tablespoons olive oil, divided

1½ pounds beef chuck roast,
trimmed of excess fat and
cut into 1½-inch cubes

2 cups sliced onions

2 garlic cloves, minced
(about 2 teaspoons)

Kosher salt, for seasoning

¼ cup sweet paprika

2 teaspoons caraway seeds

2 teaspoons dried marjoram
or oregano

3 cups Beef Stock (page 264)
or low-sodium broth

1 (14-ounce) can diced
tomatoes, drained

2 large carrots, peeled and
cut into 1-inch rounds
(about 1½ cups)

2 medium red bell peppers,
cut into 1-inch pieces
(about 1½ cups)

½ pound small red potatoes,
left whole if less than
1½ inches in diameter,
halved if larger

Sour cream, for garnish
(optional)

Many Americans think of goulash as a catchall term for any kind of stew, and many of us grew up with what's often called "American goulash"— a ground-beef-and-tomato mixture tossed with macaroni. But true Hungarian goulash bears no relation to that dish. It's beef, lots of paprika, and a selection of vegetables that usually includes potatoes, onions, carrots, and sometimes cabbage or parsnips. It can be thin like soup or thick like stew, but it never contains macaroni. This version, while not entirely authentic Hungarian, comes close.

1. In a stove-top pressure cooker set over medium heat, or an electric cooker set to "brown," heat 1 tablespoon of olive oil until it shimmers and flows like water. Add the beef, and sear on two sides, working in batches if necessary so as not to crowd the pan. Remove the beef from the cooker, and set aside. Add the remaining 1 tablespoon of olive oil to the pan; then add the onions and garlic, and sprinkle with a pinch or two of kosher salt. Cook, stirring, for about 3 minutes, or until the onions and garlic soften. Add the paprika, caraway seeds, and marjoram. Stir to coat the onions. Cook for about 1 minute, or until fragrant.

2. Pour the Beef Stock into the pressure cooker, and stir to dissolve the spices. Return the beef to the pot. Add the tomatoes, carrots, red bell peppers, and red potatoes.

3. Lock the lid in place, and bring the pot to high pressure (15 psi for stove top or 9 to 11 psi for electric).

STOVE TOP: Maintain pressure for 25 minutes, adjusting the burner as necessary.

ELECTRIC: Cook at high pressure for 25 minutes. When the timer goes off, turn the cooker off. Do not let it switch to the "warm" setting.

4. After cooking, use the ***natural method*** to release pressure.

5. Unlock and remove the lid. Let the goulash sit for 1 minute to allow any fat to rise to the surface. Spoon or blot off as much as possible.

6. Ladle into bowls, and serve topped with a little sour cream (if using).

PER SERVING: CALORIES: 563; FAT: 38G; SODIUM: 508MG; CARBOHYDRATES: 21G; FIBER: 6G; PROTEIN: 35G

Tomato-Glazed Meatloaf

SERVES 4

PRESSURE: High
TIME UNDER PRESSURE: 25 minutes
RELEASE: Quick

1 tablespoon olive oil

1 cup chopped onion

2 garlic cloves, minced

¾ pound meatloaf mix, or
    ½ pound ground chuck and
    ¼ pound ground pork

3 tablespoons chopped
    fresh parsley

1 teaspoon kosher salt

½ teaspoon freshly ground
    black pepper

¼ teaspoon dried thyme

12 saltine crackers, sealed in
    a zip–top bag and crushed
    to crumbs

¼ cup whole milk

2 large eggs

1 teaspoon Creole (or other
    grainy) mustard

1½ teaspoons Worcestershire
    sauce, divided

1 cup water, for steaming

¼ cup Tomato Relish
    (page 275)

¼ cup ketchup

My mother was a fabulous cook, but she couldn't make good meatloaf. Hers was dense and dry, made palatable only by the tomato sauce she served with it. So I grew up thinking I didn't like it. Then I tried this recipe, and I revised my opinion. It takes a little time to make, but it's well worth the effort. And in a pressure cooker, it cooks in half the time required in the oven, while still staying extra juicy.

Note: Before you form your meatloaf, measure the interior of your pressure cooker. If it's less than 8½ inches in diameter, form the meatloaf into a smaller loaf so it fits.

1. In a stove-top pressure cooker set over medium heat, or an electric cooker set to "brown," heat the olive oil until it shimmers and flows like water. Add the onion and garlic, and cook for about 2 minutes, stirring, until the onions soften. Remove from the heat.

2. In a large bowl, break the meatloaf mix into small pieces. Over the meat, sprinkle the parsley, kosher salt, pepper, and thyme. Add the sautéed onion and garlic, and sprinkle the crushed saltines over all.

3. In a small bowl, whisk together the milk, eggs, mustard, and 1 teaspoon of Worcestershire sauce. Pour the mixture over the cracker crumbs. Using your hands or a large spoon, gently mix the ingredients. Everything should be thoroughly combined, but avoid overworking the mixture, or it may toughen as it cooks. ➡

4. Make an aluminum foil "sling" for the meatloaf: Tear off a 12-by-16-inch piece of heavy-duty foil, and fold it in half lengthwise to form a 12-by-8-inch rectangle. Form the meatloaf mixture into an 8-by-4-inch loaf on the middle of the foil.

5. Pour the water into the pressure cooker. Then, using the foil on either side of the loaf as handles, move the meatloaf and foil into the cooker.

6. Lock the lid in place, and bring the pot to high pressure (15 psi for stove top or 9 to 11 psi for electric).

STOVE TOP: Maintain pressure for 25 minutes, adjusting the burner as necessary.
ELECTRIC: Cook at high pressure for 25 minutes.

7. After cooking, use the *quick method* to release pressure.

8. Unlock and remove the lid. Using oven mitts, carefully lift the foil sling out of the pressure cooker, and place it on a cutting board. Slide the meatloaf off the foil, and use the foil to tent the meatloaf while you prepare the glaze.

9. Pour the water out of the pressure cooker. Add the tomato relish and ketchup to the cooker. Set it over medium heat (if stove top) or set to "brown" (if electric), and bring to a simmer.

10. While the food simmers, preheat the broiler. Place the meatloaf on a small cookie sheet or oven-proof pan. When the glaze is hot, spread it over the meatloaf and place the meatloaf under the broiler for 5 to 6 minutes, or until the glaze is bubbling. Remove the meatloaf from the broiler, slice, and serve.

TIP *If you like a glazed meatloaf but are not a fan of ketchup, use the mustard glaze from the sparerib recipe on page 46 instead.*

PER SERVING: CALORIES: 307; FAT: 12G; SODIUM: 965MG; CARBOHYDRATES: 15G; FIBER: 1G; PROTEIN: 3G

Beef Bourguignon

SERVES 2

PRESSURE: High
TIME UNDER PRESSURE: 35 or
40 minutes
RELEASE: Natural

GLUTEN FREE

¾ pound beef chuck roast,
    trimmed of excess fat and
    cut into 2-inch chunks

½ teaspoon kosher salt

1 teaspoon unsalted butter

2 bacon slices, sliced crosswise
    into ½-inch pieces

2 teaspoons tomato paste

1 cup dry red wine (preferably
    Pinot Noir), divided

½ cup low-sodium beef broth

1 very small onion,
    cut into eighths

1 medium carrot, peeled and
    cut into ¼-inch slices
    (about ½ cup)

1 garlic clove, smashed

1 bay leaf

1 fresh thyme sprig

½ cup frozen pearl
    onions, thawed

½ cup "Sautéed" Mushrooms
    (page 200)

1 tablespoon fresh
    minced parsley

Freshly ground black pepper

The classic French stew *boeuf bourguignon* **typically takes hours to make and involves many steps. Like many classic French dishes, it's excellent made the traditional way, but it can still be very good with a few shortcuts. I like to think my version stays true to the spirit of the original while putting the dish within reach of the typical home cook on a schedule.**

1. Season the beef with the kosher salt.

2. In a stove-top pressure cooker set over medium heat, or an electric cooker set to "brown," add the butter and bacon. Cook, stirring, for about 4 minutes, or until the bacon renders most of its fat and is crisp. Remove the bacon, and set aside. Blot the beef chunks dry, and add them to the pressure cooker. Brown on all sides, about 10 minutes total, working in batches if necessary so as not to crowd the pan. Remove the beef from the pot, and set aside.

3. Add the tomato paste to the pot, and cook, stirring, for about 1 minute, or until the paste has darkened slightly. Add ½ cup of red wine, and cook, stirring, to release the browned bits from the bottom of the pan. Add the remaining ½ cup of red wine and the beef broth, onion, carrot, garlic, bay leaf, and thyme. Return the beef to the pot, and stir to combine.

4. Lock the lid in place, and bring the pot to high pressure (15 psi for stove top or 9 to 11 psi for electric).

STOVE TOP: Maintain pressure for 35 minutes, adjusting the burner as necessary.
ELECTRIC: Cook at high pressure for 40 minutes. When the timer goes off, turn the cooker off. Do not let it switch to the "warm" setting.

5. After cooking, use the **natural method** to release pressure.

6. Unlock and remove the lid. Using tongs, remove the beef chunks to a bowl while you finish the sauce. Pour the sauce and vegetables through a strainer or colander into a fat separator. Discard the vegetables, bay leaf, and thyme sprig. When the fat has risen to the top of the separator, pour the defatted sauce back into the cooker, and add the pearl onions. Over medium heat for a stove-top cooker, or with the electric cooker turned to "brown," simmer the sauce for about 3 minutes, or until slightly thickened. Stir in the reserved bacon. Add the "Sautéed" Mushrooms and parsley, and season with pepper.

TIP *If you're cooking mushrooms just for this dish, follow the instructions for "Sautéed" Mushrooms (page 200). When the mushrooms are browned, add the thawed and drained pearl onions. Cook for 2 to 3 minutes over medium-high heat, stirring occasionally, until they start to brown. They'll have a better texture and more flavor with the extra browning step.*

PER SERVING: CALORIES: 806; FAT: 50G; SODIUM: 869MG; CARBOHYDRATES: 16G; FIBER: 3G; PROTEIN: 48G

Mustard-Glazed Spareribs

SERVES 2

PRESSURE: High
TIME UNDER PRESSURE: 20 minutes
RELEASE: Natural

GLUTEN FREE

½ rack (about 1½ pounds)
    spareribs

1 teaspoon kosher salt

Freshly ground black pepper

1 cup Beef Stock (page 264)
    or low-sodium broth

3 tablespoons Dijon mustard

3 tablespoons packed
    brown sugar

Gone are the days when you needed all afternoon to spend in front of the grill cooking spareribs. Starting the ribs in the pressure cooker means you can enjoy these on the spur of the moment, but with all the flavor of those lovingly grilled ones. Twenty minutes in the pressure cooker will yield meat that comes off the bones easily but with a bit of resistance. If you want the meat falling off the bones, cook them for 30 minutes.

1. Cut the spareribs into two or three pieces so they'll fit in the pressure cooker. Sprinkle the ribs on both sides with the kosher salt, and season with pepper.

2. Pour the Beef Stock into the pressure cooker, and place the steamer trivet or basket in the cooker. Place the ribs on the steamer insert.

3. Lock the lid in place, and bring the pot to high pressure (15 psi for stove top or 9 to 11 psi for electric).

STOVE TOP: Maintain pressure for 20 minutes, adjusting the burner as necessary.
ELECTRIC: Cook at high pressure for 20 minutes. When the timer goes off, turn the cooker off. Do not let it switch to the "warm" setting.

4. After cooking, use the *natural method* to release pressure.

5. Unlock and remove the lid. Using tongs, transfer the ribs, bone-side up, to a rack placed on an aluminum foil–lined sheet pan.

6. Degrease the stock by using a fat separator or letting it sit for several minutes to allow the fat to rise to the surface, then spooning it off and discarding it. If using a fat separator, pour the defatted stock back into the cooker. →

7. Preheat the broiler, and move an oven rack to the top or second position, depending on the strength of your broiler.

8. Place the stove-top cooker over medium heat, or turn the electric cooker to "brown," and bring the stock to a vigorous simmer, cooking for 8 to 10 minutes, or until the stock is reduced by about two-thirds. Stir in the mustard and brown sugar, and continue simmering for about 6 minutes more, or until the sauce resembles a thick syrup. Baste the bottom (bone) side of the ribs with some sauce, and place them under the broiler for about 4 minutes, or until the sauce is bubbling. Remove the sheet from the oven, and turn the ribs over. Baste with the remaining glaze, and return to the broiler for about 6 minutes more.

9. Cut the ribs into 1-rib or 2-rib sections, and serve.

TIP *For a change of pace, try these ribs with the glaze for the Honey-Chipotle Chicken Wings (page 86). Discard the cooking liquid, and just brush on the sauce before broiling.*

PER SERVING: CALORIES: 967; FAT: 75G; SODIUM: 2,317MG; CARBOHYDRATES: 15G; FIBER: 1G; PROTEIN: 52G

Beef Stroganoff

SERVES 4

PRESSURE: High
TIME UNDER PRESSURE:
10 minutes total
RELEASE: Quick

ONE POT

2½ teaspoons kosher salt, divided

1 pound flatiron steak or beef "shoulder tenders," sliced ½ inch thick (see Tip)

1 pound cremini or white button mushrooms, washed and stemmed (see Tip)

2 tablespoons unsalted butter, divided

1½ cups water, divided

½ cup sliced shallot or onion

½ cup brandy, dry sherry, or dry red wine

1½ tablespoons all-purpose flour

2 cups Beef Stock (page 264) or low-sodium broth

6 ounces egg noodles

¼ cup sour cream

2 tablespoons fresh dill or parsley (optional)

When I was growing up, Beef Stroganoff was something my mother made only when we had guests. The ingredients—expensive steak, fresh mushrooms (exotic back then), brandy, and sour cream—made it company fare, not an everyday meal. With a pressure cooker, though, you can cut the expense of the dish because you no longer have to use filet or rib eye to get the tender meat that's a hallmark of this dish. Plus, cooking the noodles in the sauce means you can skip a step and use just one pot.

1. Using ½ teaspoon of kosher salt, season the beef. Set aside.

2. Cut medium-size mushrooms into quarters and large mushrooms into eighths. To a stove-top or electric pressure cooker, add the mushrooms, 1 tablespoon of butter, and ½ teaspoon of kosher salt. Pour ½ cup of water into the cooker.

3. Lock the lid in place, and bring the pot to high pressure (15 psi for stove top or 9 to 11 psi for electric).

STOVE TOP: Maintain pressure for 5 minutes, adjusting the burner as necessary.
ELECTRIC: Cook at high pressure for 5 minutes.

4. After cooking, use the *quick method* to release pressure.

5. Unlock and remove the lid. Turn the heat to medium-high under the stove-top pressure cooker, or turn the electric cooker to "brown." Bring to a boil, and cook for about 5 minutes, or until all the water evaporates. The mushrooms will begin to sizzle in the remaining butter. Brown them for about 1 minute; then stir them to brown the other sides, 1 to 2 minutes more. Once completely browned, remove the mushrooms to a bowl and set aside. →

6. Add the remaining 1 tablespoon of butter to the cooker. Still over medium-high heat, or on "brown," melt the butter. When it stops foaming, add the meat to the pot in a single layer, working in batches if necessary so as not to crowd the pan. Cook for 2 to 3 minutes to brown. Turn the slices, and cook for 2 to 3 minutes more to brown the other side. When the beef is completely browned, remove it to a bowl and set aside.

7. Add the shallot to the cooker. Cook, stirring, for about 2 minutes, or until the shallot starts to soften. Deglaze the cooker by adding the brandy and stirring to scrape up all the browned bits from the bottom. Simmer the brandy for 3 to 4 minutes, or until it's reduced by about two-thirds.

8. In a small bowl, whisk the flour into the remaining 1 cup of water. To the cooker, add the Beef Stock, the remaining 1 cup of water mixed with the flour, the remaining 1½ teaspoons of kosher salt, the noodles, and the seared beef.

9. Lock the lid in place, and bring the pot to high pressure (15 psi for stove top or 9 to 11 psi for electric).

STOVE TOP: Maintain pressure for 5 minutes, adjusting the burner as necessary.
ELECTRIC: Cook at high pressure for 5 minutes.

10. After cooking, use the *quick method* to release pressure.

11. Unlock and remove the lid. Check one of the noodles for doneness; if they're not quite done, place the stovetop cooker over medium heat, or turn the electric cooker to "simmer," and simmer for 1 to 2 minutes, or until the noodles are completely tender. Meanwhile, ladle 1 cup of the sauce (with no noodles or beef) into a small bowl. Cool for 1 minute; then stir in the sour cream. When the noodles are done, turn off the heat and add the reserved mushrooms. Once the mixture stops simmering, stir in the sour cream sauce. Serve in bowls, garnished with dill (if using).

TIP *I almost always make this dish when we have leftover steak or leftover "Sautéed" Mushrooms (page 200). If you have leftover mushrooms, skip steps 2 through 5 and just add the mushrooms at the end as directed. If you have leftover steak, begin the recipe with the cooking of the shallots. Either way, the recipe is much faster and easier (and more economical) when prepared with leftovers.*

PER SERVING: CALORIES: 496; FAT: 28G; SODIUM: 1,777MG; CARBOHYDRATES: 23G; FIBER: 2G; PROTEIN: 31G

Corned Beef *and* Cabbage

SERVES 6

FOR THE CORNED BEEF
PRESSURE: High
TIME UNDER PRESSURE: 1 hour,
30 minutes or 1 hour, 45 minutes
RELEASE: Natural

FOR THE VEGETABLES
PRESSURE: High
TIME UNDER PRESSURE: 12 minutes
RELEASE: Quick

**GLUTEN FREE, ONE POT,
PALEO FRIENDLY**

1 (3- to 4-pound) corned beef
   brisket

1 bay leaf (optional)

4 or 5 whole peppercorns
   (optional)

1 teaspoon dried thyme
   (optional)

3 or 4 whole allspice berries, or
   ⅛ teaspoon ground allspice
   (optional)

3 cups Chicken Stock (page 262)
   or low-sodium broth

3 cups water, plus additional
   as needed

6 medium carrots, peeled and
   cut into 2-inch pieces

1 small head green cabbage,
   root end trimmed,
   cut into 8 wedges

½ pound small red potatoes,
   left whole if less than
   1½ inches in diameter,
   halved if larger

Almost certainly, the corned beef brisket you can buy in the store is, technically, half a brisket. It's still a big hunk of meat, which means, for most of us, corned beef is a dish for company. Additionally, with conventional cooking methods, it takes three hours or longer to cook—it's no wonder most of us cook corned beef only once a year. Cooking it in a pressure cooker cuts the time in half, so while it might still be a special-occasion dish, many more occasions can be opportunities to enjoy this meal.

1. In a stove-top or electric pressure cooker, place the corned beef, and add the contents of the spice packet. If your beef did not include a spice packet, add the bay leaf, peppercorns, thyme, and allspice. Pour in the Chicken Stock and water, adding more water if necessary to cover the brisket.

2. Lock the lid in place, and bring the pot to high pressure (15 psi for stove top or 9 to 11 psi for electric).

STOVE TOP: Maintain pressure for 1 hour, 30 minutes, adjusting the burner as necessary.
ELECTRIC: Cook at high pressure for 1 hour, 45 minutes. When the timer goes off, turn the cooker off. Do not let it switch to the "warm" setting.

3. After cooking, use the *natural method* to release pressure.

4. Unlock and remove the lid. Transfer the corned beef to a cutting board, and tent it with aluminum foil. Spoon or blot off most of the fat from the surface of the cooking liquid and discard. Add the carrots, cabbage wedges, and red potatoes to the cooker.

5. Lock the lid in place, and bring the pot to high pressure (15 psi for stove top or 9 to 11 psi for electric).

STOVE TOP: Maintain pressure for 12 minutes, adjusting the burner as necessary.
ELECTRIC: Cook at high pressure for 12 minutes.

6. After cooking, use the *quick method* to release pressure.

7. While the vegetables cook, slice the corned beef against the grain into thick slices.

8. When the vegetables are done, unlock and remove the lid. Using a slotted spoon, transfer the vegetables to a serving platter. Place the corned beef slices on top of the vegetables, pour a little of the cooking liquid over the food on the platter, and serve.

PER SERVING: CALORIES: 486; FAT: 29G; SODIUM: 1,767MG; CARBOHYDRATES: 20G; FIBER: 5G; PROTEIN: 36G

Pot Roast *with* Root Vegetables

SERVES 4

PRESSURE: High
TIME UNDER PRESSURE: 1 hour
RELEASE: Natural

GLUTEN FREE, ONE POT, PALEO FRIENDLY

1 (2½-pound) beef chuck (shoulder) roast

1 teaspoon kosher salt, plus additional for seasoning

Freshly ground black pepper

1 tablespoon olive oil

2 tablespoons tomato paste

2 cups Beef Stock (page 264) or low-sodium broth

1 teaspoon Worcestershire sauce, plus additional as needed

½ pound boiling onions (about 2 inches in diameter), peeled and root ends trimmed

4 large carrots, peeled and cut into 2-inch lengths

1 pound small red or Yukon gold potatoes (1 to 3 inches in diameter)

Like Corned Beef and Cabbage (page 52), pot roast is true comfort food and an all-in-one meal you can cook on a Sunday afternoon. Unlike corned beef, though, it's relatively easy to scale pot roast down to make fewer servings. This recipe makes enough to serve four generously. You can buy a smaller piece of chuck roast and halve the amounts of vegetables to serve two or three without a refrigerator full of leftovers. A 1½-pound roast will cook in about 40 minutes.

1. Season the roast on all sides with 1 teaspoon of kosher salt and a generous grinding of pepper.

2. In a stove-top pressure cooker set over medium heat, or an electric cooker set to "brown," heat the olive oil until it shimmers and flows like water. Add the meat, and brown on all sides, about 8 minutes total. Remove the roast to a plate, and set aside. Add the tomato paste. Cook for about 1 minute, stirring, until the paste darkens slightly. Stir in the Beef Stock and Worcestershire sauce, and stir, scraping the bottom of the cooker to release any browned bits. Return the roast to the liquid, and cover with the onions, carrots, and red potatoes.

3. Lock the lid in place, and bring the pot to high pressure (15 psi for stove top or 9 to 11 psi for electric).

STOVE TOP: Maintain pressure for 1 hour, adjusting the burner as necessary.

ELECTRIC: Cook at high pressure for 1 hour. When the timer goes off, turn the cooker off. Do not let it switch to the "warm" setting.

4. After cooking, use the *natural method* to release pressure.

5. Unlock and remove the lid. Transfer the vegetables to a bowl, and cover with aluminum foil. Transfer the roast to a cutting board, and tent it with foil. Let it rest for 15 minutes.

6. If there is a large amount of fat in the sauce, pour it into a fat separator and let the fat rise to the surface; then return the defatted sauce to the pan. If it's very thin, you may want to simmer it to reduce it slightly. Taste and adjust the seasoning, adding kosher salt, pepper, or more Worcestershire sauce if necessary.

7. Slice the roast against the grain into thick pieces. Arrange the vegetables and meat on a serving platter, pour the sauce over the top, and serve.

PER SERVING: CALORIES: 905; FAT: 42G; SODIUM: 1,249MG; CARBOHYDRATES: 35G; FIBER: 5G; PROTEIN: 94G

Garlic-Rosemary Baby Back Ribs

SERVES 2

PRESSURE: High
TIME UNDER PRESSURE: 30 minutes
RELEASE: Natural

GLUTEN FREE, PALEO FRIENDLY

½ rack (about 1½ pounds) baby back ribs

1 teaspoon kosher salt, plus additional for seasoning

Freshly ground black pepper

1 tablespoon olive oil

1 cup chopped onion

2 large garlic cloves, minced

1 tablespoon tomato paste, or 2 tablespoons tomato sauce

½ cup white wine

1 tablespoon minced fresh rosemary

1 cup Chicken Stock (page 262) or low-sodium broth

2 tablespoons honey

Much as I like a good barbecue sauce on ribs, it's nice to try something new. This subtle sauce, with hints of rosemary and garlic, complements the pork so well it made me wonder why it took me so long to make the change. Baby back ribs can stand up to longer cooking times than spareribs, so I give them an extra 10 minutes in the pressure cooker to make sure they're nice and tender.

1. Cut the ribs into 2 or 3 pieces so they'll fit in the pressure cooker. Sprinkle the ribs on both sides with 1 teaspoon of kosher salt, and season with pepper.

2. In a stove-top pressure cooker set over medium heat, or an electric cooker set to "brown," heat the olive oil until it shimmers and flows like water. Add the onion, and sprinkle with a pinch or two of kosher salt. Cook for about 3 minutes, stirring, until the onions just begin to brown. Add the garlic, and continue to cook for 2 to 3 minutes more, or until the onions are golden brown. Add the tomato paste, and cook for about 2 minutes, stirring, until the paste darkens slightly.

3. Pour the white wine into the pressure cooker, and add the rosemary. Cook for about 3 minutes, until the wine has reduced by half, scraping the bottom of the cooker to release the browned bits. Add the Chicken Stock, and stir to combine. Place the steamer trivet or basket in the cooker. The liquid will probably come up over the steamer trivet. Place the ribs on the steamer insert.

4. Lock the lid in place, and bring the pot to high pressure (15 psi for stove top or 9 to 11 psi for electric).

STOVE TOP: Maintain pressure for 30 minutes, adjusting the burner as necessary.

ELECTRIC: Cook at high pressure for 30 minutes. When the timer goes off, turn the cooker off. Do not let it switch to the "warm" setting.

5. After cooking, use the *natural method* to release pressure.

6. Unlock and remove the lid. Using tongs, transfer the ribs, bone-side up, to a rack placed on an aluminum foil–lined sheet pan.

7. Degrease the sauce by straining it into a fat separator or by letting it sit for several minutes so the fat rises to the surface, then spooning it off and discarding. If using a fat separator, pour the defatted sauce back into the cooker.

8. Preheat the broiler, and move an oven rack to the top or second position, depending on the strength of your broiler.

9. Place the stove-top cooker over medium heat, or turn the electric cooker to "brown." Stir in the honey, and bring to a vigorous simmer. Reduce the sauce for 8 to 10 minutes, or until it resembles moderately thick syrup. Baste the bottom (bone) side of the ribs, and place them under the broiler for about 4 minutes, or until the sauce is bubbling. Remove the pan from the oven, and turn the ribs over. Baste with the remaining glaze, and return to the broiler for about 6 minutes more.

10. Cut the ribs into 1-rib or 2-rib sections, and serve.

TIP *You can easily double this recipe by using a whole rack of ribs. It's okay to pile them up in the cooker. You don't have to double the sauce; you'll have enough for the whole rack. On the other hand, who doesn't like extra sauce?*

PER SERVING: CALORIES: 990; FAT: 50G; SODIUM: 1,401MG; CARBOHYDRATES: 28G; FIBER: 2G; PROTEIN: 93G

Pulled Pork *with* Mustardy Barbecue Sauce

SERVES 2

PRESSURE: High
TIME UNDER PRESSURE: 25 minutes
RELEASE: Natural

1 tablespoon yellow mustard

1 tablespoon Dijon mustard

1 tablespoon honey

3 tablespoons ketchup

1½ teaspoons cider vinegar

½ teaspoon Worcestershire sauce

¼ teaspoon kosher salt

½ teaspoon ground cayenne pepper

¾ pound boneless pork shoulder, trimmed of as much visible fat as possible, cut into 2-inch chunks

Buns or lettuce leaves, for serving

True pulled pork is a masterpiece, but it takes hours and hours over low heat and smoke. I love it when someone else makes it, but it's too much work for me. This cheater's version can be made—and enjoyed—on a weeknight, so that counts for a lot. I hope you will think so, too.

1. In the pressure cooker, stir together the yellow mustard, Dijon mustard, honey, ketchup, cider vinegar, Worcestershire sauce, kosher salt, and cayenne pepper until thoroughly mixed. Add the pork, and toss to coat.

2. Lock the lid in place, and bring the pot to high pressure (15 psi for stove top or 9 to 11 psi for electric).

STOVE TOP: Maintain pressure for 25 minutes, adjusting the burner as necessary.
ELECTRIC: Cook at high pressure for 25 minutes. When the timer goes off, turn the cooker off. Do not let it switch to the "warm" setting.

3. After cooking, use the **natural method** to release pressure.

4. Unlock and remove the lid. Pour the pork and sauce through a coarse sieve; set the pork aside to cool. Return the sauce to the cooker, and let it sit for 1 to 2 minutes so any fat rises to the surface. Skim or blot off as much fat as possible and discard.

5. Put the stove-top cooker over medium heat, or turn the electric cooker to "brown." Simmer the sauce for about 5 minutes, or until it's the consistency of a thick tomato sauce.

6. While the sauce thickens, shred the pork, discarding any fat or gristle. Add the shredded pork to the sauce, and heat through. Serve on buns, or use as a filling for lettuce wraps.

PER SERVING: CALORIES: 307; FAT: 7G; SODIUM: 841MG; CARBOHYDRATES: 13G; FIBER: 1G; PROTEIN: 46G

Asian Pork Sliders

SERVES 2

PRESSURE: High
TIME UNDER PRESSURE: 25 or
35 minutes
RELEASE: Natural

¼ cup hoisin sauce

2 tablespoons rice vinegar

1 tablespoon minced
    fresh ginger

2 teaspoons minced garlic

1 teaspoon Asian chili-garlic
    sauce, plus additional
    as desired

¾ pound pork shoulder,
    trimmed of as much visible
    fat as possible, cut into
    2-inch cubes

4 slider buns or soft dinner rolls

Pork shoulder is my quintessential choice of meat when it comes to pressure cooking. It turns meltingly soft and succulent in a fraction of the time it takes to cook with conventional methods. Using boneless shoulder "country ribs" saves time, since the meat is already cut into strips. The combination of ginger and hoisin sauce adds Asian flavors that get a kick of heat from the chili-garlic sauce. If you're concerned about the preservatives and other additives in some brands of hoisin sauce, choose a brand such as Wok Mei that contains more natural ingredients.

1. In the pressure cooker, stir together the hoisin sauce, rice vinegar, ginger, garlic, and chili-garlic sauce until thoroughly mixed. Add the pork, and toss to coat.

2. Lock the lid in place, and bring the pot to high pressure (15 psi for stove top or 9 to 11 psi for electric).

STOVE TOP: Maintain pressure for 25 minutes, adjusting the burner as necessary.
ELECTRIC: Cook at high pressure for 35 minutes. When the timer goes off, turn the cooker off. Do not let it switch to the "warm" setting.

3. After cooking, use the *natural method* to release pressure.

4. Unlock and remove the lid. Pour the pork and sauce through a coarse sieve; set the pork aside to cool. Return the sauce to the cooker, and let it sit for 1 to 2 minutes so any fat rises to the surface. Skim or blot off as much fat as possible and discard.

5. Put the cooker over medium heat, or turn the electric cooker to "brown," and simmer the sauce for about 5 minutes, or until it's the consistency of a thick tomato sauce.

6. While the sauce thickens, shred the pork, discarding any fat or gristle. Add the shredded pork to the sauce, and heat through. Serve on buns or over rice.

TIP *These sandwiches are especially good served with an Asian-style slaw on top of the pork, and it's easy to make one. Combine 1 cup of shredded red or green cabbage with 1 chopped scallion and 1 shredded carrot. Sprinkle with ¼ teaspoon of kosher salt. Add 1 tablespoon of unseasoned rice vinegar and ½ teaspoon of grated fresh ginger, and toss to combine.*

PER SERVING: CALORIES: 680; FAT: 31G; SODIUM: 1,188MG; CARBOHYDRATES: 60G; FIBER: 3G; PROTEIN: 38G

Pork Tenderloin *with* Braised Apples *and* Onions

SERVES 4

PRESSURE: High
TIME UNDER PRESSURE: 5 minutes
RELEASE: Quick

GLUTEN FREE, ONE POT

FOR THE BRINE (OPTIONAL)

½ cup Diamond Crystal kosher
    salt, or ¼ cup fine table salt

¼ cup granulated sugar

2 cups very hot tap water

2 cups ice water

FOR THE PORK AND APPLES

1 (1-pound) pork tenderloin,
    trimmed of silver skin and
    halved crosswise

Kosher salt, for salting
    and seasoning

2 tablespoons unsalted butter

1 cup thinly sliced onion

1 medium Granny Smith apple,
    or other tart apple, peeled
    and cut into ¼-inch slices

¾ cup apple juice, cider,
    or hard cider

½ cup low-sodium
    chicken broth

2 tablespoons heavy
    (whipping) cream

1 teaspoon Dijon mustard,
    plus additional as needed

Apples are a popular accompaniment to pork in much European cooking, and this recipe will prove why. While it's more common to see the preparation with pork chops, loin chops will overcook and toughen in a pressure cooker, and it can be difficult to find shoulder chops. Pork tenderloin not only works well but also cooks very quickly, so it's perfect for making a quick weeknight dinner something special to linger over.

To make the brine (if using)

In a large stainless steel or glass bowl, dissolve the salt and sugar in the hot water; then stir in the ice water. Submerge the pork in the brine, and refrigerate for 2 to 3 hours. Drain and pat dry.

To make the pork and apples

1. If you choose not to brine the pork, sprinkle it liberally with kosher salt.

2. In a stove-top pressure cooker set over medium heat, or an electric pressure cooker set to "brown," heat the butter just until it stops foaming. Add the pork halves, browning on all sides, about 4 minutes total. Transfer to a plate or rack, and set aside.

3. Add the onion slices to the cooker, and cook, stirring, for 2 to 3 minutes, or until they just start to brown. Add the apple slices, and cook for 1 minute. Add the apple juice, and scrape the browned bits from the bottom of the pot. Bring to a simmer, and cook for 2 to 3 minutes, or until the juice has reduced by about one-third. Add the chicken broth, and return the pork tenderloin to the cooker, placing the pieces on top of the apples and onions.

4. Lock the lid in place, and bring the pot to high pressure (15 psi for stove top or 9 to 11 psi for electric).

STOVE TOP: Maintain pressure for 5 minutes, adjusting the burner as necessary.
ELECTRIC: Cook at high pressure for 5 minutes.

5. After cooking, use the *quick method* to release pressure.

6. Unlock and remove the lid. Transfer the pork to a plate or rack, and tent it with aluminum foil while you finish the sauce.

7. In the stove-top cooker set over medium-high heat, or the electric cooker on "brown," simmer for about 6 minutes, or until the liquid is reduced by about half. Stir in the heavy cream and mustard, and taste, adding kosher salt or more mustard as needed.

8. Slice the pork into ¾-inch pieces, and place on a serving platter. Spoon the apples, onions, and sauce over the pork, and serve.

PER SERVING: CALORIES: 321; FAT: 13G; SODIUM: 754MG; CARBOHYDRATES: 21G; FIBER: 2G; PROTEIN: 32G

Chili Verde

SERVES 2

PRESSURE: High
TIME UNDER PRESSURE: 25 minutes
RELEASE: Natural

PALEO

1 large poblano chile, stemmed, cored, seeded, and cut into 2 to 3 strips

1 large jalapeño pepper, stemmed, cored, seeded, and cut into 2 to 3 strips

¾ pound tomatillos, husks removed and rinsed

1 tablespoon olive oil, plus additional as needed

¾ pound boneless country-style pork shoulder ribs

½ cup thinly sliced onion

1 large garlic clove, smashed or minced

Kosher salt

½ cup low-sodium chicken broth

½ teaspoon ground cumin

2 tablespoons minced fresh cilantro (optional)

Cooked rice, optional

I've seen recipes for chili verde that start with a jar of green salsa from the store; in fact, I've made it that way when tomatillos were nowhere to be found. It's perfectly acceptable, but starting with fresh tomatillos and chiles cuts down on the processed foods you're eating and results in a complexity and depth of flavor not found in the simpler version. Since you save so much cooking time using a pressure cooker, I think the extra prep time and effort are worth it.

1. Place the poblano chile and jalapeño pepper pieces on an aluminum foil–lined baking sheet, skin-side up. Add the tomatillos to the sheet.

2. Preheat the broiler. Place the baking sheet close to the broiler element. Broil until the peppers' skins are blackened and the tomatillos begin to char in places. This can take anywhere from 3 to 10 minutes, depending on the strength of the broiler element. When the peppers are blackened, remove the pan from the oven and use tongs to transfer the tomatillos to a blender jar. Fold the foil up around the chile strips and seal. Let sit for 5 minutes. When cool enough to handle, peel and discard the skin from the strips. Add the chile strips to the blender jar, and purée the vegetables until mostly smooth.

3. In a stove-top pressure cooker set over medium heat, or an electric cooker set to "brown," heat the olive oil until it shimmers and flows like water. Add the pork, sear on two sides, and remove from the cooker. If necessary, add a little more olive oil to the pot; then add the onion and garlic, and sprinkle with a pinch or two of kosher salt. Cook for about 5 minutes, stirring, until the onions and garlic are quite browned.

4. Pour the chicken broth into the cooker, scraping the bottom to dissolve the browned bits. Pour the tomatillo mixture from the blender into the pressure cooker, and add the pork and cumin.

5. Lock the lid in place, and bring the pot to high pressure (15 psi for stove top or 9 to 11 psi for electric).

STOVE TOP: Maintain pressure for 25 minutes, adjusting the burner as necessary.
ELECTRIC: Cook at high pressure for 25 minutes. When the timer goes off, turn the cooker off. Do not let it switch to the "warm" setting.

6. After cooking, use the *natural method* to release pressure.

7. Unlock and remove the lid. Using tongs or a large fork, break the pork into bite-size pieces; it should break apart very easily. Let the chili sit for a few minutes to allow the fat to come to the surface, and blot or spoon off as much as possible and discard. If you prefer a thicker sauce, simmer the pork for several minutes over medium heat in a stove-top cooker, or in the electric cooker on "brown." Stir in the cilantro (if using).

8. Serve over rice, or use as a filling for tacos or burritos.

PER SERVING: CALORIES: 544; FAT: 41G; SODIUM: 198MG;
CARBOHYDRATES: 14G; FIBER: 4G; PROTEIN: 41G

Pork Ragu

SERVES 6

PRESSURE: High
TIME UNDER PRESSURE: 25 minutes
RELEASE: Natural

PALEO

1 pound boneless pork
shoulder country ribs,
cut into 2-inch chunks

½ teaspoon kosher salt

1 tablespoon olive oil

¼ pound Italian sausage, sweet
or hot, casings removed

1½ cups diced onion

1 medium carrot, diced
(about ½ cup)

1 small celery stalk, diced
(about ½ cup)

2 garlic cloves, minced or
crushed in a garlic press

½ cup dry red wine

1 (28-ounce) can crushed
tomatoes

2 tablespoons tomato paste

Pinch red pepper flakes

2 teaspoons dried Italian herbs
(thyme, oregano, basil,
or a combination)

1 tablespoon minced
fresh parsley

This recipe, based on one from author and *Los Angeles Times* food editor Russ Parsons, originally called for pork necks. That cheap but tasty cut used to be easy to find, but I hardly ever see it at the markets where I shop. Country ribs from the shoulder make a good substitute. If you can find pork necks, try them. You'll need about 2½ pounds and will have to spend some time picking the meat off the bones, but it's fabulous.

1. Sprinkle the ribs with ½ teaspoon of kosher salt.

2. In a stove-top pressure cooker set over medium heat, or an electric cooker set to "brown," heat the olive oil until it shimmers and flows like water. Add half the pork (don't crowd the pan), and brown on two sides. Remove the pork to a plate. You can brown the remaining pork for more intense flavor, but it's not necessary if you want to save time.

3. Add the Italian sausage, and cook for 2 to 3 minutes, stirring to break it up a little, until most of the pink is gone and some fat renders. Add the onion, carrot, celery, and garlic. Cook for about 3 minutes, stirring, until the vegetables soften. Stir in the red wine, and scrape up any browned bits. Cook for 2 to 3 minutes, or until the wine has reduced by at least half. Add the tomatoes, tomato paste, red pepper flakes, Italian herbs, and parsley.

4. Lock the lid in place, and bring the pot to high pressure (15 psi for stove top or 9 to 11 psi for electric).

STOVE TOP: Maintain pressure for 25 minutes, adjusting the burner as necessary.

ELECTRIC: Cook at high pressure for 25 minutes. When the timer goes off, turn the cooker off. Do not let it switch to the "warm" setting.

5. After cooking, use the *natural method* to release pressure.

6. Unlock and remove the lid. Let the ragu sit for several minutes to allow the fat to rise to the surface, then spoon or blot it off and discard. Using a large spoon or fork, break up the meat. If the sauce is too thin, simmer it over medium-low heat in a stove-top cooker, or in the electric cooker on "simmer," until you reach the desired consistency. Serve over polenta or pasta.

PER SERVING: CALORIES: 384; FAT: 23G; SODIUM: 669MG; CARBOHYDRATES: 17G; FIBER: 5G; PROTEIN: 24G

Italian Stuffed Peppers

SERVES 2

PRESSURE: High
TIME UNDER PRESSURE: 13 minutes
RELEASE: Quick

2 large bell peppers
(red, yellow, or green),
tops removed and reserved,
cored and seeded

2 teaspoons olive oil

¼ pound hot or mild Italian
sausage, casing removed

⅓ cup diced onion

⅓ small fennel bulb, trimmed
and chopped (about ⅓ cup)

1 garlic clove, minced

Kosher salt

⅓ cup diced fresh or
canned tomato

½ cup cooked mushrooms,
roughly chopped

¾ cup cooked rice

8 tablespoons (½ cup)
grated part-skim mozzarella
cheese, divided

4 tablespoons (¼ cup) grated
Parmigiano-Reggiano or
similar cheese, divided

1 cup water

If you're like me, stuffed peppers conjure thoughts of those overcooked, bland, tomato-sauce-drenched versions I remember from my college dining hall— but that needn't be the case. It's easy to make this updated version that's both healthy and delicious. Vegetables and rice make up the bulk of the stuffing, with a little Italian sausage and cheese for richness and flavor. They take a little time to prepare, but your time and effort are rewarded with a tasty, wholesome meal. Choose peppers with flat bottoms so they'll stand up. If needed, slice a very thin piece from the bottom to flatten.

1. Using a paring knife and your fingers, remove as much of the ribs as possible from the peppers, leaving a hollow shell. Cut the flesh of the reserved pepper tops from the stem. Trim off any white pith, and dice the flesh. You should have ⅓ to ½ cup. Discard the stems.

2. In a stove-top pressure cooker set over medium heat, or an electric cooker set to "brown," heat the olive oil until it shimmers and flows like water. Add the Italian sausage, and cook for 2 to 3 minutes, breaking it up into small pieces with a spatula or spoon, until no pink remains. Add the onion, chopped pepper tops, fennel, and garlic, and sprinkle with a pinch or two of kosher salt. Cook for about 6 minutes, stirring, until the vegetables are very soft.

3. To a medium bowl, transfer the sausage and vegetables. Cool for 3 minutes. Add the tomato, mushrooms, and rice, and stir to combine. Mix in 5 tablespoons plus 1 teaspoon of mozzarella cheese and 2 tablespoons of Parmigiano-Reggiano. Fill the hollow bell peppers with equal amounts of the stuffing mixture, packing it in and heaping it slightly over the tops.

4. Wash or wipe out the pressure cooker. To a stove-top or electric pressure cooker, add the water, and insert the steamer basket or trivet. Place the stuffed peppers on the steamer insert.

5. Lock the lid in place, and bring the pot to high pressure (15 psi for stove top or 9 to 11 psi for electric).

STOVE TOP: Maintain pressure for 13 minutes, adjusting the burner as necessary.
ELECTRIC: Cook at high pressure for 13 minutes.

6. After cooking, use the *quick method* to release pressure.

7. Unlock and remove the lid. Sprinkle the remaining 2 tablespoons plus 2 teaspoons of mozzarella cheese and the remaining 2 tablespoons of Parmigiano-Reggiano over the top of the peppers, and place the lid back on the cooker *without* locking it. Let sit for about 2 minutes, or until the cheese melts, and serve.

8. If you want the tops of the peppers browned, carefully transfer the peppers to a small baking sheet before sprinkling with the remaining cheeses. Preheat the broiler, place the peppers under the broiler and cook for 2 to 3 minutes, or until the cheese is bubbling and the tops are browned, and serve.

TIP *The cooking time in this recipe results in peppers that are fully cooked but firm; if you prefer softer peppers, cook for 14 minutes.*

PER SERVING: CALORIES: 610; FAT: 32G; SODIUM: 807MG; CARBOHYDRATES: 53G; FIBER: 7G; PROTEIN: 30G

Pork Tenderloin *with* Rice Pilaf

SERVES 4

PRESSURE: High
TIME UNDER PRESSURE: 5 minutes
RELEASE: Quick

GLUTEN FREE, ONE POT

FOR THE BRINE (OPTIONAL)

½ cup Diamond Crystal kosher
  salt, or ¼ cup fine table salt

¼ cup granulated sugar

2 cups very hot tap water

2 cups ice water

FOR THE PORK AND RICE

1 (1-pound) pork tenderloin,
  trimmed of silver skin
  and halved

½ teaspoon kosher salt, plus
  additional for seasoning

2 tablespoons olive oil

½ cup chopped onion

¼ cup chopped red bell pepper

¼ cup chopped green
  bell pepper

1 large garlic clove, minced

¾ cup long-grain white rice

1¼ cup plus 2 tablespoons
  low-sodium vegetable broth
  or chicken broth

⅔ cup frozen green peas,
  thawed

The USDA has finally confirmed what countless chefs have suspected for years: Pork is perfectly safe cooked to 145°F. Pork tenderloin, especially, is certainly more delicious with a hint of pink in the center. It stays juicy and tender, and brining increases that effect. Don't worry that the pork will be too salty; it absorbs just enough salt to season the meat to the center.

To make the brine (if using)

In a large stainless steel or glass bowl, dissolve the salt and sugar in the hot water; then stir in the ice water. Submerge the pork in the brine, and refrigerate for 2 to 3 hours. Drain and pat dry.

To make the pork and rice

1. If you choose not to brine the pork, sprinkle it liberally with kosher salt.

2. In a stove-top pressure cooker set over medium heat, or an electric pressure cooker set to "brown," heat the olive oil until it shimmers. Add the pork tenderloin pieces, browning on all sides, about 4 minutes total. Transfer to a plate or rack.

3. Add the onion, red bell pepper, green bell pepper, and garlic to the pressure cooker. Cook for about 2 minutes, stirring occasionally, until the onion pieces separate and the vegetables soften. Add the rice, and stir briefly just to coat with the olive oil. Add the vegetable broth and ½ teaspoon of kosher salt, and bring to a simmer. Stir to make sure the rice isn't clumping, and cook for 1 minute. →

4. Lock the lid in place, and bring the pot to high pressure (15 psi for stove top or 9 to 11 psi for electric).

STOVE TOP: Maintain pressure for 5 minutes, adjusting the burner as necessary.

ELECTRIC: Cook at high pressure for 5 minutes.

5. After cooking, use the **quick method** to release pressure.

6. Unlock and remove the lid. Quickly remove the pork to a plate or rack. Stir the peas into the rice, and replace but *do not lock* the lid. Let the rice steam for 8 minutes more. Cover the pork loosely with aluminum foil while the rice steams. When the rice is almost finished, slice the pork against the grain. When the rice is steamed, fluff lightly with a fork and serve with the pork.

TIP *For a southwestern version, sprinkle the tenderloin with chili powder, and add the ingredients in Arroz Verde (page 178).*

PER SERVING: CALORIES: 416; FAT: 12G; SODIUM: 988MG; CARBOHYDRATES: 40G; FIBER: 2G; PROTEIN: 36G

Lamb Curry

SERVES 4

PRESSURE: High
TIME UNDER PRESSURE: 40 minutes
RELEASE: Natural

GLUTEN FREE, ONE POT

2 small onions

2 garlic cloves, peeled
and smashed

1¼ cups plain yogurt

2 teaspoons kosher salt

1 tablespoon freshly squeezed
lemon juice

1 tablespoon ground coriander

2 teaspoons ground cumin

1 teaspoon ground allspice

1½ teaspoons freshly ground
black pepper

½ teaspoon ground ginger

2 tablespoons cornstarch

½ teaspoon red pepper flakes
(optional)

1½ pounds boneless lamb
shoulder, cut into
1½-inch cubes

Cooked rice or couscous,
for serving

¼ cup chopped fresh mint

This recipe is based on one from the first cookbook I ever bought: *Sunset* **magazine's** *Cooking with Spices and Herbs.* **It was exotic and different and, for a time, the only dish I made for company. I've since moved on and expanded my repertoire, but this dish remains one of my favorite ways to cook lamb.**

1. Cut one of the onions into chunks. Place it, along all ingredients except for the lamb, rice, and mint, into a blender jar or food processor. Blend until mostly smooth.

2. In a large bowl, pour the yogurt mixture over the lamb cubes. Stir to coat the meat evenly; then cover with plastic wrap or aluminum foil and marinate for 2 hours at room temperature, or in the refrigerator overnight.

3. Into a pressure cooker, pour the meat and marinade. Slice the remaining onion, and add it to the pot, stirring to combine.

4. Lock the lid in place, and bring the pot to high pressure (15 psi for stove top or 9 to 11 psi for electric).

STOVE TOP: Maintain pressure for 40 minutes, adjusting the burner as necessary.
ELECTRIC: Cook at high pressure for 40 minutes. When the timer goes off, turn the cooker off. Do not let it switch to the "warm" setting.

5. After cooking, use the *natural method* to release pressure.

6. Unlock and remove the lid. Let the lamb sit for a few minutes to allow the fat to rise, and spoon off and discard the fat. Serve over rice or couscous, and garnish with the mint.

PER SERVING: CALORIES: 411; FAT: 14G; SODIUM: 1,351MG; CARBOHYDRATES: 14G; FIBER: 1G; PROTEIN: 53G

Lamb *and* Bulgur-Stuffed Acorn Squash

SERVES 2

PRESSURE: High
TIME UNDER PRESSURE: 20 minutes
RELEASE: Quick

½ cup medium or coarse
    bulgur wheat

1 tablespoon olive oil

½ cup chopped onion

2 tablespoons minced red or
    green bell pepper

1 tablespoon minced garlic

2 teaspoons kosher salt, plus
    additional for seasoning

1 pound ground lamb

2 teaspoons ground cumin

½ teaspoon ground coriander

½ cup finely chopped
    fresh parsley

¼ cup minced fresh mint

1 large egg white,
    lightly beaten

1 medium acorn squash, halved
    and seeded

1 cup water, for steaming
    (double-check the pressure
    cooker manual to confirm
    amount, and follow
    the manual if there is
    a discrepancy)

This hearty main dish is based in part on Middle Eastern *kofta*, highly spiced ground lamb formed into long patties on sticks and grilled. Stuffing it into acorn squash might not be authentic, but it makes for a lovely presentation and a delicious meal.

1. In a medium bowl, soak the bulgur wheat in very hot tap water for about 15 minutes, or until softened but still slightly chewy.

2. In a stove-top pressure cooker set over medium heat, or an electric cooker set to "brown," heat the olive oil until it shimmers and flows like water. Add the onion, red bell pepper, and garlic, and sprinkle with a pinch or two of kosher salt. Cook, stirring, for about 2 minutes, or until the vegetables soften.

3. Drain the bulgur, and return it to the bowl. Transfer the cooked vegetables to the bowl. Add the lamb, 2 teaspoons of kosher salt, and the cumin, coriander, parsley, mint, and egg white. Stir just to combine; don't overwork the meat, or it may become tough.

4. Make sure the two squash halves will sit level and fit in the pressure cooker in one layer, trimming if necessary. Evenly divide the meat mixture and stuff it into the squash halves.

5. Add the water to a stove-top or electric pressure cooker, and insert the steamer basket or trivet. Place the squash halves on the steamer insert.

6. Lock the lid in place, and bring the pot to high pressure (15 psi for stove top or 9 to 11 psi for electric).

STOVE TOP: Maintain pressure for 20 minutes, adjusting the burner as necessary.

ELECTRIC: Cook at high pressure for 20 minutes.

7. After cooking, use the *quick method* to release pressure.

8. Unlock and remove the lid. Using a large slotted spatula, carefully remove the squash halves (they'll be quite soft), and serve.

TIP *If you can't find acorn squash, or simply don't like it, you can form the meat mixture into a meatloaf and cook it separately. Use the foil sling as described in the Tomato-Glazed Meatloaf recipe (see page 41) to transfer it in and out of the cooker.*

PER SERVING: CALORIES: 734; FAT: 25G; SODIUM: 2,546MG; CARBOHYDRATES: 56G; FIBER: 12G; PROTEIN: 73G

Lamb Shanks Provençal

SERVES 2

PRESSURE: High
TIME UNDER PRESSURE: 40 minutes
RELEASE: Natural

GLUTEN FREE

2 large (12-ounce) lamb shanks

1 teaspoon kosher salt, plus
  additional for seasoning

Freshly ground black pepper

1 tablespoon olive oil

1 cup sliced onion

2 garlic cloves, finely minced

2 medium plum tomatoes,
  coarsely chopped,
  or ½ cup diced canned
  tomatoes, drained

½ cup dry white wine or
  dry white vermouth

1 cup Chicken Stock (page 262)
  or low-sodium broth

1 bay leaf

1 lemon, sliced very thin

⅓ cup pitted Kalamata olives

2 tablespoons coarsely
  chopped fresh parsley

When I was growing up, my exposure to eating lamb was very limited. Mom cooked a roast occasionally, and I'd sometimes order rib chops at restaurants, but that was about it. So I never knew how great lamb shanks were until I had them at a French bistro in San Francisco, and even after that, I never cooked them—at least not until I got a pressure cooker. Pressure cooking turns them meltingly tender and amazingly flavorful in about a third of the time it takes in the oven.

1. Sprinkle the lamb shanks with 1 teaspoon of kosher salt and several grinds of pepper. The longer ahead of the cooking time you can do this, the better. Cover and let sit for 20 minutes to 2 hours at room temperature or refrigerate for up to 24 hours.

2. In a stove-top pressure cooker set over medium heat, or an electric cooker set to "brown," heat the olive oil until it shimmers and flows like water. Add the lamb shanks, and brown on all sides, about 6 minutes total. Remove them to a plate. Add the onion and garlic, and sprinkle with a pinch or two of kosher salt. Cook, stirring, for about 3 minutes, or until the onions just begin to brown. Add the tomatoes, and cook until most of their liquid evaporates.

3. Add the white wine, and stir, scraping up the browned bits from the bottom of the cooker. Cook for 2 to 3 minutes, or until the wine reduces by about half; then add the Chicken Stock and bay leaf. Return the lamb shanks to the cooker, and place the lemon slices over them.

4. Lock the lid in place, and bring the pot to high pressure (15 psi for stove top or 9 to 11 psi for electric).

STOVE TOP: Maintain pressure for 40 minutes, adjusting the burner as necessary.

ELECTRIC: Cook at high pressure for 40 minutes. When the timer goes off, turn the cooker off. Do not let it switch to the "warm" setting.

5. After cooking, use the ***natural method*** to release pressure.

6. Unlock and remove the lid. Transfer the lamb to a cutting board or plate, and tent it with aluminum foil. Strain the sauce into a fat separator, and let it rest until the fat rises to the surface. If you don't have a fat separator, let the sauce sit for a few minutes, then spoon or blot off any excess fat from the top and discard. Pour the defatted sauce back into the cooker along with the strained vegetables. If you want a thicker sauce, simmer the liquid for about 5 minutes, or until it reaches the desired consistency.

7. Stir in the olives and parsley. Place the shanks in shallow bowls, pour the sauce and vegetables over the lamb, and serve.

TIP *Lamb shanks benefit from salting in advance, which makes them much more flavorful and helps them brown beautifully. If you have the time, salt them up to 24 hours in advance. Place them on a tray and refrigerate, covered loosely with foil.*

PER SERVING: CALORIES: 835; FAT: 36G; SODIUM: 2,039MG; CARBOHYDRATES: 19G; FIBER: 5G; PROTEIN: 101G

Poultry

CHAPTER THREE

With poultry and pressure cookers, thighs rule. That's not to say you can't get moist, flavorful pressure-cooked dishes using turkey or chicken breast; you just shouldn't substitute breast meat for thigh meat in these recipes. Use the method for Curried Chicken Salad for cooking bone-in chicken breasts any time you want cooked chicken for a recipe, and use the Turkey Tenderloin with Sun-Dried-Tomato Pesto recipe with your favorite sauce for a fast, healthy, tasty entrée.

One thing you won't find here is a recipe for a whole cooked chicken or even a Cornish game hen. I know cooks who use their pressure cookers for whole birds, and I've seen plenty of recipes for them. Personally, I find the results disappointing. By the time the thighs are done, the breast is overcooked, and you don't even get the pleasure of the crisp skin, which is the whole point of roasted chicken.

Braised Turkey *in* Red Wine

SERVES 2

PRESSURE: High
TIME UNDER PRESSURE: 30 minutes
RELEASE: Natural

1 large or 2 small turkey thighs
    (1½ pounds total),
    skin removed
¼ teaspoon kosher salt, plus
    additional as needed
Freshly ground black pepper
1 cup dry red wine
1 cup low-sodium turkey or
    chicken broth
½ cup tawny port
1 bay leaf
1 fresh thyme sprig, or
    ½ teaspoon dried thyme
1 fresh rosemary sprig
1 tablespoon cold
    unsalted butter

My teaching partner and I developed this recipe for a "nontraditional" Thanksgiving dinner menu. It's a great choice if you're only cooking for two; it's elegant and worthy of a holiday but won't leave your refrigerator full of leftovers.

1. Sprinkle the turkey with ¼ teaspoon of kosher salt, and season with a few grinds of pepper. Into a pressure cooker, place the turkey and pour over it the red wine, turkey broth, and port. Add the bay leaf, thyme, and rosemary.

2. Lock the lid in place, and bring the pot to high pressure (15 psi for stove top or 9 to 11 psi for electric).

STOVE TOP: Maintain pressure for 30 minutes, adjusting the burner as necessary.
ELECTRIC: Cook at high pressure for 30 minutes. When the timer goes off, turn the cooker off. Do not let it switch to the "warm" setting.

3. After cooking, use the *natural method* to release pressure.

4. Unlock and remove the lid. Remove the thighs from the liquid, and set aside. Strain the cooking liquid into a fat separator. If you don't have a fat separator, strain the liquid into a shallow bowl, and allow the liquid to settle. When the fat rises to the surface, spoon or blot it off and discard.

5. Pour 1¼ cups of the defatted braising liquid back into the pressure cooker, discarding the rest. Bring the liquid to a boil, and cook for 7 to 10 minutes, until reduced by about two-thirds, or until thickened to a sauce consistency. Reduce the heat to low for a stove-top cooker, or "warm" for an electric cooker. The liquid should end up being warm to the touch, about 130°F.

6. While the liquid reduces, remove the turkey meat from the bone, and shred it into large pieces.

7. When you're ready to serve the dish, whisk the cold butter into the sauce 1 teaspoon at a time, adding each piece only after the previous one has been incorporated. Adjust the seasoning with kosher salt and pepper, as needed. Add the turkey to the sauce to warm it before serving.

PER SERVING: CALORIES: 577; FAT: 18G; SODIUM: 787MG; CARBOHYDRATES: 6G; FIBER: 0G; PROTEIN: 67G

Onion-Thyme Smothered Chicken

SERVES 2

PRESSURE: High
TIME UNDER PRESSURE: 12 minutes
RELEASE: Natural

½ teaspoon kosher salt, plus additional as needed

2 (8-ounce) or 4 (4-ounce) bone-in, skin-on chicken thighs

1 tablespoon olive oil

2 medium onions, peeled and cut into ¼-inch wedges (about 1½ cups)

1 large or 2 small garlic cloves, minced

½ cup dry white wine

1 tablespoon white wine vinegar

1 teaspoon honey, plus additional as needed

½ teaspoon dried thyme

2 teaspoons fresh thyme leaves, divided

1 small bay leaf

Freshly ground black pepper

2 teaspoons all-purpose flour

½ cup low-sodium chicken broth

Traditionally, smothered chicken is coated in flour, fried, and topped with a gravy and onions or mushrooms. This version, based loosely on a recipe from Edna Lewis, one of the queens of southern cooking, is much lighter but packed with flavor. Using both fresh and dried thyme adds complexity. Use only dried thyme if you can't find or don't have fresh, increasing the amount to 1 teaspoon.

1. Using ½ teaspoon of kosher salt, sprinkle the chicken thighs on both sides. In a stove-top pressure cooker set over medium heat, or an electric cooker set to "brown," heat the olive oil until it shimmers and flows like water. Add the chicken thighs, skin-side down, and cook, undisturbed, for about 6 minutes, or until the skin is dark golden brown and most of the fat under the skin has rendered. Turn the thighs to the other side, and cook for about 3 minutes more, or until that side is light golden brown. Remove the thighs.

2. Carefully pour off almost all the fat and discard, leaving just enough (about 1 tablespoon) to cover the bottom of the pressure cooker with a thick coat. Add the onions, and cook for 3 to 4 minutes, stirring, until they brown slightly. Add the garlic, and cook for 1 minute, until fragrant.

3. Add the white wine, and scrape the bottom of the pan to release the browned bits. Boil for about 2 minutes, or until the wine reduces by about half. Add the white wine vinegar, honey, dried thyme, 1 teaspoon of fresh thyme leaves, the bay leaf, and several grinds of pepper. In a small bowl, whisk together the flour and chicken broth, and add to the pressure cooker. Bring the sauce to a boil, and cook for 1 minute. Add the chicken thighs, skin-side up, to the pressure cooker.

4. Lock the lid in place, and bring the pot to high pressure (15 psi for stove top or 9 to 11 psi for electric).

STOVE TOP: Maintain pressure for 12 minutes, adjusting the burner as necessary.
ELECTRIC: Cook at high pressure for 12 minutes. When the timer goes off, turn the cooker off. Do not let it switch to the "warm" setting.

5. After cooking, use the *natural method* to release pressure.

6. Unlock and remove the lid. Remove the chicken thighs from the pot. Strain the sauce into a fat separator, and let it rest until the fat rises to the surface. If you don't have a fat separator, let the sauce sit for a few minutes; then spoon or blot off any excess fat from the top and discard. Pour the defatted sauce back into the cooker, and add the chicken thighs and the strained solids. If you prefer a thicker sauce, place the stove-top cooker over medium-high heat, or turn the electric cooker to "brown," and simmer the sauce for several minutes until it's reduced to the consistency you like.

7. Adjust the seasoning, adding more salt if necessary or a little more honey if the sauce is too acidic. Spoon the onions and sauce over the chicken, sprinkle the remaining 1 teaspoon of thyme leaves on top, and serve.

PER SERVING: CALORIES: 612; FAT: 38G; SODIUM: 1,296MG; CARBOHYDRATES: 19G; FIBER: 3G; PROTEIN: 37G

Chicken *with* Artichoke Hearts *and* Mushrooms

SERVES 2

PRESSURE: High
TIME UNDER PRESSURE: 12 minutes
RELEASE: Natural

ONE POT

½ teaspoon kosher salt

2 (8-ounce) or 4 (4-ounce) bone-in, skin-on chicken thighs

1 tablespoon olive oil

¼ cup sliced onion

4 ounces white button or cremini mushrooms, trimmed and quartered

½ cup dry white wine

1 bay leaf

¼ teaspoon dried thyme

½ cup frozen artichoke hearts, thawed

⅓ cup low-sodium chicken broth

Freshly ground black pepper

This recipe was an accident. I was going to make the Chicken Thighs in Sherry Vinegar Sauce (page 90), but when I started sautéing the chicken, I realized I didn't have the can of tomatoes I thought I did. Neither did I have sherry vinegar, or in fact, any sherry at all. I did have a package of artichoke hearts in the freezer and some mushrooms and white wine in the refrigerator. The substitutions were serendipitous, and this dish has been in regular rotation ever since.

1. Using ½ teaspoon of kosher salt, sprinkle the chicken thighs on both sides. In a stove-top pressure cooker set over medium heat, or an electric cooker set to "brown," heat the olive oil until it shimmers and flows like water. Add the chicken thighs, skin-side down, and cook, undisturbed, for about 6 minutes, or until the skin is dark golden brown and most of the fat under the skin has rendered. Turn the thighs to the other side, and cook for about 3 minutes more, or until that side is light golden brown. Remove the thighs.

2. Carefully pour off almost all the fat, leaving just enough (about 1 tablespoon) to cover the bottom of the pressure cooker with a thick coat. Add the onion and mushrooms, and cook for about 5 minutes, or until softened. Add the white wine, and cook for 3 to 5 minutes, or until reduced by half. Add the bay leaf, thyme, artichokes, and chicken broth, and bring to a simmer. Return the chicken to the pot, skin-side up.

3. Lock the lid in place, and bring the pot to high pressure (15 psi for stove top or 9 to 11 psi for electric).

STOVE TOP: Maintain pressure for 12 minutes, adjusting the burner as necessary.
ELECTRIC: Cook at high pressure for 12 minutes. When the timer goes off, turn the cooker off. Do not let it switch to the "warm" setting.

4. After cooking, use the *natural method* to release pressure.

5. Unlock and remove the lid. Remove the chicken thighs from the pan, and set aside. Remove the bay leaf. Strain the sauce into a fat separator, and let it rest until the fat rises to the surface. If you don't have a fat separator, let the sauce sit for a few minutes; then spoon or blot off any excess fat from the top and discard. Pour the defatted sauce back into the cooker, and add the chicken thighs and the solids from the sauce. If you prefer a thicker sauce, place the stove-top cooker over medium-high heat or turn the electric cooker to "brown," and simmer the sauce for several minutes until it's reduced to the consistency you like.

6. Adjust the seasoning, adding more salt if necessary and several grinds of pepper, and serve.

PER SERVING: CALORIES: 612; FAT: 38G; SODIUM: 1,269MG; CARBOHYDRATES: 19G; FIBER: 3G; PROTEIN: 37G

Honey-Chipotle Chicken Wings

SERVES 2

PRESSURE: High
TIME UNDER PRESSURE: 10 minutes
RELEASE: Quick

6 whole chicken wings, or 12 wing segments

1 cup water, for steaming (double-check the pressure cooker manual to confirm amount, and follow the manual if there is a discrepancy)

3 tablespoons Mexican hot sauce (such as Valentina brand)

2 tablespoons honey

1 teaspoon minced canned chipotle in adobo sauce

Forget Buffalo wings! Steaming chicken wings instead of frying them cuts calories and results in delicious meat with a silky texture. An easy sweet-and-spicy sauce plus a little time under the broiler give them an equally great exterior.

1. If using whole wings, cut off the tips and discard. Cut the wings at the joint into two pieces each, the "drumette" and the "flat."

2. To a stove-top or electric pressure cooker, add the water and insert the steamer basket or trivet. Place the wings on the steamer insert.

3. Lock the lid in place, and bring the pot to high pressure (15 psi for stove top or 9 to 11 psi for electric).

STOVE TOP: Maintain pressure for 10 minutes, adjusting the burner as necessary.
ELECTRIC: Cook at high pressure for 10 minutes.

4. After cooking, use the *quick method* to release pressure.

5. While the wings are cooking, make the sauce. In a large bowl, whisk together the hot sauce, honey, and minced chipotle. Preheat the broiler, and place an oven rack in the top or second position.

6. Unlock and remove the lid. Using tongs, carefully transfer the wing segments to the bowl with the sauce. Toss gently to coat. Transfer the wing segments to a baking rack placed over a sheet pan, or to a baking sheet lined with nonstick aluminum foil.

7. Place the baking sheet under the broiler for 4 to 5 minutes, or until the wings start to brown, and serve.

PER SERVING: CALORIES: 434; FAT: 27G; SODIUM: 1,152MG; CARBOHYDRATES: 19G; FIBER: 1G; PROTEIN: 31G

Turkey Tenderloin *with* Sun-Dried-Tomato Pesto

SERVES 2

PRESSURE: High
TIME UNDER PRESSURE: 10 minutes
RELEASE: Quick

GLUTEN FREE, PALEO FRIENDLY

FOR THE BRINE (OPTIONAL)

½ cup Diamond Crystal kosher salt, or ¼ cup fine table salt

2 cups very hot tap water

2 cups ice water

FOR THE PESTO

½ cup oil-packed sun-dried tomatoes, plus 3 tablespoons of the olive oil

1 cup packed basil leaves (about ½ ounce)

¼ cup grated Parmigiano-Reggiano (about 1 ounce)

1 garlic clove, minced

1 tablespoon toasted pine nuts (optional) (see Tip)

FOR THE TURKEY

Kosher salt

1 (12-ounce) turkey tenderloin

3 tablespoons sun-dried-tomato pesto, divided

1 cup water, for steaming (double-check the pressure cooker manual to confirm amount, and follow the manual if there is a discrepancy)

Coating turkey tenderloins, which are cut from the breast, with sun-dried-tomato pesto helps keep them juicy and flavorful. While pesto is undeniably high in fat, you don't need much in this easy, delicious recipe. Use a commercial brand if you prefer. The recipe here makes extra, but it's a great condiment to have on hand. Add some to the Penne with Chicken, Peppers, and Arugula (page 97) or to the salad dressing for the Warm French Potato Salad (page 224).

To make the brine (if using)

In a large stainless steel or glass bowl, dissolve the salt in the hot water; then stir in the ice water. Submerge the turkey in the brine, and refrigerate for 1 hour. Drain and pat dry.

To make the pesto

In the bowl of a small food processor or in a small blender jar, pulse the tomatoes, oil, basil, Parmigiano-Reggiano, garlic, and pine nuts (if using) until a coarse paste forms, adding 1 to 2 tablespoons of water, if necessary, to get a loose enough consistency. You should have about ¾ cup of pesto. The leftovers can be refrigerated for about 1 week, or frozen for several months.

To make the turkey

1. If you haven't brined the turkey, salt it generously on both sides. Carefully cut the turkey lengthwise almost all the way through, stopping about ½ inch from the other side. Open the turkey like a book, and spread about 2 tablespoons of pesto over the cut side. Fold the tenderloin together, and spread the remaining 1 tablespoon of pesto over the top.

2. To a stove-top or electric pressure cooker, add the water and insert the steamer basket or trivet. Place the turkey tenderloin on the steamer insert.

3. Lock the lid in place, and bring the pot to high pressure (15 psi for stove top or 9 to 11 psi for electric).

STOVE TOP: Maintain pressure for 10 minutes, adjusting the burner as necessary.
ELECTRIC: Cook at high pressure for 10 minutes.

4. After cooking, use the *quick method* to release pressure.

5. Unlock and remove the lid. Using a large slotted spatula, transfer the turkey to a cutting board. Slice into ¾-inch-thick pieces, and serve.

TIP *To toast nuts, preheat the oven to 350°F. Spread the nuts on a baking sheet in an even layer. Both pine nuts and walnuts take 10 to 15 minutes, while almonds take 7 to 10 minutes to brown nicely. Stir halfway through toasting time to ensure even browning, and check frequently near the end to avoid burning. Shorten toasting times if nuts are in pieces.*

PER SERVING: CALORIES: 289; FAT: 14G; SODIUM: 1,832MG; CARBOHYDRATES: 8G; FIBER: 1G; PROTEIN: 30G

Chicken Thighs *in* Sherry Vinegar Sauce

SERVES 2

PRESSURE: High
TIME UNDER PRESSURE: 12 minutes
RELEASE: Natural

GLUTEN FREE

½ teaspoon kosher salt, plus
   additional as needed

2 (6-ounce) or 4 (3-ounce)
   bone-in, skin-on
   chicken thighs

1 tablespoon olive oil

¼ cup sliced onion

⅓ cup dry sherry

3 tablespoons sherry vinegar

⅓ cup chicken broth

½ cup canned diced tomatoes,
   drained thoroughly

1½ teaspoons Dijon mustard

½ teaspoon packed brown
   sugar, plus additional
   as needed

Freshly ground black pepper

Whenever I mention this recipe, I get pretty much the same reaction: "Vinegar sauce?" It sounds mouth puckering, but the braising time mellows the vinegar's acid, resulting in an absolutely mouth-watering dish.

1. Using ½ teaspoon of kosher salt, sprinkle the chicken thighs on both sides. In a stove-top pressure cooker set over medium heat, or an electric cooker set to "brown," heat the olive oil until it shimmers and flows like water. Add the chicken thighs, skin-side down, and cook, undisturbed, for about 6 minutes, or until the skin is dark golden brown and most of the fat under the skin has rendered. Turn the thighs to the other side, and cook for about 3 minutes more, or until that side is light golden brown. Remove the thighs.

2. Carefully pour off almost all the fat, leaving just enough (about 1 tablespoon) to cover the bottom of the pressure cooker with a thick coat. Add the onion, and cook for about 3 minutes, stirring, until the onions begin to brown. Add the sherry, and scrape the bottom of the pan to release the browned bits. Boil for about 2 minutes, or until the sherry reduces by about half. Add the sherry vinegar, and boil for about 2 minutes more, or until the liquid in the pan has reduced by about half. Add the chicken broth, tomatoes, mustard, brown sugar, and a few grinds of pepper. Bring the sauce to a boil, and cook for 1 minute. Add the chicken thighs, skin-side up, to the sauce.

3. Lock the lid in place, and bring the pot to high pressure (15 psi for stove top or 9 to 11 psi for electric).

STOVE TOP: Maintain pressure for 12 minutes, adjusting the burner as necessary.

ELECTRIC: Cook at high pressure for 12 minutes. When the timer goes off, turn the cooker off. Do not let it switch to the "warm" setting.

4. After cooking, use the *natural method* to release pressure.

5. Unlock and remove the lid. Remove the chicken thighs from the pot. Strain the sauce into a fat separator, and let it rest until the fat rises to the surface. If you don't have a fat separator, let the sauce sit for a few minutes; then spoon or blot off any excess fat from the top and discard. Pour the defatted sauce back into the cooker. Add the chicken thighs and the strained solids. If you prefer a thicker sauce, place the stove-top cooker over medium-high heat, or turn the electric cooker to "brown," and simmer the sauce for several minutes until it's reduced to the consistency you like.

6. Adjust the seasoning, adding more salt if necessary or a little more brown sugar if the sauce is too acidic, and serve.

TIP *Chicken thighs can vary wildly in size. Large thighs can weigh 6 or more ounces, while small thighs might be half that. Let your appetite and the size of the thighs be your guide when choosing the number to cook.*

PER SERVING: CALORIES: 579; FAT: 30G; SODIUM: 1,286MG; CARBOHYDRATES: 6G; FIBER: 1G; PROTEIN: 27G

Coq au Vin

SERVES 2

PRESSURE: High
TIME UNDER PRESSURE: 15 minutes
RELEASE: Natural

GLUTEN FREE

½ teaspoon kosher salt, plus additional as needed

2 chicken leg-thigh quarters, skin on

1 bacon slice, diced

¼ cup sliced onion

1 cup dry red wine, divided

⅓ cup chicken broth

1½ teaspoons tomato paste

½ teaspoon packed brown sugar, plus additional as needed

Freshly ground black pepper

Authentic French coq au vin is made with a rooster (*coq*), which has to marinate in wine for a day or so to become tender enough to eat. Then it cooks forever, and after that, several garnishes are prepared separately. Finally, several days later, you can eat. This very modern version keeps the traditional flavors of coq au vin but turns it into a dish you can make on a weeknight. If you want to be more authentic and spend a little more time, you can add mushrooms and pearl onions as prepared in the tip for Beef Bourguignon (see page 45). Add them after the sauce is reduced at step 6.

1. Using ½ teaspoon of kosher salt, sprinkle the chicken thighs on both sides. To a stove-top pressure cooker set over medium heat, or an electric cooker set to "brown," add the bacon, and cook for about 4 minutes, or until most of the fat renders and the bacon begins to crisp. Remove the bacon, and set aside, leaving the fat in the pan.

2. Add the chicken quarters, skin-side down, and cook, undisturbed, for about 6 minutes, or until the skin is dark golden brown and most of the fat under the skin has rendered. Turn the quarters to the other side, and cook for about 3 minutes more, or until that side is light golden brown. Remove the chicken to a plate.

3. Carefully pour off almost all the fat, leaving just enough (about 1 tablespoon) to cover the bottom of the pressure cooker with a thick coat. Add the onions, and cook for about 3 minutes, stirring, until they begin to brown. Add ½ cup of red wine, and scrape the bottom of the pan to release the browned bits. Boil for about 2 minutes, or until the wine reduces by about one-third. Add the remaining

½ cup of red wine and the chicken broth, tomato paste, brown sugar, and a few grinds of pepper. Bring the sauce to a boil, and cook for 1 minute, stirring to make sure the tomato paste is incorporated. Add the chicken pieces, skin-side up.

4. Lock the lid in place, and bring the pot to high pressure (15 psi for stove top or 9 to 11 psi for electric).

STOVE TOP: Maintain pressure for 15 minutes, adjusting the burner as necessary.
ELECTRIC: Cook at high pressure for 15 minutes. When the timer goes off, turn the cooker off. Do not let it switch to the "warm" setting.

5. After cooking, use the ***natural method*** to release pressure.

6. Unlock and remove the lid. Remove the chicken pieces from the pot. Strain the sauce into a fat separator, and let the sauce sit for about 5 minutes, or until the fat rises to the surface. If you don't have a fat separator, let the sauce sit for a few minutes; then spoon or blot off any excess fat from the top and discard. Return the defatted sauce to the cooker. Place the stove-top cooker over medium-high heat, or turn the electric cooker to "brown," and simmer the sauce for several minutes, until it's reduced to the consistency of gravy.

7. Adjust the seasoning, adding more kosher salt if necessary or a little more brown sugar if the sauce is too acidic. Return the chicken to the sauce, and serve with the bacon sprinkled over the top.

PER SERVING: CALORIES: 233; FAT: 5G; SODIUM: 743MG;
CARBOHYDRATES: 6G; FIBER: 2G; PROTEIN: 19G

Chicken *and* Dumplings

SERVES 4

PRESSURE: High
TIME UNDER PRESSURE: 5 minutes
(chicken), 3 minutes (dumplings)
RELEASE: Quick (chicken), Combination
(dumplings)

ONE POT

FOR THE DUMPLINGS

1 cup all-purpose flour

2 teaspoons baking powder

½ teaspoon kosher salt

⅛ teaspoon freshly ground
    black pepper

½ teaspoon dried thyme

1 tablespoon melted butter

1 egg

⅓ cup whole milk

FOR THE CHICKEN AND VEGETABLES

3 tablespoons all-purpose flour

½ teaspoon kosher salt

¼ teaspoon garlic powder

⅛ teaspoon ground
    cayenne pepper

⅛ teaspoon freshly ground
    black pepper

4 (4-ounce) boneless, skinless
    chicken thighs

2 tablespoons olive oil

3½ cups Chicken Stock
    (page 262) or low-sodium
    broth, divided

3 large carrots, peeled and cut
    into 1-inch lengths

2 large celery stalks, sliced
    ½ inch thick

1 cup frozen pearl onions

⅔ cup frozen peas

At first glance, chicken and dumplings, while comforting and delicious, might not seem all that healthy. But this modern version contains lots of vegetables, flavorful stock instead of a cream-thickened sauce, and fewer dumplings. You'll be satisfied without being stuffed.

To make the dumplings

In a medium bowl, whisk together the flour, baking powder, kosher salt, pepper, and thyme. In a measuring cup, whisk together the butter, egg, and milk. Pour the wet ingredients into the flour mixture, and stir until just incorporated. Place the bowl in the refrigerator while you prepare the chicken and vegetables.

To make the chicken and vegetables

1. In a small bowl or jar with a shaker top, mix together the flour, kosher salt, garlic, cayenne pepper, and black pepper. Sprinkle half the flour mixture over both sides of the chicken thighs, coating as evenly as possible.

2. In a stove-top pressure cooker set over medium heat, or an electric cooker set to "brown," heat the olive oil until it shimmers and flows like water. Add the chicken thighs, and cook for 5 minutes, or until golden brown. Turn the thighs, and cook the other side for 5 minutes more, or until that side is also golden brown. Remove the thighs to a rack or cutting board, and cool for 2 minutes. Cut into bite-size pieces.

3. With the stove-top cooker over medium heat, or the electric cooker set to "brown," add the remaining half of the flour mixture to the olive oil in the cooker, and stir to combine. Cook for about 2 minutes, or until the flour mixture begins to brown. ➡

4. Add 1 cup of Chicken Stock, and stir to combine with the flour roux, scraping up any browned flour mixture from the bottom. Stir in the remaining 2½ cups of stock, half a cup at a time, until all the stock has been added and the sauce is smooth. Add the carrots, celery, pearl onions, and chicken to the sauce in the cooker.

5. Lock the lid in place, and bring the pot to high pressure (15 psi for stove top or 9 to 11 psi for electric).

STOVE TOP: Maintain pressure for 5 minutes, adjusting the burner as necessary.
ELECTRIC: Cook at high pressure for 5 minutes.

6. After cooking, use the *quick method* to release pressure.

7. Unlock and remove the lid. Add the peas to the cooker.

8. Remove the dumpling dough from the refrigerator. Using two spoons, scoop rounded tablespoons of dough onto the surface of the chicken and vegetables in the cooker. Don't make larger dumplings; they won't cook evenly.

9. Lock the lid in place, and bring the pot to high pressure (15 psi for stove top or 9 to 11 psi for electric).

STOVE TOP: Maintain pressure for 3 minutes, adjusting the burner as necessary.
ELECTRIC: Cook at high pressure for 3 minutes. When the timer goes off, turn the cooker off. Do not let it switch to the "warm" setting.

10. After cooking, use the *natural method* to release pressure for 5 minutes, then the *quick method* to release the remaining pressure.

11. Unlock and remove the lid. Ladle into bowls, and serve.

PER SERVING: CALORIES: 564; FAT: 22G; SODIUM: 1,463MG; CARBOHYDRATES: 44G; FIBER: 5G; PROTEIN: 45G

Penne *with* Chicken, Peppers, *and* Arugula

SERVES 4

PRESSURE: High
TIME UNDER PRESSURE: 5 minutes
RELEASE: Quick

ONE POT

1 tablespoon all-purpose flour

1 teaspoon kosher salt, divided

⅛ teaspoon granulated garlic
   or garlic powder

½ teaspoon dried Italian herbs,
   divided (or ¼ teaspoon
   dried oregano and
   ¼ teaspoon dried basil)

⅛ teaspoon freshly ground
   black pepper

3 (4-ounce) boneless, skinless
   chicken thighs

1 tablespoon olive oil

1 cup thinly sliced onion

1 small green bell pepper,
   seeded and cut into 1-inch
   chunks (about 1½ cups)

3 garlic cloves, minced
   or pressed (about
   1 tablespoon)

½ cup dry white or red wine

1½ cups Quick Marinara
   Sauce (page 270) or plain
   tomato sauce

2 tablespoons minced sun-dried
   tomatoes (optional)

1¾ cups water

½ pound penne or similar
   pasta shape

3 cups arugula or baby spinach

Parmigiano-Reggiano or a
   similar cheese, for garnish

I based this recipe on one for penne with Italian sausage and peppers. While the chicken is lower in fat, it lacks the complex flavor of the sausage. Dredging the chicken in seasoned flour and frying it in a little oil adds layers of flavor and helps ensure that the chicken is tender by the time the pasta is cooked.

1. In a small bowl or jar with a shaker top, mix together the flour, ½ teaspoon of kosher salt, the granulated garlic, ¼ teaspoon of Italian herbs, and the pepper. Sprinkle the flour mixture over both sides of the chicken thighs, coating as evenly as possible.

2. In a stove-top pressure cooker set over medium heat, or an electric cooker set to "brown," heat the olive oil until it shimmers and flows like water. Add the chicken thighs, and cook for 5 minutes, or until golden brown. Turn the thighs over, and cook the other side for 5 minutes more, or until that side is also golden brown. Remove the thighs to a rack or cutting board, and cool for 3 minutes.

3. With the stove-top cooker still over medium heat, or the electric cooker on "brown," add the onion, green bell pepper, and garlic. Cook for about 3 minutes, stirring, until the onions just start to brown. Pour in the wine, and scrape the bottom of the pan to release the browned bits, cooking until the wine is almost completely evaporated. Add the Quick Marinara Sauce, the remaining ½ teaspoon of kosher salt, the sun-dried tomatoes (if using), the remaining ¼ teaspoon of Italian herbs, the water, the chicken, and the penne.

4. Lock the lid in place, and bring the pot to high pressure (15 psi for stove top or 9 to 11 psi for electric). ➡

STOVE TOP: Maintain pressure for 5 minutes, adjusting the burner as necessary.

ELECTRIC: Cook at high pressure for 5 minutes.

5. After cooking, use the *quick method* to release pressure.

6. Unlock and remove the lid. The penne should be almost done, and the sauce will be a little thin. Add the arugula, and stir. With the stove-top cooker on medium-low heat, or the electric cooker set to "simmer," cook for 3 to 4 minutes, or until the pasta is done to your liking, the arugula is wilted, and the sauce has thickened. Serve topped with grated Parmigiano-Reggiano.

PER SERVING: CALORIES: 510; FAT: 14G; SODIUM: 1,040MG; CARBOHYDRATES: 63G; FIBER: 6G; PROTEIN: 35G

Curried Chicken Salad

SERVES 2

PRESSURE: High
TIME UNDER PRESSURE: 15 or
18 minutes
RELEASE: Quick

GLUTEN FREE

FOR THE BRINE (OPTIONAL)

½ cup Diamond Crystal kosher
    salt, or ¼ cup fine table salt

2 cups very hot tap water

2 cups ice water

FOR THE CHICKEN AND SALAD

1 medium (12- to 16-ounce)
    bone-in chicken breast

½ teaspoon kosher salt, plus
    additional for seasoning

1 cup water, for steaming
    (double-check the pressure
    cooker manual to confirm
    amount, and follow
    the manual if there is
    a discrepancy)

¼ cup plain whole-milk yogurt

2 tablespoons mayonnaise

1 or 2 teaspoons curry powder

⅛ teaspoon freshly ground
    black pepper

Pinch ground cayenne pepper

2 medium scallions, sliced on
    the bias (about ⅓ cup)

½ cup sliced celery

¼ cup chopped red bell pepper

½ cup chopped fresh cilantro

⅓ cup blanched slivered
    almonds, toasted

Salad greens, for serving
    (optional)

2 hollowed-out tomatoes
    (optional)

Growing up, I wasn't much of a chicken salad fan. I changed my mind when I tried a curried chicken salad at a sandwich shop near my office in San Francisco—I was never one to pass up curried anything at that time. The salad contained toasted almonds, scallions, cilantro, and red bell pepper, and, of course, curry. This is my version; naturally, I think it's even better than the original. If you've never tried anything like this, I think it will become your favorite version, too.

To make the brine (if using)

In a large stainless steel or glass bowl, dissolve the salt in the hot water; then stir in the ice water. Submerge the chicken breast in the brine, and refrigerate for 1 to 2 hours. Drain and pat dry.

To make the chicken and salad

1. If you choose not to brine the chicken, sprinkle it generously on both sides using ½ teaspoon of kosher salt. To a stove-top or electric pressure cooker, add the water and insert the steamer basket or trivet. Place the chicken breast on the steamer insert.

2. Lock the lid in place, and bring the pot to high pressure (15 psi for stove top or 9 to 11 psi for electric).

STOVE TOP: Maintain pressure for 15 minutes, adjusting the burner as necessary.
ELECTRIC: Cook at high pressure for 18 minutes.

3. After cooking, use the *quick method* to release pressure.

4. Unlock and remove the lid. Transfer the chicken breast to a plate or cutting board to cool. →

Curried Chicken Salad,
continued

5. While the chicken cools, make the dressing. In a small bowl, whisk together the yogurt, mayonnaise, curry powder, black pepper, and cayenne pepper.

6. When the chicken is cool enough to handle, remove the skin and pull the meat off the bones. Chop coarsely, and place in a large bowl. Add the scallions, celery, red bell pepper, and cilantro, and toss gently. Pour the dressing over the chicken and vegetables, and toss to coat. Season with kosher salt, keeping in mind that some curry powders contain salt; if yours does, you may need only a pinch of salt. Right before serving, stir in the toasted almonds. Serve over salad greens or in hollowed-out tomatoes.

TIP *While I prefer my chicken salad without fruit, raisins or apples are popular additions to recipes like this. If you like them, add ¼ cup of raisins or ½ cup chopped Granny Smith apple.*

PER SERVING: CALORIES: 465; FAT: 18G; SODIUM: 922MG; CARBOHYDRATES: 13G; FIBER: 4G; PROTEIN: 61G

Turkey Sloppy Joes

SERVES 2

PRESSURE: High
TIME UNDER PRESSURE: 30 minutes
RELEASE: Natural

1 tablespoon olive oil

¼ cup chopped onion

¼ small red or green bell pepper, chopped (about 2 tablespoons)

1 garlic clove, minced or pressed

Kosher salt

⅔ cup tomato sauce

¼ cup beer or water

1 tablespoon cider or wine vinegar, plus additional as needed

1 tablespoon packed brown sugar

2 teaspoons ancho or New Mexico chili powder

1 teaspoon Dijon mustard

½ teaspoon Worcestershire sauce

1 large or 2 small turkey thighs (1½ pounds total), skin removed

2 hamburger buns

We all loved sloppy joes as kids. Braising turkey thighs in tangy sauce results in that great sloppy-joe flavor, but with less fat for the grown-up you.

1. In a stove-top pressure cooker set over medium heat, or an electric cooker set to "brown," heat the olive oil until it shimmers and flows like water. Add the onion, bell pepper, and garlic, and sprinkle with a pinch or two of kosher salt. Cook for about 5 minutes, stirring, until the onions just begin to brown. Add the tomato sauce, beer, cider vinegar, brown sugar, chili powder, mustard, and Worcestershire sauce. Bring to a simmer. Stir to make sure the brown sugar is dissolved. Place the turkey thigh in the cooker.

2. Lock the lid in place, and bring the pot to high pressure (15 psi for stove top or 9 to 11 psi for electric).

STOVE TOP: Maintain pressure for 30 minutes, adjusting the burner as necessary.
ELECTRIC: Cook at high pressure for 30 minutes. When the timer goes off, turn the cooker off.

3. After cooking, use the *natural method* to release pressure.

4. Unlock and remove the lid; transfer the turkey to a plate or cutting board to cool.

5. Put the stove-top cooker over medium heat, or the electric cooker on "brown," and simmer the sauce for about 5 minutes, or until it's the consistency of a thick tomato sauce. Skim any visible fat from the surface and discard. Taste and adjust the seasoning.

6. When the turkey is cool enough to handle, shred or chop the meat, discarding any fat or gristle. Add the meat to the sauce, and heat through. Serve on the hamburger buns.

PER SERVING: CALORIES: 532; FAT: 20G; SODIUM: 1,253MG; CARBOHYDRATES: 36G; FIBER: 5G; PROTEIN: 53G

Indian-Style Chicken *in* Yogurt Sauce

SERVES 4

PRESSURE: High
TIME UNDER PRESSURE: 8 minutes
RELEASE: Natural

1 cup plain whole-milk yogurt

1 teaspoon kosher salt

1 teaspoon ground ginger

1 teaspoon ground paprika, smoked or sweet

½ teaspoon ground turmeric

1 teaspoon curry powder

¼ teaspoon ground cayenne pepper (optional)

1 teaspoon cornstarch

1¼ pounds boneless, skinless chicken thighs (4 to 6 thighs), trimmed of excess fat

Cooked rice, for serving

This chicken is based on an Indian tandoori-inspired dish in which chicken thighs marinate in spiced yogurt for several hours and are then grilled or broiled. When I forgot to marinate the chicken and ran out of time, this was the result. The cornstarch in the sauce keeps the yogurt from separating, so don't omit it. Add the cayenne pepper if you like a bit more spice to your chicken.

1. In a stove-top or electric pressure cooker, stir together the yogurt, kosher salt, ginger, paprika, turmeric, curry powder, cayenne (if using), and cornstarch. Let the sauce sit for 5 minutes so the cornstarch hydrates fully.

2. Add the chicken thighs to the cooker, and stir to coat. Distribute them in a single layer as much as possible.

3. Lock the lid in place, and bring the pot to high pressure (15 psi for stove top or 9 to 11 psi for electric).

STOVE TOP: Maintain pressure for 8 minutes, adjusting the burner as necessary.
ELECTRIC: Cook at high pressure for 8 minutes. When the timer goes off, turn the cooker off. Do not let it switch to the "warm" setting.

4. After cooking, use the *natural method* to release pressure.

5. Unlock and remove the lid. Serve the chicken and sauce over brown or white rice.

PER SERVING: CALORIES: 322; FAT: 12G; SODIUM: 747MG; CARBOHYDRATES: 6G; FIBER: 1G; PROTEIN: 45G

Chicken, Rice, and Mushroom Casserole

SERVES 4

PRESSURE: High
TIME UNDER PRESSURE: 12 minutes
RELEASE: Combination

GLUTEN FREE, ONE POT

1 tablespoon olive oil

½ cup chopped onion

1 garlic clove, minced

½ teaspoon kosher salt, plus additional for seasoning

1 small carrot, peeled and diced (about ¼ cup)

8 ounces white button or cremini mushrooms, sliced

¾ cup brown rice

1 pound boneless chicken thighs, cut into chunks

1¼ cups low-sodium chicken broth

½ teaspoon dried thyme

⅔ cup frozen peas, thawed

¼ cup heavy (whipping) cream

While I usually cook mushrooms according to the method on page 200 used for the "Sautéed" Mushrooms, for this casserole, it's easier and almost as good to sauté them with the other vegetables and let them flavor the rice. This all-in-one dinner is practically as easy as the old cream-of-mushroom-soup casseroles—but so much better that you'll never go back.

1. In a stove-top pressure cooker set over medium heat, or an electric cooker set to "brown," heat the olive oil until it shimmers and flows like water. Add the onion and garlic, and sprinkle with a pinch or two of kosher salt. Cook for about 3 minutes, stirring, until the onions just begin to brown. Add the carrot and mushrooms, and cook for 5 minutes, or until the carrots soften somewhat and the mushrooms give off most of their liquid and start to brown. Add the rice, and stir to coat with the olive oil.

2. Add the chicken, chicken broth, ½ teaspoon of kosher salt, and the thyme, and stir to combine.

3. Lock the lid in place, and bring the pot to high pressure (15 psi for stove top or 9 to 11 psi for electric).

STOVE TOP: Maintain pressure for 12 minutes, adjusting the burner as necessary.
ELECTRIC: Cook at high pressure for 12 minutes. When the timer goes off, turn the cooker off. Do not let it switch to the "warm" setting.

4. After cooking, use the *natural method* to release pressure for 10 minutes, then the *quick method* to release the remaining pressure.

5. Unlock and remove the lid. Gently stir the peas and heavy cream into the rice, and replace but *do not lock* the lid. Let the rice steam for 5 minutes more. Test the rice and make sure it's tender; it may take another 2 minutes or more. Ladle into bowls, and serve.

PER SERVING: CALORIES: 380; FAT: 13G; SODIUM: 351MG; CARBOHYDRATES: 37G; FIBER: 4G; PROTEIN: 29G

Duck Quarters *with* Apricots *and* Prunes

SERVES 2

PRESSURE: High
TIME UNDER PRESSURE: 35 minutes
RELEASE: Quick

1 teaspoon kosher salt, plus
    additional for seasoning
2 duck leg-thigh quarters
    (about 1¼ pounds)
1 tablespoon olive oil
½ cup sliced onion
½ cup red wine
1 tablespoon all-purpose flour
1½ cups low-sodium
    chicken broth
¼ cup prunes, halved
¼ cup dried apricots, halved
2 tablespoons brandy (optional)

Duck quarters aren't very common in American cuisine, but they make a delicious change from the more typical chicken thighs or quarters. If you can find them, I urge you to give this recipe a try. Pressure cooking ensures they'll be meltingly tender, and the fruit lends a sweetness to the sauce that pairs beautifully with the slightly gamy flavor of the duck.

1. Using 1 teaspoon of kosher salt, season the duck on both sides. Let sit for 20 minutes, or up to 1 hour. Blot off any moisture with paper towels before searing.

2. In a stove-top pressure cooker set over medium heat, or an electric cooker set to "brown," heat the olive oil until it shimmers and flows like water. Add the duck, skin-side down, and cook, undisturbed, for 5 to 6 minutes, or until golden brown. Turn the duck over, and cook on the other side for about 4 minutes more, or until brown. Remove the duck to a plate.

3. Pour off all but about 1 tablespoon of the fat in the cooker. Add the onion to the cooker, and sprinkle with a pinch or two of kosher salt. Cook for about 3 minutes, stirring, or until the onions just begin to brown. Pour in the red wine, and scrape the bottom of the pan to release the browned bits. Cook for 3 to 4 minutes, or until the wine is reduced by half.

4. In a small bowl, whisk together the flour and chicken broth. Pour the mixture into the cooker. Add the prunes and apricots. Place the duck over the fruit in the cooker.

5. Lock the lid in place, and bring the pot to high pressure (15 psi for stove top or 9 to 11 psi for electric).

STOVE TOP: Maintain pressure for 35 minutes, adjusting the burner as necessary.
ELECTRIC: Cook at high pressure for 35 minutes.

6. After cooking, use the *quick method* to release pressure.

7. Unlock and remove the lid. Remove the duck pieces to a serving platter, and tent them with aluminum foil. Degrease the sauce by straining it into a fat separator or by letting it sit for several minutes to let the fat rise to the surface, then spooning it off and discarding. If using a fat separator, pour the defatted sauce back into the cooker. Place the stove-top cooker over medium heat, or turn the electric cooker to "brown," and add the brandy (if using). Simmer the sauce for several minutes; then pour it over the duck, and serve.

PER SERVING: CALORIES: 665; FAT: 21G; SODIUM: 1,465MG; CARBOHYDRATES: 24G; FIBER: 3G; PROTEIN: 69G

Fish and Seafood

CHAPTER FOUR

Pressure cooking with fish and seafood gets a bit more complicated. On one hand, the steamy environment inside a pressure cooker can be ideal for the right type of seafood, like the Poached Salmon with Dill Sauce, Clams Steamed in Lemon-Garlic Broth, or Steamed Mussels in Porter Cream Sauce. On the other hand, much shellfish and finfish overcooks if you even look at it wrong; even the shortest cooking time turns shrimp and scallops rubbery. You can get around this in many ways, such as by adding delicate shrimp to a dish after the pressure is released or by cooking a dish most of the way through and adding fish fillets for a short blast of pressure to finish. Much more so than in the previous chapters, *for the best results, it's crucial to abide by the cooking time and pressure-release details for these recipes.*

109

Cioppino

SERVES 2

PRESSURE: High
TIME UNDER PRESSURE:
25 or 26 minutes
RELEASE: Quick

PALEO

2 tablespoons olive oil

½ cup chopped onion

1 small carrot, peeled, trimmed, and chopped

½ celery stalk, chopped

½ small fennel bulb, trimmed and chopped

1 small garlic clove, minced

½ teaspoon kosher salt, plus additional for seasoning

½ cup dry white wine

1 (14-ounce) can diced tomatoes, undrained

¾ cup seafood broth or water

1 bay leaf

¾ teaspoon dried Italian herbs

¼ teaspoon freshly ground black pepper

⅛ teaspoon ground cayenne pepper

3 to 6 ounces cleaned calamari rings (thawed if frozen) (optional)

8 to 12 mussels or clams (optional)

3-6 ounces firm white fish, such as tilapia, cod, halibut, or snapper, cut into bite-size chunks

3-6 ounces raw medium shrimp, or large shrimp, halved and peeled

1 or 2 tablespoons chopped fresh fennel fronds, parsley, or a combination

A San Francisco Italian specialty, cioppino was originally a humble soup made with fish scraps. Today it's a more spectacular fish and seafood dish. At the minimum, I call for a combination of fish and shrimp, but if you want more variety, you can add calamari, mussels, or clams. Whichever you use, plan on about 12 ounces of seafood total. While the list of ingredients is long, the soup goes together quickly.

1. In a stove-top pressure cooker set over medium heat, or an electric cooker set to "brown," heat the olive oil until it shimmers and flows like water. Add the onion, carrot, celery, fennel, and garlic, and sprinkle with a pinch or two of kosher salt. Cook for about 5 minutes, stirring, until the vegetables soften and begin to brown.

2. Add the white wine, tomatoes with their juice, seafood broth, bay leaf, Italian herbs, ½ teaspoon of kosher salt, black pepper, and cayenne pepper to the pressure cooker. If using calamari rings, add them now.

3. Lock the lid in place, and bring the pot to high pressure (15 psi for stove top or 9 to 11 psi for electric).

STOVE TOP: Maintain pressure for 25 minutes, adjusting the burner as necessary.
ELECTRIC: Cook at high pressure for 25 minutes.

4. After cooking, use the *quick method* to release pressure.

5. Unlock and remove the lid. If using mussels or clams, add them and replace the lid.

6. Lock the lid in place, and bring the pot to high pressure again.

STOVE TOP: Maintain pressure for 1 minute, adjusting the burner as necessary.

ELECTRIC: Cook at high pressure for 1 minute.

7. After cooking, use the **quick method** to release pressure.

8. Unlock and remove the lid. With the stove-top cooker set over medium-low heat, or the electric cooker set to "simmer," add the white fish and shrimp, and replace but do not lock the lid. Simmer for 3 to 4 minutes, or until the fish and shrimp are cooked through. Taste and adjust the seasoning, as needed. Serve topped with the fennel fronds.

PER SERVING: CALORIES: 381; FAT: 16G; SODIUM: 841MG; CARBOHYDRATES: 15G; FIBER: 4G; PROTEIN: 37G

Halibut *and* Bok Choy *with* Ginger Broth

SERVES 4

PRESSURE: High
TIME UNDER PRESSURE: 3 minutes
RELEASE: Quick

ONE POT

1 (20-ounce) halibut fillet, or 2 (10-ounce) fillets

½ teaspoon kosher salt

Freshly ground black pepper

3 or 4 baby bok choys, root ends trimmed

1 cup Mushroom Stock (page 268) or low-sodium vegetable stock

¾ cup water

2 tablespoons unseasoned rice vinegar

2 teaspoons soy sauce

2 tablespoons dry sherry or rice wine

1 tablespoon minced fresh ginger

2 or 3 large garlic cloves, minced or pressed (about 1 tablespoon)

8 ounces shiitake, white button, or cremini mushrooms, stemmed and sliced

2 scallions, sliced thin, divided

1 tablespoon toasted sesame oil, divided

Steamed whole fish topped with a flavorful mixture of vegetables, herbs, and spices is a classic Chinese dish, but a whole fish isn't always practical for the home cook. This recipe combines fish fillets and vegetables with aromatic broth for a delicious adaptation of the classic.

1. Season the halibut with the kosher salt and a generous amount of pepper.

2. Quarter the bok choys through the base; the core should keep the quarters intact.

3. To a stove-top or electric pressure cooker, add the Mushroom Stock, water, rice vinegar, soy sauce, sherry, ginger, and garlic, and stir to combine. Arrange the bok choy quarters in a single layer, as much as possible, in the cooker, and scatter the mushrooms over them. Place the fish on top.

4. Lock the lid in place, and bring the pot to high pressure (15 psi for stove top or 9 to 11 psi for electric).

STOVE TOP: Maintain pressure for 3 minutes.
ELECTRIC: Cook at high pressure for 3 minutes.

5. After cooking, use the *quick method* to release pressure.

6. Unlock and remove the lid. Using a large slotted spatula, gently cut the halibut into 4 pieces. If it is not quite done in the center, replace but *do not lock* the lid and steam for 2 minutes more, or until done. Using the spatula, divide the bok choy and mushrooms among 4 bowls, and top each with 1 piece of fish. Ladle the broth over the fish and vegetables. Garnish with the scallions, drizzle with the sesame oil, and serve.

PER SERVING: CALORIES: 466; FAT: 8G; SODIUM: 2,875MG; CARBOHYDRATES: 71G; FIBER: 8G; PROTEIN: 55G

Steamed Mussels *in* Porter Cream Sauce

SERVES 2 AS A MAIN COURSE OR 4 AS AN APPETIZER

PRESSURE: High
TIME UNDER PRESSURE: 1 minute
RELEASE: Quick

ONE POT

1 tablespoon olive oil

2 garlic cloves, minced

2 scallions, minced (about ⅓ cup)

1 (12-ounce) bottle porter or other dark beer

⅛ teaspoon red pepper flakes

2 pounds mussels, scrubbed and debearded

2 tablespoons heavy (whipping) cream

I have nothing against a nice lemon-and-garlic broth for steamed mussels; in fact, I often use the broth from the Clams Steamed in Lemon-Garlic Broth recipe (page 114) for mussels. But this easy sauce is an unusual, easy change. Have a baguette on hand to sop up the sauce—you won't want to leave any on the plate.

1. In a stove-top pressure cooker set over medium heat, or an electric cooker set to "brown," heat the olive oil until it shimmers and flows like water. Add the garlic and scallions, and cook for about 3 minutes, stirring, until the scallions just begin to brown. Pour in the beer, stirring for 1 minute, or until the foam dissipates. Add the red pepper flakes and mussels, and stir to coat with the liquid.

2. Lock the lid in place, and bring the pot to high pressure (15 psi for stove top or 9 to 11 psi for electric).

STOVE TOP: Maintain pressure for 1 minute, adjusting the burner as necessary.
ELECTRIC: Cook at high pressure for 1 minute.

3. After cooking, use the *quick method* to release pressure.

4. Unlock and remove the lid. The mussels should be opened; if not, replace *but don't lock* the lid, and cook over medium-high heat in a stove-top cooker, or on "brown" for an electric cooker, for 1 to 2 minutes more. *Discard any mussels that still have not opened.* Stir in the heavy cream; then pour the mussels with their sauce into a large serving bowl, and enjoy.

PER SERVING (MAIN COURSE): CALORIES: 584; FAT: 23G; SODIUM: 1,313MG; CARBOHYDRATES: 25G; FIBER: 0G; PROTEIN: 56G

Clams Steamed *in* Lemon-Garlic Broth

SERVES 2 AS A MAIN COURSE
OR 4 AS AN APPETIZER

PRESSURE: High
TIME UNDER PRESSURE: 2 minutes
RELEASE: Quick

ONE POT, PALEO FRIENDLY

2 tablespoons unsalted butter,
    divided

2 garlic cloves, minced

½ cup dry white wine

2 pounds littleneck clams,
    thoroughly scrubbed

1 tablespoon freshly squeezed
    lemon juice, plus additional
    as needed

2 tablespoons chopped
    fresh parsley

Like mussels, clams take well to a pressure cooker. Their more delicate flavor is a good match for this classic lemon-and-garlic broth, but feel free to experiment with bolder flavors as well.

1. In a stove-top pressure cooker set over medium heat, or an electric cooker set to "brown," heat 1 tablespoon of butter until it stops foaming. Add the garlic, and cook for 1 to 2 minutes, or until fragrant. Pour in the white wine. Add the clams, and stir to coat with the liquid.

2. Lock the lid in place, and bring the pot to high pressure (15 psi for stove top or 9 to 11 psi for electric).

STOVE TOP: Maintain pressure for 2 minutes, adjusting the burner as necessary.
ELECTRIC: Cook at high pressure for 2 minutes.

3. After cooking, use the *quick method* to release pressure.

4. Unlock and remove the lid. The clams should be opened; if not, replace *but don't lock* the lid, and cook over medium-high in a stove-top cooker, or on "brown" for an electric cooker, for 1 to 2 minutes more. *Discard any clams that still have not opened.* Cut the remaining 1 tablespoon of butter into 4 to 6 small pieces. Stir in the butter pieces, lemon juice, and parsley. When the butter has melted, pour the clams with their sauce into a large serving bowl, and enjoy.

TIP *The clams and sauce from this recipe are also great tossed with cooked linguine; simmer the sauce to reduce it slightly to thicken and intensify the flavors.*

PER SERVING (MAIN COURSE): CALORIES: 745; FAT: 20G; SODIUM: 596MG; CARBOHYDRATES: 35G; FIBER: 0G; PROTEIN: 91G

Snapper Veracruz

SERVES 2

PRESSURE: High
TIME UNDER PRESSURE: 6 minutes total
RELEASE: Combination

PALEO

¼ teaspoon kosher salt, plus additional for seasoning

2 (7-ounce) snapper fillets

Freshly ground black pepper

2 tablespoons olive oil

½ cup sliced onion

2 large garlic cloves, minced

1 small jalapeño pepper, seeded and minced (about 1 tablespoon)

1 (14.5-ounce) can diced tomatoes, drained

¼ cup sliced green olives

1 bay leaf

½ teaspoon dried oregano

2 tablespoons chopped fresh parsley, divided

3 tablespoons capers, divided

Steamed rice, for serving

Traditionally made with a whole red snapper, this dish features the definite Spanish influence common to Veracruz (Mexico) cooking: olives, capers, and parsley. This scaled-down version uses fish fillets for two servings. If you can't find snapper fillets, substitute tilapia or cod. Because the fish overcooks so easily, it's important to keep it refrigerated until you add it to the pressure cooker and pay very close attention to the cooking and release times.

1. Using ¼ teaspoon of kosher salt, sprinkle the fish fillets, and season them with pepper. Refrigerate while you make the sauce.

2. In a stove-top pressure cooker set over medium heat, or an electric cooker set to "brown," heat the olive oil until it shimmers and flows like water. Add the onion, and sprinkle with a pinch or two of kosher salt. Cook for about 5 minutes, stirring, until the onions begin to brown. Add the garlic and jalapeño, and cook for 1 or 2 minutes more, until the garlic is fragrant and the onions are mostly browned.

3. Add the tomatoes, olives, bay leaf, oregano, 1 tablespoon of parsley, and 1½ tablespoons of capers to the cooker.

4. Lock the lid in place, and bring the pot to high pressure (15 psi for stove top or 9 to 11 psi for electric).

STOVE TOP: Maintain pressure for 5 minutes, adjusting the burner as necessary.
ELECTRIC: Cook at high pressure for 5 minutes.

5. After cooking, use the *quick method* to release pressure.

6. Unlock and remove the lid. Remove the fish from the refrigerator, and lay the fillets on top of the sauce in the pressure cooker.

7. Lock the lid in place again, and bring the pot to high pressure (15 psi for stove top or 9 to 11 psi for electric).

STOVE TOP: Maintain pressure for 1 minute, adjusting the burner as necessary.
ELECTRIC: Cook at high pressure for 1 minute. When the timer goes off, turn the cooker off. Do not let it switch to the "warm" setting.

8. After cooking, use the *natural method* to release pressure for 4 minutes, then the *quick method* to release the remaining pressure.

9. Unlock and remove the lid. Using a large spatula, carefully remove the fish fillets and transfer them to two plates. Spoon the sauce over the fish. Garnish with the remaining 1 tablespoon of parsley and 1½ tablespoons of capers. Serve with the steamed white or brown rice.

TIP *This sauce freezes very well; if you like it, make a double batch (through step 5) and divide it in half. Freeze or refrigerate the portions of sauce. To finish the dish, place one portion of the sauce in the pressure cooker, and heat it to a boil. Finish the dish starting at step 6, and serve.*

PER SERVING: CALORIES: 374; FAT: 18G; SODIUM: 871MG; CARBOHYDRATES: 18G; FIBER: 4G; PROTEIN: 43G

Fish *and* Vegetable "Tagine" *with* Chermoula

SERVES 2

PRESSURE: High
TIME UNDER PRESSURE: 6 minutes total
RELEASE: Combination

GLUTEN FREE, ONE POT

FOR THE CHERMOULA
4 large garlic cloves
1 cup fresh cilantro leaves
1 cup fresh parsley leaves
¼ cup freshly squeezed lemon
    juice (about 2 lemons)
1½ teaspoons kosher salt
1 heaping teaspoon ground
    sweet paprika
¼ teaspoon ground cumin
¼ teaspoon ground
    cayenne pepper
2 tablespoons olive oil

FOR THE FISH AND VEGETABLES
2 (7-ounce) tilapia fillets
¼ teaspoon kosher salt
10 ounces Yukon gold potatoes
    (about 2 medium or
    3 small), peeled and sliced
    ¼ inch thick
½ medium red bell pepper,
    cut into bite-size chunks
½ medium green bell pepper,
    cut into bite-size chunks
1 very small onion, sliced
¼ cup water
1 large tomato, seeded
    and diced

In Morocco, whole fish and vegetables are often cooked in a *tagine*, a special baking dish designed to keep food moist while it cooks slowly. Fortunately, you don't need the special dish to make this traditional recipe. The *chermoula*—a traditional Moroccan herb sauce—flavors the fish and vegetables and keeps them from drying out.

To make the chermoula

1. Into the chute of a small running food processor, drop the garlic cloves, one at a time, and process until minced. Add the cilantro, parsley, lemon juice, kosher salt, paprika, cumin, and cayenne pepper, and process until mostly smooth. With the processor still running, slowly drizzle in the olive oil, and process until the sauce is emulsified.

2. If you don't have a food processor, finely mince the garlic, cilantro, and parsley. Transfer to a small bowl, and stir in the lemon juice, kosher salt, paprika, cumin, and cayenne pepper. Slowly whisk in the olive oil. The sauce won't be as smooth as if prepared in a food processor, but it will taste good.

To make the fish and vegetables

1. Sprinkle both sides of the fish fillets lightly with the kosher salt, and brush with 3 tablespoons of chermoula. Refrigerate the fish.

2. To a stove-top or electric pressure cooker, add the potato slices, red bell pepper, green bell pepper, and onion. Pour in ⅓ cup of chermoula, and gently toss the vegetables to coat. Pour the water over the vegetables.

3. Lock the lid in place, and bring the pot to high pressure (15 psi for stove top or 9 to 11 psi for electric).

STOVE TOP: Maintain pressure for 5 minutes, adjusting the burner as necessary.
ELECTRIC: Cook at high pressure for 5 minutes.

4. After cooking, use the *quick method* to release pressure.

5. Unlock and remove the lid. Sprinkle the tomato over the vegetables in the pressure cooker, and lay the fillets on top. Drizzle with the remaining chermoula.

6. Lock the lid in place again, and bring the pot to high pressure (15 psi for stove top or 9 to 11 psi for electric).

STOVE TOP: Maintain pressure for 1 minute, adjusting the burner as necessary.
ELECTRIC: Cook at high pressure for 1 minute. When the timer goes off, turn the cooker off. Do not let it switch to the "warm" setting.

7. After cooking, use the *natural method* to release pressure for 4 minutes, then the *quick method* to release the remaining pressure.

8. Unlock and remove the lid. Using a large spatula, carefully remove the fish fillets and vegetables and divide them between 2 plates. Spoon any residual sauce over the fish, and serve.

PER SERVING: CALORIES: 479; FAT: 17G; SODIUM: 2,157MG; CARBOHYDRATES: 43G; FIBER: 7G; PROTEIN: 44G

Salmon *and* Vegetables "en Papillote"

SERVES 2

PRESSURE: High
TIME UNDER PRESSURE: 4 minutes
RELEASE: Quick

GLUTEN FREE, ONE POT

1 teaspoon unsalted butter, at room temperature

½ teaspoon kosher salt, plus additional for seasoning

1 (12-ounce) skinless salmon fillet

Freshly ground black pepper

2 tablespoons very finely minced scallions

1 small tomato, seeded and diced (about ½ cup)

⅓ cup sugar snap peas, trimmed

¼ cup "Sautéed" Mushrooms (page 200)

2 or 3 whole flat-leaf parsley leaves

1 cup water, for steaming (double-check the pressure cooker manual to confirm amount, and follow the manual if there is a discrepancy)

The culinary term "en papillote" literally means "in paper"—the traditional envelope for such dishes being parchment paper. Since parchment won't survive the steam of a pressure cooker very well, aluminum foil makes a good substitute. The butter under the fish and vegetables forms a light sauce as the fish steams, so there's no need to make a separate sauce. You can use any vegetables you like, so long as they're cooked in advance or will cook in the time it takes to steam the salmon (see Pressure Cooking Time Charts, page 277).

1. Take a piece of aluminum foil, 15 by 20 inches or larger, and smear the butter in the center, spreading it out so the salmon will fit on the buttered portion. Using ½ teaspoon of kosher salt, season each side of the salmon. Add several grinds of pepper. You may find it easiest to season the less attractive side of the salmon and lay it down on the butter, then season the top side.

2. Sprinkle the scallions over the fish; then do the same with the tomato. Scatter the peas and mushrooms around the salmon, and top with the parsley leaves.

3. Lift the shorter sides of the foil, and bring the edges together right above the salmon, like a tent. Fold them over several times, leaving some air space over the fish and vegetables. Then fold the ends together, crimping the folds tightly with your fingers.

4. To a stove-top or electric pressure cooker, add the water and insert the steamer basket or trivet. Place the salmon packet on top of the steamer insert.

5. Lock the lid in place, and bring the pot to high pressure (15 psi for stove top or 9 to 11 psi for electric).

STOVE TOP: Maintain pressure for 4 minutes, adjusting the burner as necessary.
ELECTRIC: Cook at high pressure for 4 minutes.

6. After cooking, use the *quick method* to release pressure.

7. Unlock and remove the lid. Using tongs or a large slotted spatula, remove the salmon packet to a cutting board. Open the foil, and carefully slide the salmon and vegetables onto a serving plate, pour the sauce over everything, and enjoy.

PER SERVING: CALORIES: 337; FAT: 20G; SODIUM: 699MG; CARBOHYDRATES: 4G; FIBER: 1G; PROTEIN: 34G

Smoked Salmon Chowder

SERVES 2

PRESSURE: High
TIME UNDER PRESSURE: 6 minutes total
RELEASE: Combination

ONE POT

1 tablespoon unsalted butter

2 large scallions, chopped

½ teaspoon kosher salt, plus additional for seasoning

1 tablespoon all-purpose flour

¼ cup dry white wine, dry vermouth, or dry sherry

2½ cups whole milk

2 small (or 1 medium) red or Yukon gold potatoes (about 5 ounces), peeled and cut into ½-inch cubes

1 (4- or 5-ounce) salmon fillet, skinned

1½ ounces hot-smoked salmon, chopped or flaked into small chunks

3 teaspoons chopped fresh dill, divided

1 teaspoon lemon zest

Freshly ground black pepper

With family in the Pacific Northwest, I'm often the recipient of smoked salmon as a gift. This is one of my favorite ways to use the last of a can or package. It doesn't take much to turn a really good chowder into something extraordinary.

1. In a stove-top pressure cooker set over medium heat, or an electric pressure cooker set to "brown," melt the butter. When the butter is foaming, add the scallions and sprinkle with ½ teaspoon of kosher salt. Cook for 1 minute, stirring, until softened. Add the flour, and cook for 2 to 3 minutes, or until it turns a very light tan color. Add the white wine, and cook for about 2 minutes, or until the mixture has thickened. Add the milk, and whisk until the mixture is smooth. Add the potatoes.

2. Lock the lid in place, and bring the pot to high pressure (15 psi for stove top or 9 to 11 psi for electric).

STOVE TOP: Maintain pressure for 5 minutes, adjusting the burner as necessary.
ELECTRIC: Cook at high pressure for 5 minutes.

3. After cooking, use the *quick method* to release pressure.

4. Unlock and remove the lid. Add the raw salmon fillet, and replace the lid.

5. Lock the lid in place, and bring the pot to high pressure (15 psi for stove top or 9 to 11 psi for electric).

STOVE TOP: Maintain pressure for 1 minute, adjusting the burner as necessary.
ELECTRIC: Cook at high pressure for 1 minute. When the timer goes off, turn the cooker off. Do not let it switch to the "warm" setting. →

6. After cooking, use the ***natural method*** to release pressure for 4 minutes, then the ***quick method*** to release the remaining pressure.

7. Unlock and remove the lid. Using a large slotted spoon or fish spatula, remove the salmon fillet to a plate or cutting board. Use a fork to break it into chunks. Don't worry if the fish is not completely cooked; it will finish cooking later.

8. Place the stove-top pressure cooker over low heat, or turn the electric cooker to "brown." Add the salmon chunks, smoked salmon, 2 teaspoons of dill, and the lemon zest, and simmer for 1 to 2 minutes, or until the fish is heated through. Adjust the seasoning with additional kosher salt and pepper. Sprinkle the remaining 1 teaspoon of dill over the soup just before serving.

TIP *This soup is a great way to use leftover cooked salmon, which typically doesn't reheat well. Simply cook the soup at step 2 for 7 minutes for a stove-top cooker or 9 minutes for an electric cooker. Skip steps 4, 5, and 6, and add the chunked cooked salmon at step 8, along with the smoked salmon and other ingredients.*

PER SERVING: CALORIES: 531; FAT: 21G; SODIUM: 955MG; CARBOHYDRATES: 48G; FIBER: 4G; PROTEIN: 32G

Poached Salmon *with* Dill Sauce

SERVES 4

PRESSURE: High
TIME UNDER PRESSURE: 4 minutes
RELEASE: Quick

1 (20-ounce) center-cut salmon fillet

½ teaspoon kosher salt

Freshly ground black pepper

Zest of 1 small lemon (about 2 teaspoons)

Juice of 1 small lemon (about 2 tablespoons)

½ cup dry white wine

2 cups low-sodium chicken broth or fish broth

1 bay leaf

4 scallions, chopped

3 or 4 fresh dill sprigs, plus 3 tablespoons minced fresh dill

2 tablespoons heavy (whipping) cream

When I first read about poaching salmon in the pressure cooker, I was dubious. Now that I've tried it, I'll never poach salmon any other way. Sure, it's fast, but it also results in a fabulous texture—velvety and moist without being mushy at all. Plus, you can turn the braising liquid into a quick, delicious sauce.

1. Season the salmon with the kosher salt and a generous amount of pepper. To a stove-top or electric pressure cooker, add the lemon zest, lemon juice, white wine, chicken broth, and bay leaf. Place the steamer trivet or basket in the pressure cooker, and then place the salmon on top of it. The fish should be partly submerged in the liquid. Scatter the scallions and dill sprigs over the salmon.

2. Lock the lid in place, and bring the pot to high pressure (15 psi for stove top or 9 to 11 psi for electric).

STOVE TOP: Maintain pressure for 4 minutes, adjusting the burner as necessary.
ELECTRIC: Cook at high pressure for 4 minutes.

3. After cooking, use the *quick method* to release pressure.

4. Unlock and remove the lid. Using a large slotted spatula, remove the salmon to a serving platter and tent it with a piece of aluminum foil to keep it warm. ➞

5. Remove the steamer trivet or basket, and place the stove-top cooker over medium-high heat, or turn the electric cooker to "brown." Bring the liquid to a boil, and cook for about 5 minutes, or until the liquid is reduced to about one-third of its original volume. Remove the bay leaf and the dill sprigs, and add the heavy cream. Return to a simmer for 1 to 2 minutes to thicken the sauce. Pour the sauce over the salmon, and serve.

TIP *If you're cooking for two only, make the full recipe and use the leftovers in Smoked Salmon Chowder (page 123).*

PER SERVING: CALORIES: 250; FAT: 12G; SODIUM: 395MG; CARBOHYDRATES: 3G; FIBER: 0G; PROTEIN: 29G

Succotash *with* Shrimp

SERVES 2

PRESSURE: High
TIME UNDER PRESSURE: 6 minutes
RELEASE: Quick

GLUTEN FREE, ONE POT

1 tablespoon plus ¼ teaspoon
   kosher salt, divided

1 quart water

¼ pound dried lima beans

1 tablespoon olive oil

8 ounces raw medium shrimp,
   peeled and deveined

1 garlic clove, minced

1 cup fresh corn kernels
   (about 1 ear) or frozen corn

½ medium green bell pepper,
   cut into ½-inch pieces
   (about ½ cup)

½ cup onion, chopped

¼ teaspoon ground
   cayenne pepper

1 bay leaf

1¼ cups low-sodium
   chicken broth

1 large tomato, seeded
   and chopped

¼ cup chopped fresh parsley,
   basil, or a combination

Usually a side dish, succotash easily becomes a healthy main course here with the addition of shrimp. Once the beans are soaked, the dish goes together in less than 20 minutes, making it a perfect busy weeknight dinner.

1. In a large bowl, dissolve 1 tablespoon of kosher salt in the water. Add the lima beans, and soak at room temperature for 8 to 24 hours. Drain and rinse.

2. In a stove-top pressure cooker set over medium heat, or an electric cooker set to "brown," heat the olive oil until it shimmers and flows like water. Add the shrimp and the garlic, and cook for about 2 minutes, stirring, until the shrimp begin to turn pink and opaque but are not quite done. Remove the shrimp to a bowl, and set aside.

3. To the pressure cooker, add the drained, soaked lima beans, corn, green bell pepper, onion, cayenne pepper, bay leaf, chicken broth, and the remaining ¼ teaspoon of kosher salt.

4. Lock the lid in place, and bring the pot to high pressure (15 psi for stove top or 9 to 11 psi for electric).

STOVE TOP: Maintain pressure for 6 minutes, adjusting the burner as necessary.
ELECTRIC: Cook at high pressure for 6 minutes.

5. After cooking, use the *quick method* to release pressure.

6. Unlock and remove the lid. Place the stove-top cooker over medium heat, or turn the electric cooker to "brown," and bring to a simmer. Add the tomato and reserved shrimp, and cook for about 2 minutes, or until the tomato is warmed through and the shrimp have finished cooking. Right before serving, stir in the parsley.

PER SERVING: CALORIES: 371; FAT: 10G; SODIUM: 624G;
CARBOHYDRATES: 37G; FIBER: 7G; PROTEIN: 35G

Soups, Stews, and Chilies

CHAPTER FIVE

If there's a cliché about pressure cookers, it's that their best and highest use is for soups and stews. Like most clichés, this one contains a core of truth. From hearty stews to delicate, broth-based soups, almost all are naturals for the accelerated reactions of pressure cooking. Stew meats tenderize quickly, so stews that usually take hours to cook are done in less than half the time. And flavor reactions are practically instantaneous, so a soup that ordinarily needs to simmer for 30 minutes can be finished in 10. Because there's virtually no evaporation in pressure cooking, you'll start with less liquid than in recipes that use traditional cooking methods; resist the urge to add more.

French Onion Soup

SERVES 2

PRESSURE: High
TIME UNDER PRESSURE:
35 minutes total
RELEASE: Quick

2 tablespoons unsalted butter,
    divided

4 cups thinly sliced white or
    yellow onions, divided

½ teaspoon kosher salt, plus
    additional for seasoning

¼ cup dry sherry

2 cups low-sodium
    chicken broth

½ cup Beef Stock (page 264),
    Mushroom Stock (page 268),
    or low-sodium broth

½ teaspoon
    Worcestershire sauce

¼ teaspoon dried thyme

1 teaspoon sherry vinegar
    or red wine vinegar, plus
    additional as needed

1 ounce Gruyère or other
    Swiss-style cheese, coarsely
    grated (about ⅓ cup)

2 thin slices French or
    Italian bread

French onion soup recipes seem to fall into two camps. Most are all about the bread and cheese on top, sometimes to the point where you feel like you're eating a soggy grilled cheese sandwich. Not only does a giant raft of bread and cheese add lots of calories, but it also overpowers the soup, which seems almost like an afterthought. I prefer the soup to be the star of the show. My conventionally cooked onion soup gets a deep color from long-cooked onions, which have a chance to brown slowly in an open pan. Since onions in the pressure cooker never develop that dark color, I use mushroom or beef stock to deepen not only the color but also the flavor.

1. In a stove-top pressure cooker set over medium-high heat, or an electric cooker set to "brown," heat 1 tablespoon of butter until it stops foaming, and then add 1 cup of onions. Sprinkle with a pinch or two of kosher salt, and stir to coat with the butter. Cook the onions in a single layer for about 4 minutes, or until browned. Resist the urge to stir them until you see them browning. Stir them to expose the other side to the heat, and cook for 4 minutes more. The onions should be quite browned but still slightly firm. Remove the onions from the pan, and set aside.

2. Pour the sherry into the pot, and stir to scrape up the browned bits from the bottom. When the sherry has mostly evaporated, add the remaining 1 tablespoon of butter, and let it melt. Stir in the remaining 3 cups of onions, and sprinkle with ½ teaspoon of kosher salt.

3. Lock the lid in place, and bring the pot to high pressure (15 psi for stove top or 9 to 11 psi for electric).

STOVE TOP: Maintain pressure for 25 minutes, adjusting the burner as necessary.
ELECTRIC: Cook at high pressure for 25 minutes.

4. After cooking, use the *quick method* to release pressure.

5. Unlock and remove the lid.

6. The onions should be pale and very soft, with a lot of liquid in the pot. Add the chicken broth, Beef Stock, Worcestershire sauce, and thyme.

7. Lock the lid in place, and bring the pot to high pressure (15 psi for stove top or 9 to 11 psi for electric).

STOVE TOP: Maintain pressure for 10 minutes, adjusting the burner as necessary.
ELECTRIC: Cook at high pressure for 10 minutes.

8. After cooking, use the *quick method* to release pressure.

9. Unlock and remove the lid. Stir in the sherry vinegar, and taste. The soup should be balanced between the sweetness of the onions, the savory stock, and the acid from the vinegar. If it seems bland, add a pinch or two of kosher salt or a little more vinegar. Stir in the reserved cup of onions, and keep warm while you prepare the cheese toasts.

10. Preheat the broiler. Reserve 2 tablespoons of the cheese, and sprinkle the remaining cheese evenly over the 2 bread slices. Place the bread slices on a sheet pan under the broiler for 2 to 3 minutes, or until the cheese melts.

11. Place 1 tablespoon of the reserved cheese in each of 2 bowls. Ladle the soup into the bowls, float a toast slice on top of each, and serve.

PER SERVING: CALORIES: 366; FAT: 17G; SODIUM: 1,122MG; CARBOHYDRATES: 40G; FIBER: 6G; PROTEIN: 14G

Mushroom Soup *with* Snow Peas *and* Scallions

SERVES 2

PRESSURE: High
TIME UNDER PRESSURE: 5 minutes
RELEASE: Quick

GLUTEN FREE, ONE POT, PALEO FRIENDLY, VEGAN

8 ounces white button or cremini mushrooms, washed and stems trimmed

2 teaspoons sesame oil

¼ teaspoon kosher salt

¼ cup plus 1 tablespoon water, divided

1 teaspoon cornstarch

2 cups Mushroom Stock (page 268) or low-sodium broth

1 tablespoon soy sauce (choose a wheat-free brand for a gluten-free soup)

½ teaspoon Chinese five-spice powder

1 cup snow peas, trimmed, strings removed

2 scallions, sliced thin

If your idea of mushroom soup is the thick, creamy style made popular by the canned soup of the casserole crowd, this recipe may come as a surprise. Mushroom stock and an unusual method for cooking mushrooms result in a simple yet intense soup that needs only a little spice and a couple of garnishes to finish it off.

1. Cut medium-size mushrooms into quarters and large mushrooms into eighths.

2. To a stove-top or electric pressure cooker, add the mushrooms, sesame oil, and kosher salt. Pour in ¼ cup of water.

3. Lock the lid in place, and bring the pot to high pressure (15 psi for stove top or 9 to 11 psi for electric).

STOVE TOP: Maintain pressure for 5 minutes, adjusting the burner as necessary.
ELECTRIC: Cook at high pressure for 5 minutes.

4. After cooking, use the *quick method* to release pressure.

5. Unlock and remove the lid. Because the mushrooms exude water as they cook, there will be more liquid in the pot and the mushrooms will be smaller than when they started cooking. Turn the heat to medium-high under the stove-top pressure cooker, or turn the electric cooker to "brown." Bring to a boil, and cook for about 5 minutes, or until all the water evaporates. The mushrooms will begin to sizzle in the remaining sesame oil. Let them brown for 1 minute; then stir to brown the other sides.

6. In a small bowl, mix the remaining 1 tablespoon of water with the cornstarch. To the pot, add the Mushroom Stock, soy sauce, Chinese five-spice powder, and the cornstarch mixture, and bring to a simmer. Add the snow peas, and simmer for 3 to 4 minutes, or until the peas are mostly tender with a bit of crunch. Stir in the scallions, ladle into 2 bowls, and serve.

TIP *The method for cooking the mushrooms in this recipe may seem strange; in fact, it runs counter to what most chefs and authors recommend. But once you try it, I think you'll agree that it's the best. For an explanation of why it works, see the recipe description for the "Sautéed" Mushrooms (page 200).*

PER SERVING: CALORIES: 150; FAT: 6G; SODIUM: 1,497MG; CARBOHYDRATES: 13G; FIBER: 4G; PROTEIN: 12G

Borscht

SERVES 4

PRESSURE: High
TIME UNDER PRESSURE:
22 minutes total
RELEASE: Combination

**GLUTEN FREE, ONE POT,
PALEO FRIENDLY**

1 cup water, for steaming
(double-check the pressure
cooker manual to confirm
amount, and follow
the manual if there is
a discrepancy)

2 medium beets, roots and
stem ends trimmed, halved

1 tablespoon olive oil

1 cup chopped onion

2 garlic cloves, minced

1 quart Beef Stock (page 264),
Mushroom Stock (page 268),
or low-sodium broth

1 teaspoon dried marjoram
or oregano

1 bay leaf

2 cups shredded red or
green cabbage

2 celery stalks, trimmed and
cut about ¼ inch thick

1 carrot, peeled and cut about
¼ inch thick

1 teaspoon kosher salt

1 or 2 tablespoons red wine
vinegar, divided

½ teaspoon freshly ground
black pepper

2 tablespoons minced fresh dill

4 tablespoons sour cream
(optional)

Classic peasant fare, borscht has as many versions as there are cooks in Russia. It can be full of beef with the vegetables in the background, or it can be vegetarian, and everything in between. What's common to all these recipes is beets, which give the soup a beautiful color and delicious sweetness. My version is heavy on the vegetables, but beef or mushroom stock gives it a meaty depth of flavor.

1. To a stove-top or electric pressure cooker, add the water and insert the steamer basket or trivet. Add the beets to the steamer insert.

2. Lock the lid in place, and bring the pot to high pressure (15 psi for stove top or 9 to 11 psi for electric).

STOVE TOP: Maintain pressure for 9 minutes, adjusting the burner as necessary.
ELECTRIC: Cook at high pressure for 9 minutes. When the timer goes off, turn the cooker off. Do not let it switch to the "warm" setting.

3. After cooking, use the *natural method* to release pressure.

4. Unlock and remove the lid. Using tongs, remove the beets and set them aside until cool enough to handle. Using a paring knife, peel and then dice the beets. Remove the steamer from the cooker, and dump out the water.

5. In a stove-top pressure cooker set over medium heat, or an electric cooker set to "brown," heat the olive oil until it shimmers and flows like water. Add the onion and garlic. Cook, stirring, for about 5 minutes, or until the onions are browned.

6. Add the Beef Stock, marjoram, bay leaf, cabbage, celery, carrots, kosher salt, and diced beets to the pressure cooker.

7. Lock the lid in place, and bring the pot to high pressure (15 psi for stove top or 9 to 11 psi for electric).

STOVE TOP: Maintain pressure for 13 minutes, adjusting the burner as necessary.
ELECTRIC: Cook at high pressure for 13 minutes.

8. After cooking, use the *quick method* to release pressure.

9. Unlock and remove the lid. Stir in 1 tablespoon of red wine vinegar, the pepper, and the dill. Taste and adjust the seasoning, adding the remaining 1 tablespoon of red wine vinegar, if necessary. Ladle the soup into 4 bowls, top each with 1 tablespoon of sour cream (if using), and serve.

TIP *Cook extra beets when making this soup, and save them to make Beet Salad with Mint and Feta Cheese (page 214) later in the week.*

PER SERVING: CALORIES: 132; FAT: 7G; SODIUM: 1,096MG; CARBOHYDRATES: 13G; FIBER: 3G; PROTEIN: 7G

Roasted Tomato Soup

SERVES 2

PRESSURE: High
TIME UNDER PRESSURE: 10 minutes
RELEASE: Quick

ONE POT, PALEO

3 tablespoons olive oil

½ cup sliced onion

Kosher salt

1 medium garlic clove, sliced or minced

¼ cup dry or medium-dry sherry

1 (14.5-ounce) can fire-roasted tomatoes

1 small roasted red bell pepper, cut into chunks (about ¼ cup)

¾ cup Chicken Stock (page 262) or low-sodium broth

⅛ teaspoon ground cumin

⅛ teaspoon freshly ground black pepper

1 tablespoon heavy (whipping) cream (optional)

Some soups seem as though they should take forever to make, and this is one of them. When I started making it, it was a labor of love, or maybe insanity. It required first roasting tomatoes and peppers, then peeling and seeding them—and that was even before starting to make the actual soup. Then I discovered a shortcut: fire-roasted tomatoes, which meant I could make this soup anytime I wanted. Add the speed of a pressure cooker, and what used to take all day long now takes less than half an hour. You can leave the soup chunky or purée it if you prefer a smooth soup.

1. In a stove-top pressure cooker set over medium heat, or an electric cooker set to "brown," heat the olive oil until it shimmers and flows like water. Add the onions, and sprinkle with a pinch or two of kosher salt. Cook for about 5 minutes, stirring, until the onions just begin to brown. Add the garlic, and cook for 1 to 2 minutes more, or until fragrant.

2. Pour in the sherry, and simmer for 1 to 2 minutes, or until the sherry is reduced by half, scraping up any browned bits from the bottom of the pan. Add the tomatoes, roasted red bell pepper, and Chicken Stock to the pressure cooker. →

3. Lock the lid in place, and bring the pot to high pressure (15 psi for stove top or 9 to 11 psi for electric).

STOVE TOP: Maintain pressure for 10 minutes, adjusting the burner as necessary.
ELECTRIC: Cook at high pressure for 10 minutes.

4. After cooking, use the ***quick method*** to release pressure.

5. For a smooth soup, blend using an immersion or standard blender. Add the cumin and pepper, and adjust the salt, if necessary. If you like a creamier soup, stir in the heavy cream.

TIP *If using a standard blender, be careful. Steam can build up and blow the lid off if the soup is very hot. Hold the lid on with a towel, and blend in batches, if necessary; don't fill the jar more than halfway full.*

PER SERVING: CALORIES: 287; FAT: 24G; SODIUM: 641MG; CARBOHYDRATES: 16G; FIBER: 4G; PROTEIN: 4G

Carrot Soup

SERVES 2

PRESSURE: High
TIME UNDER PRESSURE: 10 minutes
RELEASE: Quick

GLUTEN FREE, ONE POT

2 teaspoons unsalted butter

⅓ cup coarsely chopped onion

8 ounces carrots, peeled and cut into ½-inch-thick coins

¼ teaspoon kosher salt, plus additional as needed

¼ cup dry sherry

1½ cups Chicken Stock (page 262) or low-sodium broth

⅛ teaspoon vanilla extract

Pinch ground cayenne pepper

¼ cup fresh or pasteurized carrot juice

3 teaspoons plain, whole-milk yogurt, divided

1 teaspoon minced fresh chives (optional)

Years ago at a San Francisco restaurant, our waiter served a complimentary *amuse-bouche*—a tall shot glass of "carrot soup with vanilla and chive oil," he explained. I was dubious, but I took a sip and was converted instantly; the soup remains, to this day, one of the best things I have ever tasted. The chef wouldn't part with the recipe, but he did give me some tips so I could make my own version.

1. In a stove-top pressure cooker set over medium heat, or an electric cooker set to "brown," heat the butter until it stops foaming and just starts to brown. Add the onion and carrots, and sprinkle with ¼ teaspoon of kosher salt. Cook for 4 to 5 minutes, stirring occasionally, until the onion starts to brown and the carrots begin to soften. Turn the heat to high, and add the sherry. Bring to a boil, and cook for 1 to 2 minutes, or until most of the sherry has evaporated. Add the Chicken Stock.

2. Lock the lid in place, and bring the pot to high pressure (15 psi for stove top or 9 to 11 psi for electric).

STOVE TOP: Maintain pressure for 10 minutes, adjusting the burner as necessary.
ELECTRIC: Cook at high pressure for 10 minutes.

3. After cooking, use the *quick method* to release pressure.

4. Unlock and remove the lid. Stir in the vanilla and cayenne pepper. Remove from the heat, and cool slightly. Using an immersion or standard blender, purée the soup completely. Stir in the carrot juice. Bring just to a simmer, and season with kosher salt, as needed. Ladle into 2 bowls, drizzle each with 1½ teaspoons of yogurt, sprinkle with the chives (if using), and serve.

PER SERVING: CALORIES: 132; FAT: 5G; SODIUM: 630MG; CARBOHYDRATES: 16G; FIBER: 4G; PROTEIN: 6G

Creole White Bean Soup

SERVES 2 AS A MAIN COURSE, OR 4 AS A FIRST COURSE

PRESSURE: High
TIME UNDER PRESSURE: 12 minutes
RELEASE: Quick

ONE POT

1 tablespoon kosher salt

1 quart water

6 ounces dried navy beans

1 tablespoon olive oil

1½ ounces ham, diced (about ⅓ cup)

⅓ cup chopped onion

1 tablespoon minced garlic (about 3 medium cloves)

1 teaspoon Creole or Cajun seasoning (for Cajun, see Tip, page 151), plus additional as needed

¼ teaspoon ground cayenne pepper (optional)

3 cups Chicken Stock (page 262) or low-sodium broth, plus additional as needed

2 tablespoons Creole or other whole-grain mustard

½ teaspoon hot pepper sauce (such as Tabasco or Crystal), plus additional as needed

1 teaspoon Worcestershire sauce

1 small tomato, seeded and diced, or ⅓ cup canned diced tomatoes

¼ cup chopped scallions

3 cups loosely packed arugula

I find most bean soups to be bland and uninteresting. But not too long ago, I tried a recipe for Creole white beans from Emeril Lagasse. The beans were a bit soupy to start with, and what was left over the next day was even better, like the best bean soup ever. So naturally, I started to work on a soup variation. This is the result.

1. In a large bowl, dissolve the kosher salt in the water. Add the beans, and soak at room temperature for 8 to 24 hours. Drain and rinse.

2. In a stove-top pressure cooker set over medium heat, or an electric cooker set to "brown," heat the olive oil until it shimmers and flows like water. Add the ham, and cook for 2 to 3 minutes, or until it just starts to brown. Add the onion and garlic, and cook for about 2 minutes, or until the onion pieces start to separate and the garlic becomes fragrant. Stir in the Creole seasoning and cayenne pepper (if using), and cook for 1 minute, stirring to coat the ham and vegetables.

3. Add the Chicken Stock; then pour in the beans.

4. Lock the lid in place, and bring the pot to high pressure (15 psi for stove top or 9 to 11 psi for electric).

STOVE TOP: Maintain pressure for 12 minutes, adjusting the burner as necessary.
ELECTRIC: Cook at high pressure for 12 minutes.

5. After cooking, use the *quick method* to release pressure.

6. Unlock and remove the lid. Place the stove-top cooker over medium heat, or turn the electric cooker to "brown." Stir in the mustard, hot pepper sauce, and Worcestershire sauce, and simmer for 3 minutes. Taste and adjust the seasoning, adding more hot sauce or Creole seasoning if you want it spicier. If the soup is too spicy or too thick, add more stock. Add the tomato, scallions, and arugula, and simmer for about 4 minutes, or until the arugula is wilted and the tomatoes are heated through. Ladle into bowls, and serve.

PER SERVING (MAIN COURSE): CALORIES: 497; FAT: 14G; SODIUM: 734MG; CARBOHYDRATES: 66G; FIBER: 25G; PROTEIN: 30G

Split Pea *and* Ham Soup

SERVES 2

PRESSURE: High
TIME UNDER PRESSURE: 8 minutes
RELEASE: Natural

GLUTEN FREE, ONE POT

1 tablespoon olive oil

½ cup diced onion

1 garlic clove, minced
   or pressed

½ pound dried split peas, rinsed

¾ cup diced ham

½ cup diced carrot

1 bay leaf

1 tablespoon minced
   fresh parsley

¼ teaspoon dried thyme

1 quart water

1 teaspoon kosher salt

1 or 2 dashes Tabasco sauce

Freshly ground black pepper

Split pea soup doesn't get faster than this. Substituting diced ham for the usual pork hock cuts down on the time and the work, so you get delicious soup with almost no effort. Eight minutes of cooking time results in split peas that have partly broken down, so the soup will be fairly thick. If you prefer a thinner soup with peas that are more intact, reduce the cooking time to 5 minutes.

1. In a stove-top pressure cooker set over medium heat, or an electric cooker set to "brown," heat the olive oil until it shimmers and flows like water. Add the onion and garlic. Cook for about 2 minutes, stirring, until the onions soften.

2. Add the split peas, ham, carrot, bay leaf, parsley, thyme, water, and kosher salt to the pressure cooker.

3. Lock the lid in place, and bring the pot to high pressure (15 psi for stove top or 9 to 11 psi for electric).

STOVE TOP: Maintain pressure for 8 minutes, adjusting the burner as necessary.
ELECTRIC: Cook at high pressure for 8 minutes. When the timer goes off, turn the cooker off. Do not let it switch to the "warm" setting.

4. After cooking, use the *natural method* to release pressure.

5. Unlock and remove the lid. Stir in the Tabasco sauce and pepper. Taste, adjust the seasoning as needed, ladle into 2 bowls, and serve.

PER SERVING: CALORIES: 555; FAT: 13G; SODIUM: 1,284MG; CARBOHYDRATES: 76G; FIBER: 31G; PROTEIN: 37G

Butternut Squash Soup

SERVES 6

PRESSURE: High
TIME UNDER PRESSURE: 13 minutes
RELEASE: Quick

PALEO, VEGAN

1 tablespoon olive oil

1 cup chopped onion

Kosher salt

1 (2-pound) butternut squash, peeled, seeded, and cut into 1-inch chunks

6 cups low-sodium vegetable broth

½ teaspoon ground ginger

¼ teaspoon ground cayenne pepper

When squash is in season, it's an inexpensive and delicious ingredient in all kinds of recipes, but one of the easiest is soup. It does take some time to cut up the squash, but after that, you're less than 20 minutes away from a warming dish on a cold evening.

1. In a stove-top pressure cooker set over medium heat, or an electric cooker set to "brown," heat the olive oil until it shimmers and flows like water. Add the onion, and sprinkle with a pinch or two of kosher salt. Cook for about 3 minutes, stirring, until the onions just begin to brown. Add the butternut squash, vegetable broth, ginger, and cayenne pepper, and stir to dissolve the spices.

2. Lock the lid in place, and bring the pot to high pressure (15 psi for stove top or 9 to 11 psi for electric).

STOVE TOP: Maintain pressure for 13 minutes, adjusting the burner as necessary.
ELECTRIC: Cook at high pressure for 13 minutes.

3. After cooking, use the *quick method* to release pressure.

4. Unlock and remove the lid. Using an immersion or regular blender, purée the soup. Taste and adjust the seasoning, if needed. Ladle into bowls, and serve.

PER SERVING: CALORIES: 111; FAT: 3G; SODIUM: 104MG; CARBOHYDRATES: 21G; FIBER: 4G; PROTEIN: 4G

Chili con Carne

SERVES 4

PRESSURE: High
TIME UNDER PRESSURE: 25 minutes
RELEASE: Natural

GLUTEN FREE, ONE POT

1 tablespoon plus ½ teaspoon kosher salt, divided, plus additional for seasoning

1 quart water

6 ounces dry pinto beans

1½ pounds beef chuck roast, trimmed and cut into 1½-inch cubes

2 tablespoons olive oil, divided

1 cup chopped onion

1 large garlic clove, minced or pressed

2 tablespoons ground ancho or New Mexico chili powder

2 teaspoons ground cumin

1 large chipotle canned in adobo sauce, minced (about 2 teaspoons)

½ cup Red Table Salsa (page 272) or crushed tomatoes

1½ cups Beef Stock (page 264) or low-sodium broth

Texas-style chili con carne is heavy on the beef and light on the beans. In fact, some Texans will argue to the death that it shouldn't have beans at all—but I'm not from Texas, so beans it is. This chili is not wildly spicy; if you want more heat, add more chipotle or a minced jalapeño pepper with the onion and garlic.

1. In a large bowl, dissolve 1 tablespoon of kosher salt with the water. Add the beans, and soak at room temperature for 8 to 24 hours. Drain and rinse.

2. Salt the beef with the remaining ½ teaspoon of kosher salt.

3. In a stove-top pressure cooker set over medium heat, or an electric cooker set to "brown," heat 1 tablespoon of olive oil until it shimmers and flows like water. Add half the beef (or as much will fit in a single layer), and sear the cubes on two sides, about 6 minutes total. Remove the beef from the cooker.

4. If necessary, add the remaining 1 tablespoon of olive oil to the cooker; then add the onion and garlic, and sprinkle with a pinch or two of kosher salt. Cook for about 3 minutes, stirring, until the onions and garlic just begin to brown. Add the chili powder and cumin, and stir to coat the onions with the spices. Cook for 1 minute, or until fragrant. Add all the beef, the minced chipotle, the Red Table Salsa, and the Beef Stock. Stir in the beans. →

5. Lock the lid in place, and bring the pot to high pressure (15 psi for stove top or 9 to 11 psi for electric).

STOVE TOP: Maintain pressure for 25 minutes, adjusting the burner as necessary.

ELECTRIC: Cook at high pressure for 25 minutes. When the timer goes off, turn the cooker off. Do not let it switch to the "warm" setting.

6. After cooking, use the ***natural method*** to release pressure.

7. Unlock and remove the lid. Let the chili sit for a minute to allow any fat to rise to the surface, then spoon or blot off as much as possible and discard. If the sauce is too thin, simmer the chili over medium heat in a stove-top cooker, or turned to "simmer" for an electric cooker, until it thickens to the desired consistency. Ladle into 4 bowls, and serve.

PER SERVING: CALORIES: 883; FAT: 56G; SODIUM: 1,047MG; CARBOHYDRATES: 36G; FIBER: 10G; PROTEIN: 57G

Sausage, Bean, and Kale Soup

SERVES 2 AS A MAIN COURSE OR 4 AS A FIRST COURSE

PRESSURE: High
TIME UNDER PRESSURE: 18 minutes
RELEASE: Quick

GLUTEN FREE, ONE POT

1 tablespoon kosher salt, plus additional for seasoning

1 quart water

½ pound dried cannellini beans

1 tablespoon olive oil

¼ pound sweet or hot Italian sausage, casings removed

½ cup chopped onion

½ cup chopped carrot

1 medium garlic clove, minced

3 cups Chicken Stock (page 262) or low-sodium broth

½ small bunch kale, cut into ½-inch ribbons (about 3 cups)

1 teaspoon red wine vinegar

TIP *If you prefer, substitute more-tender greens, like spinach or arugula, for the kale in this recipe. Add them at step 5, after the soup has come off pressure. Cook for 1 to 2 minutes, or just until wilted.*

I have a confession to make: I don't actually like kale. I don't hate it, but I'm a bit tired of all the kale salad recipes out there. If kale is so tough you have to massage it before using it in a salad, I'll pass. On the other hand, it makes a nice addition to a soup like this precisely because it is so tough that it can stand up to the (relatively) long cooking time. With the sausage and beans, it's actually quite tasty—and I'm not ashamed to admit it.

1. In a large bowl, dissolve 1 tablespoon kosher salt in the water. Add the beans, and soak at room temperature for 8 to 24 hours. Drain and rinse.

2. In a stove-top pressure cooker set over medium heat, or an electric cooker set to "brown," heat the olive oil until it shimmers and flows like water. Add the Italian sausage, breaking it up into small pieces with a spatula or spoon, and cook for 2 to 3 minutes, or until no pink remains. Add the onion, carrot, and garlic, and sprinkle with a pinch of kosher salt. Cook for about 2 minutes, stirring, until the vegetables soften slightly. Add the Chicken Stock, beans, and kale.

3. Lock the lid in place, and bring the pot to high pressure (15 psi for stove top or 9 to 11 psi for electric).

STOVE TOP: Maintain pressure for 18 minutes, adjusting the burner as necessary.
ELECTRIC: Cook at high pressure for 18 minutes.

4. After cooking, use the *quick method* to release pressure.

5. Unlock and remove the lid. Stir in the red wine vinegar, and taste the soup, adding more kosher salt if needed.

PER SERVING (MAIN COURSE): CALORIES: 694; FAT: 24G; SODIUM: 1,123MG; CARBOHYDRATES: 79G; FIBER: 30G; PROTEIN: 42G

Broccoli-Parmigiano-Reggiano Soup

SERVES 4

PRESSURE: High
TIME UNDER PRESSURE: 5 minutes
RELEASE: Quick

GLUTEN FREE, ONE POT

2 pounds broccoli, ends trimmed and tough bits peeled

3 tablespoons olive oil

2 large garlic cloves, peeled and sliced

½ teaspoon kosher salt, plus additional for seasoning

4 cups Chicken Stock (page 262) or low-sodium broth

½ cup chopped fresh parsley

1 tablespoon freshly squeezed lemon juice

Freshly ground black pepper

¾ cup grated Parmigiano-Reggiano or similar cheese, divided

Most broccoli-cheese soups I've had do a disservice to the broccoli, with so much cheese and cream added that the broccoli is definitely upstaged. This recipe puts the broccoli front and center, with a bit of lemon and Parmigiano-Reggiano to accent the soup. You can skip browning the broccoli in step 3, but it does add a more complex flavor to the soup.

1. Cut the broccoli stems into 1-inch pieces, and break the heads into florets. Reserve about 1 cup of the tiniest (finger-tip-size) florets.

2. In a stove-top pressure cooker set over medium heat, or an electric cooker set to "brown," heat the olive oil until it shimmers and flows like water. Add the garlic, and cook for about 2 minutes, without stirring, until it begins to brown. Stir the garlic, and cook for 1 minute more so it browns evenly.

3. To the cooker, add just enough of the large broccoli florets to cover the bottom in a single layer. Toss to coat with the olive oil and garlic, and sprinkle with ½ teaspoon kosher salt. Cook the broccoli florets, undisturbed, for 2 to 3 minutes, or until browned in spots. Stir and cook for 2 to 3 minutes more while more surfaces brown.

4. Add the remainder of the large pieces of broccoli (not the cup of reserved tiny florets) and the Chicken Stock to the pressure cooker.

5. Lock the lid in place, and bring the pot to high pressure (15 psi for stove top or 9 to 11 psi for electric).

STOVE TOP: Maintain pressure for 5 minutes, adjusting the burner as necessary.
ELECTRIC: Cook at high pressure for 5 minutes.

6. After cooking, use the *quick method* to release pressure.

7. Unlock and remove the lid. Add the parsley and lemon juice. Using an immersion or regular blender, blend the soup. If using a regular blender, be careful of the steam; work in batches so the top doesn't blow off.

8. Place the stove-top pressure cooker over medium heat, or turn the electric cooker to "brown," and return the soup to a simmer. Season to taste, adding pepper and more kosher salt, if necessary. Add the 1 cup of reserved florets, and simmer for 2 to 3 minutes, or until just tender. Stir in ½ cup of Parmigiano-Reggiano, and ladle the soup into 4 bowls. Top each with 1 tablespoon of the remaining Parmigiano-Reggiano, and serve.

PER SERVING: CALORIES: 256; FAT: 16G; SODIUM: 638MG; CARBOHYDRATES: 18G; FIBER: 6G; PROTEIN: 16G

Chicken *and* Sausage Gumbo

SERVES 4

PRESSURE: High
TIME UNDER PRESSURE: 20 minutes
RELEASE: Natural

ONE POT

¼ cup olive oil

⅓ cup all-purpose flour

1½ teaspoons Cajun seasoning (see Tip)

1 cup chopped onion

1 or 2 celery stalks, chopped (about ⅔ cup)

1 small red bell pepper, chopped (about ⅔ cup)

2 garlic cloves, minced

1 small jalapeño pepper, seeded and minced (optional)

2½ cups Chicken Stock (page 262) or low-sodium broth, divided

6 ounces andouille sausage, cut in ¼-inch rounds, then into half moons

1 pound boneless, skinless chicken thighs, cut into bite-size pieces

2 cups cooked white rice, divided

2 scallions, finely sliced

I'm late to the gumbo table. Never having been to New Orleans and not knowing any southern cooks, I lived most of my life without trying it. Little did I know what I was missing! Now that I've moved to the South, I've come across all kinds of recipes for gumbo, some that take all day and call for seemingly endless ingredients, and some that take so many shortcuts that the result can barely be called gumbo. I like to think this is a good compromise. If you can brave adding flour to really hot oil to make a roux, you can have a fantastic gumbo in about an hour.

1. In a stove-top pressure cooker set over medium heat, or an electric cooker set to "brown," heat the olive oil until it begins to smoke. Whisk in the flour. Switch to a wooden spoon, and cook for 3 to 5 minutes, stirring constantly, until the roux is the color of peanut butter.

2. Take the stove-top cooker off the heat, or turn off the electric cooker. Quickly add the Cajun seasoning, onion, celery, red bell pepper, garlic, and jalapeño (if using). Stir, still off the heat, for about 5 minutes, until the mixture cools a bit.

3. Place the stove-top cooker over medium heat, or turn the electric cooker to "brown." Add about 1 cup of Chicken Stock, stirring until the roux is incorporated and the mixture has thickened. Add the remaining 1½ cups of Chicken Stock, and stir to combine. Add the andouille sausage and chicken.

4. Lock the lid in place, and bring the pot to high pressure (15 psi for stove top or 9 to 11 psi for electric).

STOVE TOP: Maintain pressure for 20 minutes, adjusting the burner as necessary.

ELECTRIC: Cook at high pressure for 20 minutes. When the timer goes off, turn the cooker off. Do not let it switch to the "warm" setting.

5. After cooking, use the **natural method** to release pressure.

6. Unlock and remove the lid. Let the gumbo sit for a minute to allow the fat to rise to the surface, then spoon or blot off as much as possible and discard.

7. Scoop ½ cup of rice into each of 4 bowls. Ladle the gumbo over each, garnish with the scallions, and serve immediately.

TIP *Cajun seasoning blends are available commercially, but you can make your own by mixing together ½ teaspoon fine salt, ½ teaspoon ground white pepper, ½ teaspoon freshly ground black pepper, ½ teaspoon dried basil, ½ teaspoon dried thyme, and ¼ teaspoon ground cayenne pepper. This will give you more than the recipe calls for, but it's difficult to mix up a smaller batch, so store it in an airtight container and use for your next gumbo.*

PER SERVING: CALORIES: 641; FAT: 33G, SODIUM: 685MG; CARBOHYDRATES: 37G; FIBER: 2G; PROTEIN: 46G

Potato-Leek Soup

SERVES 4

PRESSURE: High
TIME UNDER PRESSURE: 6 minutes
RELEASE: Quick

GLUTEN FREE, ONE POT

2 tablespoons unsalted butter

2 leeks, white parts only, trimmed, cleaned, and diced

½ fennel bulb, trimmed and diced (optional)

¼ teaspoon kosher salt, plus additional as needed

½ cup dry white wine

1 pound russet potatoes (1 very large or 2 small), peeled and cut into 1-inch chunks

4 cups Chicken Stock (page 262) or low-sodium broth

¼ cup heavy (whipping) cream

Freshly ground black pepper

Potato-leek soup recipes run the gamut from chunky and rustic to smooth, creamy, and sophisticated. I like the soup to be fairly smooth, so I purée it. I also like the flavors of the vegetables to stand out, so I go easy on the cream. If you want a richer, subtler version, add an additional ¼ cup of heavy cream. Fennel isn't traditional in this classic French soup, but it adds great flavor. If you can't find it or don't want half a bulb left over, leave it out.

1. In a stove-top pressure cooker set over medium heat, or an electric pressure cooker set to "brown," heat the butter just until it stops foaming. Add the leeks and fennel (if using), and sprinkle with the kosher salt. Cook for about 3 minutes, stirring, until the vegetables begin to soften. Add the white wine, and cook for 2 to 3 minutes more, or until it has reduced by about half. Add the potatoes and Chicken Stock.

2. Lock the lid in place, and bring the pot to high pressure (15 psi for stove top or 9 to 11 psi for electric).

STOVE TOP: Maintain pressure for 6 minutes, adjusting the burner as necessary.
ELECTRIC: Cook at high pressure for 6 minutes.

3. After cooking, use the *quick method* to release pressure.

4. Unlock and remove the lid. Using an immersion or regular blender, purée the soup. If using a regular blender, be careful of the steam; work in batches so the top doesn't blow off. Stir in the heavy cream and several grinds of pepper. Adjust the seasoning, if needed. Ladle into bowls, and serve.

PER SERVING: CALORIES: 231; FAT: 9G; SODIUM: 293MG; CARBOHYDRATES: 28G; FIBER: 4G; PROTEIN: 5G

Roasted Red Pepper *and* Onion Soup

SERVES 4 AS A FIRST COURSE

PRESSURE: High
TIME UNDER PRESSURE: 40 or 45 minutes total
RELEASE: Quick

2 tablespoons unsalted butter

3 cups thinly sliced onions

1½ teaspoons kosher salt, divided, plus additional for seasoning

3 large red bell peppers, stemmed, cored, and seeded

¼ cup dry or medium-dry sherry

2 cups Chicken Stock (page 262) or low-sodium broth

When I develop recipes, I sometimes hit it on the first try, and sometimes it takes a few tries to get a winner. I started out making a respectable, but not great, roasted red pepper soup with sautéed shallots. Then I tried a version with a batch of slow-browned (a.k.a. caramelized) onions, and I knew I was onto something. Swapping sherry for my usual white wine proved to be the key to a fabulous soup. I hope you like it as much as I do.

1. In a stove-top pressure cooker set over medium heat, or an electric cooker set to "brown," heat the butter until it melts. Add the onions and 1 teaspoon of kosher salt, and stir just to distribute the salt and coat the onions with the butter.

2. Lock the lid in place, and bring the pot to high pressure (15 psi for stove top or 9 to 11 psi for electric).

STOVE TOP: Maintain pressure for 35 minutes, adjusting the burner as necessary.
ELECTRIC: Cook at high pressure for 40 minutes.

3. After cooking, use the *quick method* to release pressure.

4. While the onions cook, roast the red bell peppers. Preheat the broiler to high. Cut each pepper into 2 to 4 relatively flat pieces, and lay them, skin-side up, on an aluminum foil–lined sheet pan. Place the pan under the broiler as close to the element as possible, and broil for 6 to 8 minutes, or until the skin is blistered and blackened. When the peppers are done, removed them from the broiler. Carefully pick up the edges of the foil, and wrap the peppers in it, sealing the edges. Let sit for 10 minutes. Unwrap the peppers, scrape off, and discard the skins. Cut each pepper strip into several pieces.

5. When the onions are done, unlock and remove the lid of the pressure cooker. Add the roasted peppers, sherry, Chicken Stock, and remaining ½ teaspoon of kosher salt.

6. Lock the lid in place, and bring the pot to high pressure (15 psi for stove top or 9 to 11 psi for electric).

STOVE TOP: Maintain pressure for 5 minutes, adjusting the burner as necessary.
ELECTRIC: Cook at high pressure for 5 minutes.

7. After cooking, use the *quick method* to release pressure.

8. Unlock and remove the lid. Using an immersion or standard blender, purée the soup until smooth. Taste and adjust the seasoning, as necessary, ladle into 4 bowls, and serve.

TIP *Cooking the onions for this soup is essentially the same as making the Onion Jam (page 269). If you have that condiment on hand, you can skip steps 1 and 2 and start at step 4, adding about ½ cup of the Onion Jam to the pressure cooker at step 5 with the other ingredients.*

PER SERVING: CALORIES: 121; FAT: 6G; SODIUM: 955MG; CARBOHYDRATES: 14G; FIBER: 4G; PROTEIN: 3G

Chicken Noodle Soup

SERVES 2 AS A MAIN DISH
OR 4 AS A FIRST COURSE

PRESSURE: High
TIME UNDER PRESSURE:
17 minutes total
RELEASE: Quick

ONE POT

2 (4-ounce) skinless, bone-in
   chicken thighs

3 cups Chicken Stock
   (page 262) (see Tip)

1½ teaspoons kosher salt
   (optional)

1 medium carrot, peeled and
   cut into ¼-inch coins

1 small celery stalk, cut into
   ¼-inch-thick pieces

⅓ cup frozen peas

⅓ cup frozen pearl onions

2½ ounces egg noodles

1 tablespoon chopped fresh
   parsley or dill (optional)

Here's the dream: You cook a whole chicken in a pot of water with some vegetables, add some noodles, and end up with chicken noodle soup. Unfortunately, in my experience, that never happens. What you end up with is overcooked chicken and vegetables with broth that tastes only faintly of chicken. With the right ingredients, though, it's easy to make a quick chicken noodle soup that fulfills that dream: deeply flavored broth with tender chicken and vegetables and perfectly done noodles.

1. To a stove-top or electric pressure cooker, add the chicken and Chicken Stock. If using homemade stock from this book (page 262), add the kosher salt.

2. Lock the lid in place, and bring the pot to high pressure (15 psi for stove top or 9 to 11 psi for electric).

STOVE TOP: Maintain pressure for 12 minutes, adjusting the burner as necessary.
ELECTRIC: Cook at high pressure for 12 minutes.

3. After cooking, use the *quick method* to release pressure.

4. Unlock and remove the lid. Using tongs, remove the chicken thighs and transfer to a cutting board. When cool enough to handle, pull the meat from the bones, discarding any fat or gristle, and cut or pull the meat into bite-size pieces.

5. Add the carrot, celery, peas, pearl onions, and egg noodles to the cooker.

6. Lock the lid in place, and bring the pot to high pressure (15 psi for stove top or 9 to 11 psi for electric).

STOVE TOP: Maintain pressure for 5 minutes, adjusting the burner as necessary.
ELECTRIC: Cook at high pressure for 5 minutes.

7. After cooking, use the *quick method* to release pressure.

8. Unlock and remove the lid. Check one of the noodles for doneness; if it's not quite done, place the stove-top cooker over medium heat, or turn the electric cooker to "simmer," and simmer for 1 to 2 minutes, or until the noodles are completely tender. Ladle the soup into bowls, garnish each with parsley (if using), and serve.

TIP *For this recipe, it's important to use either homemade Chicken Stock (page 262) or a high-quality brand.*

PER SERVING (MAIN COURSE): CALORIES: 344; FAT: 16G; SODIUM: 1,096MG; CARBOHYDRATES: 16G; FIBER: 4G; PROTEIN: 25G

Beef *and* Barley Soup

SERVES 4

PRESSURE: High
TIME UNDER PRESSURE: 10 minutes
RELEASE: Natural

½ pound beef shoulder (chuck), cut into ½-inch cubes

1 teaspoon kosher salt, divided, plus additional as necessary

2 tablespoons olive oil, divided

1 cup diced onion

1 celery stalk, chopped (about ⅓ cup)

2 medium carrots, peeled and chopped (about 1 cup)

8 ounces white button or cremini mushrooms, sliced

1 tablespoon tomato paste

1 teaspoon dried thyme

1 teaspoon Worcestershire sauce

¾ cup pearl barley, rinsed and drained

3 cups Beef Stock (page 264) or low-sodium broth

1 cup water

Freshly ground black pepper

My first memory of a pressure cooker is of my mother making beef and barley soup, so this recipe brings back sweet memories. As much as I liked her soup, though, I was always a little bit afraid of the spitting pot on the stove; I think she was, too. Now that I have a modern pressure cooker, I make this version. I don't know if it's much like the soup she made, but I still think of her when I cook it.

1. Salt the beef with ½ teaspoon of kosher salt.

2. In a stove-top pressure cooker set over medium heat, or an electric cooker set to "brown," heat 1 tablespoon of olive oil until it shimmers and flows like water. Add the beef, and sear, stirring to get most of the cubes browned on at least two sides, about 6 minutes total. Remove the beef from the cooker.

3. Add the remaining 1 tablespoon of olive oil to the cooker; then add the onion, celery, carrots, and mushrooms. Cook for about 5 minutes, stirring, until the vegetables soften and just begin to brown. Add the tomato paste, and stir to coat the vegetables. Cook for about 2 minutes, or until the tomato paste darkens slightly. Add the remaining ½ teaspoon of kosher salt and the seared beef, thyme, Worcestershire sauce, barley, Beef Stock, and water to the cooker.

4. Lock the lid in place, and bring the pot to high pressure (15 psi for stove top or 9 to 11 psi for electric).

STOVE TOP: Maintain pressure for 10 minutes, adjusting the burner as necessary.
ELECTRIC: Cook at high pressure for 10 minutes. When the timer goes off, turn the cooker off. Do not let it switch to the "warm" setting.

5. After cooking, use the **natural method** to release pressure.

6. Unlock and remove the lid. Taste and adjust the seasoning, adding several grinds of pepper and more salt, if necessary. Ladle into bowls, and serve.

TIP *Cut the beef into small cubes; larger pieces won't be tender in the time it takes to cook the barley.*

PER SERVING: CALORIES: 268; FAT: 9G; SODIUM: 693MG; CARBOHYDRATES: 39G; FIBER: 8G; PROTEIN: 10G

Beans and Grains

CHAPTER SIX

If there's one reason cooks cite more often than any other in explaining why they're considering a pressure cooker, it's to cook beans and whole grains from scratch. It's no surprise. Like soups and stews, beans and grains are meant for pressure cooking. It's true that most of the bean recipes here require presoaking, but all that requires is a little foresight and 5 minutes of your time. You can start soaking beans up to 24 hours in advance or as little as 8 hours before you cook. Keep in mind that cooking beans and most grains in a pressure cooker produces a bit of foaming, which, in large batches, can interfere with the pressure gauge. With the smaller amounts in these recipes, it shouldn't be a problem. Just to be safe, I've added a bit of olive oil or butter to keep any foaming to a minimum.

Risotto *with* Peas *and* Shrimp

SERVES 4

PRESSURE: High
TIME UNDER PRESSURE: 6 minutes
RELEASE: Quick

GLUTEN FREE, ONE POT

1 tablespoon unsalted butter

½ cup chopped onion

1 cup arborio rice

⅓ cup white wine

2¾ cups Chicken Stock (page 262) or low-sodium broth, divided

½ pound raw medium shrimp, shelled and deveined

½ cup frozen peas, thawed

¼ cup grated Parmigiano-Reggiano or similar cheese

Seeing risotto made in a pressure cooker is what first sold me on the idea of buying one. I love risotto, and under the right circumstances, I don't mind standing and stirring as it cooks and thickens. But honestly, I rarely have the time to devote to the conventional method. After a little prep work, a pressure cooker gives you a huge head start on the process so you only need to stand and stir for about 6 minutes to have perfect, elegant risotto.

1. In a stove-top pressure cooker set over medium heat, or an electric cooker set to "brown," heat the butter until it stops foaming. Add the onion, and cook for about 2 minutes, stirring, until soft. Add the rice, and stir to coat with the butter. Cook for 1 minute, stirring. Stir in the white wine, and cook for 1 to 2 minutes, or until it's almost evaporated. Add 2½ cups of Chicken Stock, and stir to make sure no rice is sticking to the bottom of the cooker.

2. Lock the lid in place, and bring the pot to high pressure (15 psi for stove top or 9 to 11 psi for electric).

STOVE TOP: Maintain pressure for 6 minutes, adjusting the burner as necessary.
ELECTRIC: Cook at high pressure for 6 minutes.

3. After cooking, use the ***quick method*** to release pressure.

4. Unlock and remove the lid. Place the stove-top cooker back over medium heat, or turn the electric cooker to "brown." Continue to cook the rice, stirring, for 1 to 2 minutes more, or until the rice is firm just in the very center of the grain and the liquid has thickened slightly. Add the shrimp and peas, and continue to cook for about 4 minutes more, or until the shrimp are cooked. Stir in the Parmigiano-Reggiano. If the risotto is too thick, stir in a little of the remaining ¼ cup of Chicken Stock to loosen it up. Serve immediately.

TIP *Risotto is one of those dishes that lend themselves to almost endless variation. Leftover ham is a great addition, as is smoked salmon or trout, or go vegetarian with "Sautéed" Mushrooms (page 200), roasted peppers, or even beets.*

PER SERVING: CALORIES: 343; FAT: 6G; SODIUM: 292MG; CARBOHYDRATES: 45G; FIBER: 3G; PROTEIN: 21G

Masoor Dal

SERVES 2

PRESSURE: High
TIME UNDER PRESSURE: 10 minutes
RELEASE: Quick

GLUTEN FREE, VEGAN

2 tablespoons olive oil

1½ cups sliced onion, divided

4 garlic cloves, sliced, divided

8 ounces dried red lentils, rinsed

½ teaspoon ground turmeric

¼ teaspoon ground cumin

1 bay leaf

3 cups water

1 large tomato, seeded and
  chopped (about 1 cup)

1 serrano chile, halved

1 teaspoon kosher salt, plus
  additional as needed

2 tablespoons coarsely
  chopped fresh cilantro

Years ago, I assisted a very talented Indian instructor with a cooking class. He was just starting to market a kit of Indian spices, and he'd brought a sample with him. I was in awe. At the end of the class, he generously gave me the sample kit. I swore I'd start making Indian food more often, but I'm afraid I never got very far with that promise. I did learn how to make this delicious lentil dish, though, so his gift was not in vain.

1. In a stove-top pressure cooker set over medium-high heat, or an electric cooker set to "brown," heat the olive oil until it shimmers and flows like water. Add 1 cup of onions and half of the garlic. Stir to coat the onions and garlic with the olive oil; then cook them for about 4 minutes, in a single layer, until browned. Resist the urge to stir them until you see them browning; then stir to expose the other side to the heat. Cook for 4 minutes more. The onions should be quite browned but still slightly firm. Remove the onions and garlic from the pan, and set aside.

2. Add the remaining ½ cup of onions and remaining half of the garlic to the cooker along with the lentils, turmeric, cumin, bay leaf, water, tomato, serrano chile, and kosher salt. Stir to combine and dissolve the salt.

3. Lock the lid in place, and bring the pot to high pressure (15 psi for stove top or 9 to 11 psi for electric).

STOVE TOP: Maintain pressure for 10 minutes, adjusting the burner as necessary.
ELECTRIC: Cook at high pressure for 10 minutes.

4. After cooking, use the *quick method* to release pressure.

5. Unlock and remove the lid. Remove the bay leaf and serrano chile. Add the reserved browned onions and garlic, and stir. Let the dal sit for 2 to 3 minutes to heat the onions through, and adjust the seasoning, if needed. Serve alone or over rice, garnished with the cilantro.

PER SERVING: CALORIES: 591; FAT: 16G; SODIUM: 886MG; CARBOHYDRATES: 83G; FIBER: 38G; PROTEIN: 32G

Red Beans *and* Rice

SERVES 4

PRESSURE: High
TIME UNDER PRESSURE: 25 minutes
RELEASE: Quick

GLUTEN FREE

1 tablespoon kosher salt, plus additional for seasoning

1 quart water

⅓ pound small dried red beans

1 tablespoon olive oil

1½ cups chopped onion

2 celery stalks, chopped (about 1½ cups)

1½ cups chopped green or red bell pepper

4 garlic cloves, minced (about 1 tablespoon)

1 teaspoon freshly ground black pepper

¾ teaspoon ground cayenne pepper

¾ teaspoon dried oregano

1½ teaspoons dried thyme

2½ cups Chicken Stock (page 262) or low-sodium broth

8 ounces andouille sausage, sliced into ¼-inch pieces, then cut into half moons

1 bay leaf

2 cups cooked white rice

Tradition has it that red beans and rice is what cooks made on laundry day in New Orleans. Since Monday was usually wash day, Sunday dinner's leftover ham bone contributed to the meal, and the washing was done in the same time it took to cook this dish. If you wanted to, you could still do this, but with this streamlined version, the cooking will be done in about the time it takes to do just one load of laundry.

1. In a large bowl, dissolve 1 tablespoon of kosher salt in the water. Add the beans, and soak at room temperature for 8 to 24 hours. Drain and rinse.

2. In a stove-top pressure cooker set over medium heat, or an electric cooker set to "brown," heat the olive oil until it shimmers and flows like water. Add the onion, celery, green bell pepper, and garlic, and sprinkle with a pinch or two of kosher salt. Cook for about 3 minutes, stirring, until the vegetables just begin to brown. Add the black pepper, cayenne pepper, oregano, and thyme, and stir to coat the vegetables with the spices. Cook for 1 minute.

3. Pour the Chicken Stock into the cooker, and bring to a simmer, scraping the bottom of the pot to release any browned bits. Add the beans, andouille sausage, and bay leaf.

4. Lock the lid in place, and bring the pot to high pressure (15 psi for stove top or 9 to 11 psi for electric).

STOVE TOP: Maintain pressure for 25 minutes, adjusting the burner as necessary.
ELECTRIC: Cook at high pressure for 25 minutes.

5. After cooking, use the *quick method* to release pressure.

6. Unlock and remove the lid. Remove the bay leaf, and let the beans sit for a few minutes to allow any fat to rise to the surface. Spoon or blot off as much fat as possible and discard.

7. Place ½ cup cooked rice in each of 4 bowls, spoon the red beans over each, and serve.

TIP *If you have lots of time and can find smoked pork shanks or hocks (or even smoked turkey legs), they'll add a smoky complexity to this dish. Before starting the recipe (even the day before), place one or two shanks or hocks in the pressure cooker, and cover them with water. Cook for 30 to 40 minutes at high pressure with a quick release. Remove the shanks, and cool. Use the cooking liquid in place of some of the stock (taste it first; it can be quite salty), and shred the meat to add to the beans.*

PER SERVING: CALORIES: 454; FAT: 20G; SODIUM: 1,068MG; CARBOHYDRATES: 66G; FIBER: 27G; PROTEIN: 26G

Spicy Citrus Black Beans

SERVES 4

PRESSURE: High
TIME UNDER PRESSURE: 12 minutes
RELEASE: Quick

GLUTEN FREE, VEGETARIAN

1 tablespoon kosher salt
1 quart water
½ pound dried black beans
1 tablespoon olive oil
⅓ cup chopped onion
½ jalapeño pepper, seeded and diced (about 1 tablespoon)
¼ cup chopped red bell pepper
2 medium garlic cloves, minced
½ teaspoon dried marjoram or oregano
½ teaspoon ground cumin
1 teaspoon ground ancho chili powder or other chili powder
½ teaspoon ground chipotle pepper
1¾ cups low-sodium vegetable broth
1 bay leaf
1 tablespoon frozen orange juice concentrate
1 tablespoon freshly squeezed lime juice

Bright citrus flavors—here orange and lime—perk up these delicious black beans, which make a satisfying vegetarian entrée when served over rice.

1. In a large bowl, dissolve the kosher salt in the water. Add the black beans, and soak at room temperature for 8 to 24 hours. Drain and rinse.

2. In a stove-top pressure cooker set over medium heat, or an electric cooker set to "brown," heat the olive oil until it shimmers and flows like water. Add the onion, jalapeño, and red bell pepper, and cook for about 5 minutes, stirring, until the vegetables soften and the onion pieces separate. Stir in the garlic, and cook for 1 minute more. Add the marjoram, cumin, chili powder, and ground chipotle pepper, and cook for 1 minute, stirring to coat the vegetables with the spices.

3. Add the vegetable broth and bay leaf to the pressure cooker, and pour in the beans.

4. Lock the lid in place, and bring the pot to high pressure (15 psi for stove top or 9 to 11 psi for electric).

STOVE TOP: Maintain pressure for 12 minutes, adjusting the burner as necessary.
ELECTRIC: Cook at high pressure for 12 minutes.

5. After cooking, use the *quick method* to release pressure.

6. Unlock and remove the lid. Remove the bay leaf. If the beans are too soupy, turn the stove-top cooker to medium-low, or the electric cooker to "simmer," and simmer until some of the liquid has evaporated. Stir in the orange juice concentrate and lime juice, simmer for 2 to 3 minutes, and serve.

PER SERVING: CALORIES: 254; FAT: 5G; SODIUM: 333MG; CARBOHYDRATES: 41G; FIBER: 10G; PROTEIN: 14G

"Baked" Beans

SERVES 4

PRESSURE: High
TIME UNDER PRESSURE: 10 minutes
RELEASE: Quick

1 tablespoon kosher salt

1 quart water

½ pound dried navy beans

1 teaspoon olive oil

1 bacon or ham slice, diced

½ cup chopped onion

⅓ cup diced green bell pepper

1¾ cups Chicken Stock
   (page 262) or
   low-sodium broth

¼ cup ketchup

¼ cup packed brown sugar

2 teaspoons cider vinegar

2 teaspoons
   Worcestershire sauce

¼ teaspoon dried mustard

While beans cook beautifully in a pressure cooker using stock or water, they don't do so well with an acidic sauce. Bean lore has it that salt will toughen beans and lengthen the cooking time, but really, acid is the enemy of tender beans. It's an easy problem to overcome, though. In this recipe, the beans are cooked most of the way in broth and then simmered in a savory, tangy sauce to finish.

1. In a large bowl, dissolve 1 tablespoon of kosher salt in the water. Add the beans, and soak at room temperature for 8 to 24 hours. Drain and rinse.

2. To a stove-top pressure cooker set over medium heat, or an electric cooker set to "brown," add the olive oil and bacon. Cook for about 3 minutes, stirring, until the bacon begins to crisp. Add the onion and green bell pepper, and cook for 2 to 3 minutes, until softened. Add the Chicken Stock to the pressure cooker; then pour in the beans.

3. Lock the lid in place, and bring the pot to high pressure (15 psi for stove top or 9 to 11 psi for electric).

STOVE TOP: Maintain pressure for 10 minutes, adjusting the burner as necessary.
ELECTRIC: Cook at high pressure for 10 minutes.

4. After cooking, use the *quick method* to release pressure.

5. Unlock and remove the lid. The beans should barely be done—cooked but quite firm. Add the ketchup, brown sugar, vinegar, Worcestershire sauce, and dried mustard, and stir to combine. Place the stove-top cooker over medium-low heat, or turn the electric cooker to "simmer." Cook for about 15 minutes, uncovered, or until the sauce has thickened and the beans are completely tender, and serve.

TIP *For real baked beans, pour the beans with their sauce into a baking dish at step 5. Bake at 350°F for 25 to 40 minutes, or until the sauce has thickened and the beans are tender.*

PER SERVING: CALORIES: 281; FAT: 3G; SODIUM: 614MG; CARBOHYDRATES: 50G; FIBER: 15G; PROTEIN: 15G

Frijoles Refritos (Refried Beans)

SERVES 4

PRESSURE: High
TIME UNDER PRESSURE: 50 minutes
RELEASE: Natural

GLUTEN FREE

4 cups water

1 teaspoon kosher salt

2 bacon slices, each cut into 2 or 3 pieces, divided

1 very small onion, peeled, trimmed, and halved through the root

½ pound dried pinto beans, rinsed and picked over

2 garlic cloves, smashed

I love authentic *frijoles refritos*, but they're so rich that I reserve them for special occasions. This everyday version cooks unsoaked beans with a little bacon and lots of onion, both of which break down and become part of the sauce. That means lots of flavor with much less fat, which means we can eat them much more often.

1. To a stove-top or electric pressure cooker, add the water, kosher salt, 1 bacon slice, and the onion. Pour in the beans.

2. Lock the lid in place, and bring the pot to high pressure (15 psi for stove top or 9 to 11 psi for electric).

STOVE TOP: Maintain pressure for 50 minutes, adjusting the burner as necessary.
ELECTRIC: Cook at high pressure for 50 minutes. When the timer goes off, turn the cooker off. Do not let it switch to the "warm" setting.

3. After cooking, use the ***natural method*** to release pressure.

4. Unlock and remove the lid. Working over a large bowl, place a large sieve or colander, and drain the beans. The onion and bacon pieces will likely have dissolved into the beans, but if there are any large pieces left, remove and discard them. Reserve the liquid.

5. Place the stove-top cooker over medium-high heat, or turn the electric cooker to "brown." Add the remaining bacon slice, and cook until the pieces are crisp and the fat renders. Remove the bacon, and set aside, leaving the fat in the cooker. Add the garlic to the fat, and cook for about 6 minutes, or until well browned or a bit charred. Remove the garlic and discard.

6. Pour the beans back into the cooker. Using a large spoon or potato masher, mash the beans into the bacon fat. Stir the reserved bean liquid to redistribute the starch, and add ¼ cup of the liquid to the beans. Continue mashing the beans until they're a rough purée, or the texture you prefer. Add additional bean liquid, as necessary, to keep the beans from drying out. Chop the reserved bacon, sprinkle over the top of the beans, and serve.

PER SERVING: CALORIES: 261; FAT: 5G; SODIUM: 525MG; CARBOHYDRATES: 39G; FIBER: 9G; PROTEIN: 16G

Polenta *with* Roasted Red Peppers *and* Onion Jam

SERVES 4

PRESSURE: High
TIME UNDER PRESSURE: 10 minutes
RELEASE: Quick

VEGETARIAN

¾ cup polenta or grits (not quick cook or instant)

3 cups water

½ teaspoon kosher salt

1 tablespoon unsalted butter

3 tablespoons grated Parmigiano-Reggiano or similar cheese

½ cup diced roasted red peppers

½ cup Onion Jam (page 269)

TIP *When cooked in a pressure cooker, polenta can scorch easily, so it's important to open the cooker immediately, remove it from the heat (or turn the electric cooker off), and start stirring, scraping your wooden spoon against the bottom of the cooker.*

In my cooking classes, I'm often asked what the difference is between polenta and grits. The answer, as with many questions, is that it depends on whom you ask. Some cooks will swear up and down that the corn for polenta is ground finer than grits; others claim the opposite. Some cooks will tell you that grits is made from white corn and polenta from yellow. As I understand it, traditionally, the corn used to mill grits is different from that used for polenta, but it's not the color, it's the variety. Apparently, the two varieties have slightly different textures when cooked. That being said, don't worry about the difference. Use whatever you can find in this recipe, and it'll taste great.

1. In a stove-top or electric pressure cooker, combine the polenta, water, and kosher salt.

2. Lock the lid in place, and bring the pot to high pressure (15 psi for stove top or 9 to 11 psi for electric).

STOVE TOP: Maintain pressure for 10 minutes, adjusting the burner as necessary.
ELECTRIC: Cook at high pressure for 10 minutes. When the timer goes off, turn the cooker off; do not let it switch to the "warm" setting.

3. After cooking, use the *quick method* to release pressure.

4. Unlock and remove the lid. Quickly add the butter and Parmigiano-Reggiano, and stir vigorously with a wooden spoon or paddle until smooth and creamy. Fold in the roasted peppers and Onion Jam, and serve.

PER SERVING: CALORIES: 177; FAT: 5G; SODIUM: 500G; CARBOHYDRATES: 52G; FIBER: 1G; PROTEIN: 3G

Three-Bean Vegetarian Chili

SERVES 4

PRESSURE: High
TIME UNDER PRESSURE: 25 minutes
RELEASE: Quick

ONE POT, VEGAN

2 tablespoons olive oil

1½ cups chopped onion

4 garlic cloves, minced
  or pressed

Kosher salt

2 tablespoons ancho
  chili powder

2 teaspoons ground cumin

1 large chipotle canned in
  adobo sauce, minced (about
  2 teaspoons)

1 (14.5-ounce) can diced
  tomatoes

3 cups Mushroom Stock
  (page 268) or low-sodium
  vegetable broth

2 cups water

6 ounces dried kidney beans,
  rinsed and picked over

4 ounces dried pinto beans,
  rinsed and picked over

4 ounces dried black beans,
  rinsed and picked over

1 recipe "Sautéed" Mushrooms
  (page 200)

Unlike the beans in most recipes here, these aren't soaked before cooking. Unsoaked beans do have more of a tendency to break open, but they help thicken the sauce for this chili. The flavor and texture of the sautéed mushrooms add a meaty note to this vegan dish. If you don't have all three types of beans, use whatever combination you have or prefer.

1. In a stove-top pressure cooker set over medium heat, or an electric cooker set to "brown," heat the olive oil until it shimmers and flows like water. Add the onion and garlic, and sprinkle with a pinch or two of kosher salt. Cook for about 3 minutes, stirring, until the onions and garlic just begin to brown. Add the chili powder and cumin, and stir to coat the onion with the spices. Cook for 1 minute, or until fragrant. Add the chipotle pepper, tomatoes with their liquid, Mushroom Stock, and water, scraping the bottom of the pot to release any browned bits. Stir in the beans.

2. Lock the lid in place, and bring the pot to high pressure (15 psi for stove top or 9 to 11 psi for electric).

STOVE TOP: Maintain pressure for 25 minutes, adjusting the burner as necessary.
ELECTRIC: Cook at high pressure for 25 minutes.

3. After cooking, use the *quick method* to release pressure.

4. Unlock and remove the lid. Stir in the "Sautéed" Mushrooms. If the sauce is too thin, simmer the chili over medium heat for a stove-top cooker, or on "simmer" for an electric cooker, until it thickens to the desired consistency. Ladle into bowls, and serve.

PER SERVING: CALORIES: 468; FAT: 10G; SODIUM: 780MG; CARBOHYDRATES: 74G; FIBER: 20G; PROTEIN: 28G

Quinoa "Risotto" with Prosciutto and Asparagus

SERVES 4

PRESSURE: High
TIME UNDER PRESSURE: 5 minutes
RELEASE: Quick

GLUTEN FREE

½ pound asparagus, tough
  ends trimmed
Kosher salt
1 tablespoon olive oil
1 teaspoon unsalted butter
3 ounces prosciutto, diced
½ cup chopped onion
1½ cups quinoa, rinsed briefly
3½ cups Chicken Stock
  (page 262) or
  low-sodium broth
¼ cup dry white wine
½ cup feta cheese, crumbled
  or cut into cubes

Because it's so easy to overcook asparagus, I roast it. Roasting deepens the flavor and crisps the tips for great texture. For the risotto, quinoa takes the place of rice here for an unusual flavor twist.

1. Preheat the oven to 400°F. On a rimmed baking sheet, sprinkle the asparagus with kosher salt and drizzle with the olive oil. Stir to coat, and arrange in a single layer. Place the asparagus in the preheated oven, and roast for 8 to 12 minutes, or until the tips are crisp. Slice into 1- to 1½-inch pieces. Cover loosely with aluminum foil.

2. While the asparagus is cooking, in a stove-top pressure cooker set over medium heat, or an electric cooker set to "brown," melt the butter, and add the prosciutto. Cook for about 2 minutes, stirring, until it starts to brown. Add the onion, and cook for about 2 minutes more, stirring, until the onion pieces soften. Add the quinoa, and stir to coat with the butter. Add the Chicken Stock and white wine, and stir.

3. Lock the lid in place, and bring the pot to high pressure (15 psi for stove top or 9 to 11 psi for electric).

STOVE TOP: Maintain pressure for 5 minutes, adjusting the burner as necessary.
ELECTRIC: Cook at high pressure for 5 minutes.

4. After cooking, use the *quick method* to release pressure.

5. Unlock and remove the lid. Place the stove-top cooker back over medium heat, or turn the electric cooker to "brown." Continue to cook the quinoa for 1 to 2 minutes, stirring, until the liquid thickens slightly. Gently stir in the asparagus. Spoon the quinoa into 4 bowls, and top with the feta cheese. Serve immediately.

PER SERVING: CALORIES: 392; FAT: 13G; SODIUM: 500MG; CARBOHYDRATES: 47G; FIBER: 6G; PROTEIN: 21G

Arroz Verde

SERVES 4 TO 6

PRESSURE: High
TIME UNDER PRESSURE: 8 minutes
RELEASE: Quick

GLUTEN FREE

1 medium poblano chile, stemmed, cored, seeded, and cut into 2 or 3 strips

1 small jalapeño pepper, stemmed, cored, seeded, and cut into 2 or 3 strips (optional)

1 tablespoon olive oil

⅓ cup chopped onion

½ teaspoon kosher salt, plus additional for seasoning

¾ cup long-grain white rice

1 cup plus 2 tablespoons Chicken Stock (page 262) or low-sodium broth

12 tablespoons minced fresh cilantro, divided

If you're used to the typical tomato-based "Spanish" rice from your local Mexican restaurant, this beautiful green rice will be a welcome change. Poblanos are dark green chiles with a mild level of heat.

1. Place the poblano and jalapeño pepper (if using) pieces skin-side up on an aluminum foil–lined baking sheet.

2. Preheat the broiler. Place the baking sheet close to the broiler element. Cook for 3 to 10 minutes, depending on the strength of the broiler element, or until the skins are blackened. Remove from the broiler, carefully pull the foil up around the pepper strips, and fold over to seal. Let sit for 5 to 10 minutes, or until cool enough to handle. Peel the skin off the strips and discard. Dice the peppers.

3. In a stove-top pressure cooker set over medium heat, or an electric cooker set to "brown," heat the olive oil until it shimmers and flows like water. Add the onion, and sprinkle with a pinch or two of kosher salt. Cook for about 3 minutes, stirring, until the onions just begin to brown. Add the rice, and stir to coat with the olive oil. Pour in the Chicken Stock, and add the ½ teaspoon of kosher salt, the chopped chiles, and about 6 tablespoons of cilantro. Bring to a simmer.

4. Lock the lid in place, and bring the pot to high pressure (15 psi for stove top or 9 to 11 psi for electric).

STOVE TOP: Maintain pressure for 8 minutes, adjusting the burner as necessary.
ELECTRIC: Cook at high pressure for 8 minutes.

5. After cooking, use the **quick method** to release pressure.

6. Open the pot, and gently stir in the remaining 6 tablespoons of cilantro. Replace the lid, but *don't lock* it. Let the rice steam for 4 minutes more. Fluff gently with a fork before serving.

TIP *To save time, use a small can of chopped green chiles rather than roasting your own. They won't have the complex flavor of the poblanos, but they make this dish much easier. Rinse and drain them, then add them to the rice at step 3.*

PER SERVING: CALORIES: 168; FAT: 4G; SODIUM: 313MG; CARBOHYDRATES: 30G; FIBER: 1G; PROTEIN: 3G

Wild *and* Brown Rice Pilaf

SERVES 4

PRESSURE: High
TIME UNDER PRESSURE:
27 minutes total
RELEASE: Combination

GLUTEN FREE, VEGAN

1 tablespoon olive oil

¾ cup diced onion

1 garlic clove, minced

⅓ cup wild rice

⅔ cup water

½ teaspoon kosher salt, divided, plus additional for seasoning

½ cup brown rice

¾ cup low-sodium vegetable broth

¼ cup dry white wine

1 bay leaf

1 fresh thyme sprig, or ¼ teaspoon dried thyme

2 tablespoons chopped fresh parsley

Wild and brown rice make a great combination, and turning them into a pilaf is a natural choice. Since they cook at different rates, the wild rice is cooked partway first, and then the aromatics and brown rice go in later. This ensures that the wild rice is done, but the brown rice doesn't get mushy. To turn this into a main dish, add cooked leftover chicken at step 7.

1. In a stove-top pressure cooker set over medium heat, or an electric cooker set to "brown," heat the olive oil until it shimmers and flows like water. Add the onion and garlic, and cook for about 3 minutes, stirring, until the garlic is fragrant and the onions soften and separate. Add the wild rice, water, and ¼ teaspoon of kosher salt, and stir.

2. Lock the lid in place, and bring the pot to high pressure (15 psi for stove top or 9 to 11 psi for electric).

STOVE TOP: Maintain pressure for 15 minutes, adjusting the burner as necessary.
ELECTRIC: Cook at high pressure for 15 minutes.

3. After cooking, use the *quick method* to release pressure.

4. Unlock and remove the lid. Stir in the brown rice, vegetable broth, remaining ¼ teaspoon of kosher salt, white wine, bay leaf, and thyme.

5. Lock the lid in place, and bring the pot back to high pressure (15 psi for stove top or 9 to 11 psi for electric).

STOVE TOP: Maintain pressure for 12 minutes, adjusting the burner as necessary.
ELECTRIC: Cook at high pressure for 12 minutes. When the timer goes off, turn the cooker off. Do not let it switch to the "warm" setting.

6. After cooking, use the *natural method* to release pressure for 12 minutes, then the *quick method* to release the remaining pressure.

7. Unlock and remove the lid. Remove the bay leaf and thyme sprig, and stir in the parsley. Taste and adjust the seasoning, as needed. Replace but *do not lock* the lid. Let the rice steam for about 4 minutes, fluff gently with a fork, and serve.

PER SERVING: CALORIES: 195; FAT: 4G; SODIUM: 309MG; CARBOHYDRATES: 32G; FIBER: 2G; PROTEIN: 5G

Mediterranean Chickpea Salad

SERVES 2 AS A MAIN DISH
OR 4 AS A SIDE DISH

PRESSURE: High
TIME UNDER PRESSURE: 3 minutes
RELEASE: Combination

GLUTEN FREE, VEGAN

1 tablespoon plus 1 teaspoon
kosher salt, divided

2 quarts water, divided

6 ounces dried chickpeas
(garbanzo beans)

3 tablespoons plus 1 teaspoon
extra-virgin olive oil, divided

2 tablespoons freshly squeezed
lemon juice

½ teaspoon ground cumin

¼ teaspoon freshly ground
black pepper

½ cup coarsely chopped red or
green bell pepper

⅓ cup chopped celery

½ small red onion, sliced

1 small tomato, seeded and
chopped (about ¼ cup)

1 tablespoon minced fresh mint

2 tablespoons minced
fresh parsley

½ cup crumbled feta cheese
(optional)

I developed this recipe using canned chickpeas, and honestly, the original version is very good. It wasn't until I started developing recipes for this book that I tried it with dried, soaked beans and discovered what a difference they make. Once you discover here how fast it is to cook them from scratch, you'll never buy another can.

1. In a large bowl, dissolve 1 tablespoon of kosher salt in 1 quart of water. Add the chickpeas, and soak at room temperature for 8 to 24 hours. Drain and rinse.

2. To a stove-top or electric pressure cooker, add the chickpeas. Add 1 teaspoon of extra-virgin olive oil, and stir to coat the chickpeas. Add the remaining 1 quart of water and ½ teaspoon of kosher salt.

3. Lock the lid in place, and bring the pot to high pressure (15 psi for stove top or 9 to 11 psi for electric).

STOVE TOP: Maintain pressure for 3 minutes, adjusting the burner as necessary.
ELECTRIC: Cook at high pressure for 3 minutes. When the timer goes off, turn the cooker off. Do not let it switch to the "warm" setting.

4. After cooking, use the *natural method* to release pressure for 3 minutes, then the *quick method* to release the remaining pressure.

5. While the chickpeas cook, to a small jar with a tight-fitting lid, add the lemon juice, the remaining 3 tablespoons of extra-virgin olive oil, the cumin, the remaining ½ teaspoon of kosher salt, and the pepper and shake to mix until thoroughly combined. Alternatively, you can whisk the dressing together in a small bowl, but it's easier to make in a jar.

6. When the pressure has released completely, remove the lid. Drain the chickpeas, and pour them into a large bowl. Immediately pour the dressing over the chickpeas, and toss to coat. Cool to room temperature, stirring occasionally.

7. To the bowl with the chickpeas, add the red bell pepper, celery, scallions, red onion, and tomato. Toss gently. Add the mint and parsley right before serving, and toss to combine.

TIP *To turn this into a more substantial main-dish salad, add a can of tuna, rinsed and drained, with the vegetables in step 7.*

PER SERVING (MAIN COURSE): CALORIES: 537; FAT: 29G; SODIUM: 638MG; CARBOHYDRATES: 37G; FIBER: 17G; PROTEIN: 18G

White Beans *with* Rosemary *and* Prosciutto

SERVES 4

PRESSURE: High
TIME UNDER PRESSURE: 12 minutes
RELEASE: Quick

GLUTEN FREE

1 tablespoon kosher salt

1 quart water

½ pound dried navy beans

1 tablespoon olive oil

3 ounces prosciutto
    or ham, diced

2 medium garlic cloves, minced

1¾ cups Chicken Stock
    (page 262) or
    low-sodium broth

1 or 2 fresh rosemary sprigs

2 tablespoons dry white wine

This is one of those dishes that changed the way I thought about beans. It doesn't seem possible that a few simple ingredients can transform white beans so completely. They're creamy and so flavorful you'll want to eat every last drop of the sauce, even after the beans are gone.

1. In a large bowl, dissolve the kosher salt in the water. Add the beans, and soak at room temperature for 8 to 24 hours. Drain and rinse.

2. In a stove-top pressure cooker set over medium heat, or an electric cooker set to "brown," heat the olive oil until it shimmers and flows like water. Add the prosciutto, and cook for about 3 minutes, stirring, until the prosciutto starts to crisp. Add the garlic, and cook for 1 more minute, or until fragrant. Add the Chicken Stock and rosemary to the pressure cooker, then pour in the beans.

3. Lock the lid in place, and bring the pot to high pressure (15 psi for stove top or 9 to 11 psi for electric).

STOVE TOP: Maintain pressure for 12 minutes, adjusting the burner as necessary.
ELECTRIC: Cook at high pressure for 12 minutes.

4. After cooking, use the *quick method* to release pressure.

5. Unlock and remove the lid. Remove the rosemary sprig, but don't worry if some of the needles have fallen off; they'll be tender enough to eat. If the beans are too soupy, put the stove-top cooker over medium-low heat, or turn the electric cooker to "simmer," and simmer until some of the liquid has evaporated. Stir in the white wine, and serve.

PER SERVING: CALORIES: 271; FAT: 6G; SODIUM: 602MG; CARBOHYDRATES: 36G; FIBER: 14G; PROTEIN: 17G

Wild Rice Salad *with* Walnuts, Celery, *and* Apples

SERVES 4

PRESSURE: High
TIME UNDER PRESSURE: 18 minutes
RELEASE: Natural

GLUTEN FREE, VEGETARIAN

4 cups water

1¼ teaspoons kosher salt, divided

1 cup wild rice

⅓ cup walnut or olive oil

3 tablespoons cider vinegar

¼ teaspoon celery seed

⅛ teaspoon freshly ground black pepper

Pinch granulated sugar

½ cup walnut pieces, toasted (see Tip, page 89)

2 or 3 celery stalks, thinly sliced (about 1 cup)

1 medium Gala, Fuji, or Braeburn apple, cored and cut into ½-inch pieces

Think of this as a modern version of Waldorf salad. Nutty wild rice is the perfect complement to celery, apples, and walnuts, and the vinaigrette, replacing the mayonnaise in a typical Waldorf, lets the flavors shine through.

1. To a stove-top or electric pressure cooker, add the water and 1 teaspoon of kosher salt. Stir in the wild rice.

2. Lock the lid in place, and bring the pot to high pressure (15 psi for stove top or 9 to 11 psi for electric).

STOVE TOP: Maintain pressure for 18 minutes, adjusting the burner as necessary.

ELECTRIC: Cook at high pressure for 18 minutes. When the timer goes off, turn the cooker off. Do not let it switch to the "warm" setting.

3. After cooking, use the *natural method* to release pressure.

4. Unlock and remove the lid. The rice grains should be mostly split open. If not, simmer the rice for several minutes more, in the stove-top cooker over medium heat or in the electric cooker set to "brown," until at least half the grains have split. Drain and cool slightly.

5. To a small jar with a tight-fitting lid, add the walnut oil, cider vinegar, celery seed, the remaining ¼ teaspoon of kosher salt, the pepper, and the sugar, and shake until well combined.

6. To a medium bowl, add the cooled rice, walnuts, celery, and apple. Pour half of the dressing over the salad, and toss gently to coat, adding more dressing as desired. Serve.

PER SERVING: CALORIES: 335; FAT: 17G; SODIUM: 162MG; CARBOHYDRATES: 37G; FIBER: 5G; PROTEIN: 13G

Hummus

MAKES 6 (¼-CUP) SERVINGS

PRESSURE: High
TIME UNDER PRESSURE: 3 minutes
RELEASE: Natural

GLUTEN FREE, VEGAN

2 tablespoons plus ¼ teaspoon
   kosher salt, divided

2 quarts water, divided

¼ pound dried chickpeas
   (garbanzo beans)

2 tablespoons plus 1 teaspoon
   olive oil, divided

1 tablespoon freshly squeezed
   lemon juice, plus additional
   as needed

1 tablespoon tahini (optional)

¼ teaspoon ground cumin,
   plus additional as needed

1 large garlic clove, minced
   or pressed

2 or 3 tablespoons ice water

Hummus is a wonderful condiment to have on hand. High in protein and fiber, it's a delicious addition to sandwiches or an easy and healthy snack. Making your own is simple and lets you add the flavorings you want. While tahini (sesame paste) is a common ingredient in hummus, it's not necessary. If you can't find it or don't want to buy it, the hummus will be fine without it—although you may want to increase the olive oil to 3 tablespoons.

Note: Because salt softens vegetable cell membranes, the relatively large amount in the cooking water results in chickpeas that are very soft, which is helpful when puréeing them.

1. In a large bowl, dissolve 1 tablespoon of kosher salt in 1 quart of water. Add the chickpeas, and soak at room temperature for 8 to 24 hours. Drain and rinse.

2. To a stove-top or electric pressure cooker, add the chickpeas and 1 teaspoon of olive oil. Stir to coat the chickpeas. Add the remaining 1 quart of water and 1 tablespoon of kosher salt.

3. Lock the lid in place, and bring the pot to high pressure (15 psi for stove top or 9 to 11 psi for electric).

STOVE TOP: Maintain pressure for 3 minutes, adjusting the burner as necessary.
ELECTRIC: Cook at high pressure for 3 minutes. When the timer goes off, turn the cooker off. Do not let it switch to the "warm" setting. ➡

4. After cooking, use the **natural method** to release pressure.

5. Unlock and remove the lid. Drain the chickpeas, and put them in the bowl of a small food processor. Add the remaining 2 tablespoons of olive oil, the remaining ¼ teaspoon of kosher salt, the lemon juice, tahini (if using), cumin, and garlic, and process until a coarse paste forms. Stop the machine several times, and scrape down the sides; don't worry if the mixture contains a few chunks, but it should be mostly smooth. Remove the cover from the feed tube, and with the motor running, pour in 2 tablespoons of ice water. Process until the purée is smooth, adding another tablespoon of water if necessary.

6. While you can serve this immediately, it improves greatly if refrigerated for several hours or overnight. Place plastic wrap directly on the surface of the hummus so it doesn't dry out. It will keep for about 1 week covered and refrigerated.

PER SERVING: CALORIES: 132; FAT: 8G; SODIUM: 105MG; CARBOHYDRATES: 12G; FIBER: 4G; PROTEIN: 4G

Spanish Rice

SERVES 4

PRESSURE: High
TIME UNDER PRESSURE: 8 minutes
RELEASE: Quick

GLUTEN FREE, VEGAN

1 tablespoon olive oil

⅓ cup chopped onion

1 large garlic clove, minced

1 small jalapeño pepper,
    seeded and chopped
    (about 1 tablespoon)

½ teaspoon kosher salt, plus
    additional for seasoning

¾ cup long-grain white rice

¼ cup plus 2 tablespoons
    Red Table Salsa (page 272)

¾ cup low-sodium
    vegetable broth

1 tablespoon chopped
    fresh parsley

If you eat at Mexican-American restaurants, chances are excellent that you're familiar with this sort of rice dish; it's the standard. Making it yourself, though, will probably be an eye-opener. What may be a ho-hum side dish at most restaurants can be so good you won't just push it aside to get to your enchiladas.

1. In a stove-top pressure cooker set over medium heat, or an electric cooker set to "brown," heat the olive oil until it shimmers and flows like water. Add the onion, garlic, and jalapeño, and sprinkle with a pinch or two of kosher salt. Cook for about 3 minutes, stirring, until the vegetables just begin to brown.

2. Add the rice, and stir to coat with the olive oil. Add the Red Table Salsa, and cook for 30 seconds, stirring. Add the vegetable broth and ½ teaspoon of kosher salt, and stir to combine.

3. Lock the lid in place, and bring the pot to high pressure (15 psi for stove top or 9 to 11 psi for electric).

STOVE TOP: Maintain pressure for 8 minutes, adjusting the burner as necessary.
ELECTRIC: Cook at high pressure for 8 minutes.

4. After cooking, use the *quick method* to release pressure.

5. Unlock and remove the lid. Gently stir in the parsley, and replace but *do not lock* the lid. Let the rice sit for 4 to 5 minutes, fluff with a fork, and serve.

PER SERVING: CALORIES: 174; FAT: 4G; SODIUM: 451MG; CARBOHYDRATES: 31G; FIBER: 1G; PROTEIN: 4G

Shrimp *and* Sausage Jambalaya

SERVES 4

PRESSURE: High
TIME UNDER PRESSURE: 8 minutes
RELEASE: Quick

ONE POT

2 tablespoons olive oil, divided

1 pound raw medium shrimp, peeled and deveined

2 teaspoons Cajun seasoning (see Tip, page 151), divided

8 ounces andouille sausage, cut into ½-inch slices, then cut into half moons

½ cup chopped onion

½ cup chopped green bell pepper

1 small celery stalk, chopped (about ⅓ cup)

2 large garlic cloves, minced

1 cup long-grain white rice

¾ cup low-sodium vegetable broth

1 (14.5-ounce) can diced tomatoes, undrained

2 tablespoons chopped fresh parsley

2 scallions, chopped

Many cuisines in which rice plays a big role have a dish similar to jambalaya. In Spain, it's paella; in India, it's biriyani. Whatever the country, these dishes have one thing in common: They're a way of stretching a little bit of flavorful protein a long way with rice and vegetables. Jambalaya can be made with just about any protein available, but sweet shrimp and spicy sausage are a popular combination—and with good reason.

1. In a stove-top pressure cooker set over medium heat, or an electric cooker set to "brown," heat 1 tablespoon of olive oil until it shimmers and flows like water. Add the shrimp, and sprinkle with ½ teaspoon of Cajun seasoning. Cook for about 2 minutes, stirring, until the shrimp begin to turn pink and opaque but are not quite done. Remove the shrimp to a bowl, and set aside.

2. Add the remaining 1 tablespoon of olive oil to the cooker, and heat until it shimmers. Add the sausage, and cook for 2 to 3 minutes, stirring, until it just starts to brown. Add the onion, green bell pepper, celery, and garlic. Cook for about 2 minutes, or until the vegetables soften.

3. Add the rice to the pressure cooker, and stir to coat it with the olive oil. Add the vegetable broth, and cook for about 1 minute, scraping the bottom of the cooker to release any browned bits. Add the tomatoes with their juice and the remaining 1½ teaspoons of Cajun seasoning. Stir to combine, making sure no rice is stuck to the bottom of the cooker.

4. Lock the lid in place, and bring the pot to high pressure (15 psi for stove top or 9 to 11 psi for electric).

STOVE TOP: Maintain pressure for 8 minutes, adjusting the burner as necessary.
ELECTRIC: Cook at high pressure for 8 minutes.

5. After cooking, use the ***quick method*** to release pressure.

6. Unlock and remove the lid. Gently stir in the parsley, scallions, and reserved shrimp, and replace but *do not lock* the lid. Let the jambalaya sit for 4 to 5 minutes, fluff with a fork, and serve.

PER SERVING: CALORIES: 595; FAT: 25G; SODIUM: 988MG; CARBOHYDRATES: 48G; FIBER: 3G; PROTEIN: 42G

Black Bean *and* Sweet Potato Tacos

SERVES 4

PRESSURE: High
TIME UNDER PRESSURE: 3 minutes
(for sweet potatoes) and 12 minutes
(for beans)
RELEASE: Quick

GLUTEN FREE, VEGAN

FOR THE BEANS AND SWEET POTATOES

1 tablespoon plus ½ teaspoon
    kosher salt, divided
1 quart water, plus 1 cup water
    for steaming, divided
¼ pound dried black beans
2 large sweet potatoes, peeled
    and cut into 1-inch pieces
2 tablespoons olive oil, divided
½ teaspoon chili powder
½ cup chopped onion
1 garlic clove, minced
¼ teaspoon ground cumin
1¼ cups vegetable broth
2 tablespoons Red Table Salsa
    (page 272) or
    store-bought salsa

FOR THE GARNISH AND ASSEMBLY

2 cups shredded cabbage
1 scallion, chopped
1 jalapeño pepper, seeded
    and chopped
1 tablespoon minced
    fresh cilantro
Juice of ½ lime
¼ teaspoon kosher salt
8 corn tortillas, warmed
1 avocado, sliced

Even if you're not a vegetarian, you'll love these meatless tacos. Roasting the sweet potatoes after they're steamed concentrates the flavor and browns them a bit, which makes a great pairing with the earthy black beans. While you can garnish the tacos with any toppings you like, I think the slaw and avocado are both beautiful and delicious additions.

To make the beans and sweet potatoes

1. In a large bowl, dissolve 1 tablespoon of kosher salt in 1 quart of water. Add the beans, and soak at room temperature for 8 to 24 hours. Drain and rinse.

2. To a stove-top or electric pressure cooker, add the remaining 1 cup of water and insert the steamer basket or trivet. Place the sweet potato pieces on the steamer.

3. Lock the lid in place, and bring the pot to high pressure (15 psi for stove top or 9 to 11 psi for electric).

STOVE TOP: Maintain pressure for 3 minutes, adjusting the burner as necessary.
ELECTRIC: Cook at high pressure for 3 minutes.

4. After cooking, use the *quick method* to release pressure.

5. Unlock and remove the lid. The sweet potatoes should be barely tender when pierced with a fork or knife. Transfer the potatoes to a baking sheet, and blot them dry with a paper towel. Drizzle with 1 tablespoon of olive oil, and sprinkle with ½ teaspoon of kosher salt and the chili powder. Toss to coat with the spices. Preheat the oven to 400°F. Set aside the sweet potatoes.

6. Empty the water from the pressure cooker, and wipe it dry. In a stove-top pressure cooker set over medium heat, or an electric cooker set to "brown," heat the

TIP *Leftover Spicy Citrus Black Beans (page 168) can be used instead of the beans here. Just wait until step 10 to add them.*

remaining 1 tablespoon of olive oil until it shimmers and flows like water. Add the onion and garlic, and cook for about 2 minutes, stirring, until the onion pieces have separated. Add the cumin, and stir to coat the vegetables. Cook for 1 minute more. Add the vegetable broth to the pressure cooker; then pour in the beans.

7. Lock the lid in place, and bring the pot to high pressure (15 psi for stove top or 9 to 11 psi for electric).

STOVE TOP: Maintain pressure for 12 minutes, adjusting the burner as necessary.
ELECTRIC: Cook at high pressure for 12 minutes.

8. After cooking, use the *quick method* to release pressure.

9. Place the sweet potatoes in the preheated oven, and roast them for 12 to 15 minutes, checking occasionally and turning halfway through.

10. When the pressure has released completely, unlock and remove the lid. The beans will probably be a little soupy; turn the stove-top cooker to medium-low or the electric cooker to "simmer," and cook until some of the liquid has evaporated. Stir in the Red Table Salsa.

To make the garnish

In a medium bowl, mix together the cabbage, scallion, jalapeño, and cilantro. Add the lime juice, and sprinkle with the kosher salt. Stir to combine.

To assemble

Spoon some beans into a corn tortilla, and top with a few pieces of sweet potato. Garnish with the slaw and avocado slices.

PER SERVING: CALORIES: 397; FAT: 19G; SODIUM: 762MG; CARBOHYDRATES: 49G; FIBER: 12G; PROTEIN: 12G

Vegetables and Sides

CHAPTER SEVEN

While some vegetables are too delicate and cook too quickly for a pressure cooker, there are a surprising number that do quite well. I've tried to provide an assortment here that will please just about everyone. The recipes in this chapter range from vegetable-based side dishes to meatless main dishes; in some cases, a main dish for two can easily be transformed into a side dish for four. Like the recipes in chapter 4 for fish, most of these also require close attention to cook and release times—so it's best to stick close to the pressure cooker, especially when making them for the first time.

Spicy Vegetarian Stuffed Peppers

SERVES 2

PRESSURE: High
TIME UNDER PRESSURE: 23 minutes total
RELEASE: Combination

GLUTEN FREE, VEGETARIAN

2 red, green, or yellow bell peppers, tops removed and reserved, cored and seeded

1 tablespoon olive oil

½ onion, chopped

2 garlic cloves, finely chopped

¼ teaspoon kosher salt, plus additional for seasoning

½ cup long-grain brown or white rice

⅓ cup dried lentils

1 cup Mushroom Stock (page 268) or low-sodium vegetable broth

¼ teaspoon red pepper flakes, plus additional as needed

¼ teaspoon freshly ground black pepper

½ cup diced tomatoes, canned or fresh

¾ cup "Sautéed" Mushrooms (page 200)

8 tablespoons shredded part-skim mozzarella cheese, divided

3 tablespoons grated Parmigiano-Reggiano or similar cheese, divided

1 cup water, for steaming (double-check the pressure cooker manual to confirm amount, and follow the manual if there is a discrepancy)

Lentils and rice form the base for this spicy filling for peppers, which make a perfect main dish for vegetarians and are even hearty enough for meat eaters. If you're in a hurry, the filling alone also makes a delicious casserole; just spoon it into a baking dish instead of the peppers, and sprinkle the cheese over it. Run it under the broiler, and you've saved yourself about half the time.

1. Using a paring knife and your fingers, remove as much of the ribs from the peppers as possible, leaving a hollow shell. Cut the flesh from the stem of the reserved pepper tops. Trim off any white pithy parts, and dice the flesh. You should have ⅓ cup to ½ cup.

2. In a stove-top pressure cooker set over medium heat, or an electric cooker set to "brown," heat the olive oil until it shimmers and flows like water. Add the onion, chopped pepper tops, and garlic, and sprinkle with a pinch or two of kosher salt. Cook for about 3 minutes, stirring, until the onions just begin to brown. Add the rice and lentils, and stir to coat with the olive oil. Add the Mushroom Stock and ¼ teaspoon of kosher salt, and bring to a simmer.

3. Lock the lid in place, and bring the pot to high pressure (15 psi for stove top or 9 to 11 psi for electric).

STOVE TOP: Maintain pressure for 10 minutes, adjusting the burner as necessary.
ELECTRIC: Cook at high pressure for 10 minutes. When the timer goes off, turn the cooker off. Do not let it switch to the "warm" setting.

4. After cooking, use the ***natural method*** to release pressure.

5. Unlock and remove the lid. Stir the rice and lentils. There should be a little liquid left but not more than 2 tablespoons. If there is more than that, simmer the mixture for a few minutes to evaporate the liquid. Don't worry if the rice and lentils are slightly underdone; they'll finish cooking while stuffed in the peppers.

6. Transfer the rice and lentil mixture to a medium bowl, and cool for a few minutes. Add the red pepper flakes, pepper, tomatoes, and "Sautéed" Mushrooms, and stir to combine. Stir in about 6 tablespoons of mozzarella cheese and 2 tablespoons of Parmigiano-Reggiano. Evenly divide the stuffing mixture between the hollowed-out bell peppers, packing the filling in and heaping it slightly over the tops.

7. Wash or wipe out the pressure cooker, add the water, and insert the steamer basket or trivet. Place the stuffed peppers on the steamer insert.

8. Lock the lid in place, and bring the pot to high pressure (15 psi for stove top or 9 to 11 psi for electric).

STOVE TOP: Maintain pressure for 13 minutes, adjusting the burner as necessary.
ELECTRIC: Cook at high pressure for 13 minutes.

9. After cooking, use the *quick method* to release pressure.

10. Unlock and remove the lid. Sprinkle the remaining 2 tablespoons of mozzarella cheese and 1 tablespoon of Parmigiano-Reggiano over the tops of the peppers. Place the lid back on the cooker *without locking* it. Let sit for about 2 minutes, or until the cheese melts, and serve.

PER SERVING: CALORIES: 745; FAT: 16G; SODIUM: 575MG; CARBOHYDRATES: 111G; FIBER: 29G; PROTEIN: 35G

Bow Tie Pasta *with* Mushroom Sauce

SERVES 4

PRESSURE: High
TIME UNDER PRESSURE: 5 minutes
RELEASE: Quick

ONE POT, VEGETARIAN

1 tablespoon olive oil

1 cup thinly sliced onion

3 garlic cloves,
   minced or pressed
   (about 1 tablespoon)

½ cup dry sherry or white wine

2¼ cups Mushroom Stock
   (page 268)

1 cup water

1 teaspoon kosher salt

½ pound bow tie (farfalle) pasta

3 tablespoons sour cream

1 recipe "Sautéed" Mushrooms
   (page 200)

2 tablespoons chopped
   fresh parsley

2 tablespoons grated
   Parmigiano-Reggiano
   or similar cheese

Farfalle make a perfect complement to the mushroom sauce since they hold the sauce so well. Substitute other shapes if that's what you have on hand. Avoid long pasta like spaghetti, as it tends to get gummy in the pressure cooker.

1. In a stove-top pressure cooker set over medium heat, or an electric cooker set to "brown," heat the olive oil until it shimmers and flows like water. Add the onion and garlic, and cook for about 3 minutes, stirring, until the onions just start to brown. Pour in the sherry, and cook for 2 to 3 minutes, scraping the bottom of the pan to release the browned bits, until all the sherry is almost evaporated. Add the Mushroom Stock, water, kosher salt, and pasta.

2. Lock the lid in place, and bring the pot to high pressure (15 psi for stove top or 9 to 11 psi for electric).

STOVE TOP: Maintain pressure for 5 minutes, adjusting the burner as necessary.
ELECTRIC: Cook at high pressure for 5 minutes.

3. After cooking, use the *quick method* to release pressure.

4. Unlock and remove the lid. The pasta should be almost done with the sauce a little bit thin. Ladle 1 cup of the sauce (with no noodles) into a small bowl. Cool for 1 minute, then stir in the sour cream and set aside. Add the "Sautéed" Mushrooms to the pressure cooker. With the stove-top cooker on medium-low heat, or the electric cooker set to "simmer," cook for 3 to 4 minutes, until the pasta is done to your liking and the sauce has thickened. Stir in the sour cream mixture, parsley, and the grated Parmigiano-Reggiano, and serve.

PER SERVING: CALORIES: 255; FAT: 8G; SODIUM: 424MG; CARBOHYDRATES: 39G; FIBER: 1G; PROTEIN: 10G

Thai Sweet Potato *and* Snap Pea Curry

SERVES 2

PRESSURE: High
TIME UNDER PRESSURE: 8 minutes
RELEASE: Quick

ONE POT

1 large sweet potato, peeled
   and cut into 1-inch pieces

½ cup sliced onion

Peel of 1 lime (see Tip)

Juice of ½ lime
   (about 1 tablespoon)

1 (14-ounce) can coconut milk

1 tablespoon fish sauce or
   soy sauce

1 or 2 teaspoons Thai red
   curry paste

1 large tomato, seeded and
   cut into 8 wedges

1 cup sugar snap peas, trimmed

1 teaspoon sugar, if needed

Steamed rice, for serving

A few simple Thai ingredients transform sweet potatoes and peas into a tantalizing curry. If you want a milder sauce, start with ½ teaspoon of curry paste and add more to taste. One teaspoon will make a moderately spicy dish; use two if you like it hot.

1. To a stove-top or electric pressure cooker, add the sweet potato, onion, lime peel, lime juice, coconut milk, fish sauce, and curry paste.

2. Lock the lid in place, and bring the pot to high pressure (15 psi for stove top or 9 to 11 psi for electric).

STOVE TOP: Maintain pressure for 8 minutes, adjusting the burner as necessary.
ELECTRIC: Cook at high pressure for 8 minutes.

3. After cooking, use the *quick method* to release pressure.

4. Unlock and remove the lid. Place the stove-top cooker over medium heat, or turn the electric cooker to "brown." Add the tomato wedges and peas. Bring to a simmer, and cook for about 4 minutes, or until the peas are crisp-tender. Remove and discard the lime peel. Taste and adjust the seasoning, adding the sugar if the sauce is too acidic. Serve over steamed rice.

TIP *Use a vegetable peeler to peel the zest from the lime in strips. Avoid getting much of the white pith; a serrated peeler is great for this task. If you can't find Thai red curry paste (Mae Ploy is my favorite brand), skip it and add 1 serrano chile or jalapeño pepper, seeded and minced, 2 additional teaspoons of fish sauce or soy sauce, and 2 teaspoons of curry powder, more or less depending on your preference. The taste will be different but still excellent.*

PER SERVING: CALORIES: 581; FAT: 49G; SODIUM: 768MG; CARBOHYDRATES: 35G; FIBER: 9G; PROTEIN: 8G

"Sautéed" Mushrooms

MAKES 6 (¼-CUP) SERVINGS

PRESSURE: High
TIME UNDER PRESSURE: 5 minutes
RELEASE: Quick

GLUTEN FREE, PALEO, VEGAN

1 pound white button or
 cremini mushrooms,
 washed and stems trimmed
1 tablespoon olive oil
½ teaspoon kosher salt
½ cup water

TIP *Turn these mushrooms into an easy, delicious topping for steak or a side for roasted chicken by adding 1 or 2 sliced shallots to the mushrooms when they've finished browning. Cook, stirring, for about 2 minutes, or until the shallots soften and start to brown. Pour in ¼ cup dry sherry, red wine, or white wine to deglaze the pan, scraping the browned bits from the bottom and letting most of the sherry evaporate. Season with salt and pepper.*

The best way to cook mushrooms is to take advantage of all the water they contain. Crowd them and add even more water, and they'll cook completely as they expel much of the water they contain. Once they're cooked, boil off the remaining water, and they'll brown perfectly, with a flavor so concentrated you won't believe it. I make a batch of these at least once a week to have on hand to add to all kinds of recipes. I highly recommend it.

1. Cut medium-size mushrooms into quarters and large mushrooms into eighths.

2. To a stove-top or electric pressure cooker, add the mushrooms, olive oil, and kosher salt. Pour in the water.

3. Lock the lid in place, and bring the pot to high pressure (15 psi for stove top or 9 to 11 psi for electric).

STOVE TOP: Maintain pressure for 5 minutes, adjusting the burner as necessary.
ELECTRIC: Cook at high pressure for 5 minutes.

4. After cooking, use the *quick method* to release pressure.

5. Unlock and remove the lid. The mushrooms will be smaller than when they started cooking. Turn the heat to medium-high under the stove-top pressure cooker, or turn the electric cooker to "brown." Bring to a boil, and cook for about 5 minutes, or until all the water evaporates. The mushrooms will begin to sizzle in the remaining oil. Brown for 1 minute, and then stir them to brown the other sides for 1 minute more. At this point the mushrooms can be used in recipes or refrigerated for up to 1 week.

PER SERVING: CALORIES: 36; FAT: 3G; SODIUM: 198MG; CARBOHYDRATES: 3G; FIBER: 1G; PROTEIN: 2G

Tangy Garlic Mashed Potatoes

SERVES 2

PRESSURE: High
TIME UNDER PRESSURE: 9 minutes
RELEASE: Combination

GLUTEN FREE, VEGETARIAN

1 cup water, for steaming
(double-check the pressure
cooker manual to confirm
amount, and follow
the manual if there is
a discrepancy)

1 medium-large russet potato
(about 12 ounces), peeled
and quartered

3 large garlic cloves, peeled

2 tablespoons whole-milk
plain yogurt

1 tablespoon whole milk

1 tablespoon unsalted butter

½ teaspoon kosher salt

Freshly ground black pepper

You might think the only way to get creamy, smooth, rich-tasting mashed potatoes is to mix in tons of butter and heavy cream. Not true! In this recipe, yogurt adds a subtle tang that balances the sweetness of the garlic as well as produces a beautiful texture so you can achieve perfect potatoes with a fraction of the butter and no cream at all. Steaming the potatoes allows them to cook until completely soft without becoming waterlogged, which is crucial for the smoothest mash.

1. To a stove-top or electric pressure cooker, add the water and insert the steamer basket or trivet. Place the potato pieces and garlic cloves on the steamer insert.

2. Lock the lid in place, and bring the pot to high pressure (15 psi for stove top or 9 to 11 psi for electric).

STOVE TOP: Maintain pressure for 9 minutes, adjusting the burner as necessary.
ELECTRIC: Cook at high pressure for 9 minutes. When the timer goes off, turn the cooker off. Do not let it switch to the "warm" setting.

3. After cooking, use the *natural method* to release pressure for 9 minutes, then the *quick method* to release the remaining pressure.

4. Unlock and remove the lid. Remove the potato pieces and garlic. The potatoes should be very soft and beginning to fall apart. If they are not, return the pressure cooker to high pressure, and cook for 1 to 2 minutes more, using the quick release method. Remove the steamer basket or trivet, and empty the water from the pressure cooker. Return the stove-top pressure cooker to a burner on very low heat, or turn the electric cooker to "brown."

5. Using a potato ricer, rice the potatoes and garlic into the pot, and stir briefly to evaporate any liquid. Add the yogurt, milk, butter, and kosher salt. Stir to combine and melt the butter. Adjust the seasoning, adding pepper as needed, and serve.

TIP *For the smoothest possible mashed potatoes, it's worth investing in a potato ricer. This tool, which looks like a giant garlic press, pushes the potato flesh through small holes, breaking it up into tiny bits that are easy to combine into a smooth purée. If you don't have a potato ricer, place the potatoes in the pot along with the garlic, milk, yogurt, butter, and salt. Using a potato masher, crush the potatoes and combine with the other ingredients to form as smooth a purée as possible (you may need to add more milk or yogurt to get a smooth mixture).*

PER SERVING: CALORIES: 199; FAT: 6G; SODIUM: 637MG; CARBOHYDRATES: 32G; FIBER: 2G; PROTEIN: 5G

Mashed Sweet Potatoes *with* Rosemary *and* Parmesan

SERVES 2

PRESSURE: High
TIME UNDER PRESSURE: 9 minutes
RELEASE: Natural

GLUTEN FREE, VEGETARIAN

1 cup water, for steaming (double-check the pressure cooker manual to confirm amount, and follow the manual if there is a discrepancy)

1 large or 2 small sweet potatoes (about 12 ounces), unpeeled, halved lengthwise

2 tablespoons half-and-half

1 tablespoon unsalted butter, at room temperature

2 tablespoons grated Parmigiano-Reggiano or similar cheese

½ teaspoon very finely chopped fresh rosemary

¼ teaspoon kosher salt, plus additional as needed

⅛ teaspoon freshly ground black pepper, plus additional as needed

Cooking sweet potatoes without the usual sweet glaze or marshmallow topping lets their natural sweetness shine through. A little Parmigiano-Reggiano and fresh rosemary accents their subtle flavor. As with the Tangy Garlic Mashed Potatoes (page 202), using a potato ricer results in a smoother purée, while a potato masher will give you a more rustic dish.

1. To a stove-top or electric pressure cooker, add the water and insert the steamer basket or trivet. Place the sweet potato halves on the steamer insert.

2. Lock the lid in place, and bring the pot to high pressure (15 psi for stove top or 9 to 11 psi for electric).

STOVE TOP: Maintain pressure for 9 minutes, adjusting the burner as necessary.
ELECTRIC: Cook at high pressure for 9 minutes. When the timer goes off, turn the cooker off. Do not let it switch to the "warm" setting.

3. After cooking, use the *natural method* to release pressure.

4. Unlock and remove the lid. Remove the sweet potato halves. They should be very soft and beginning to fall apart. If not, return the pressure cooker to high pressure, and cook for 1 to 2 minutes more, using the quick release method. Remove the steamer basket or trivet and pour the water from the pressure cooker.

5. When the potato halves are cool enough to handle, slip off the skins, and cut the halves into 2 or 3 pieces. Using a potato ricer, rice the sweet potatoes into the pressure cooker, or if you don't have a ricer, place the pieces in the cooker and mash with a potato masher. Return the stove-top pressure cooker to a burner on very low heat, or turn the electric cooker to "simmer." Add the half-and-half and butter, and stir or mash to incorporate. Stir in the Parmigiano-Reggiano, rosemary, kosher salt, and pepper. Taste, adjust the seasoning, and serve.

PER SERVING: CALORIES: 295; FAT: 9G; SODIUM: 419MG; CARBOHYDRATES: 49G; FIBER: 7G; PROTEIN: 5G

Steamed Artichokes *with* Two Dipping Sauces

SERVES 2

PRESSURE: High
TIME UNDER PRESSURE: 15 minutes
RELEASE: Quick

GLUTEN FREE, PALEO FRIENDLY, VEGETARIAN

FOR THE ARTICHOKES

2 (10-ounce) artichokes

1 cup water, for steaming (double-check the pressure cooker manual to confirm amount, and follow the manual if there is a discrepancy)

FOR DIPPING SAUCE #1

2 tablespoons mayonnaise

1 teaspoon freshly squeezed lemon juice

1 very small garlic clove, pressed or mashed

⅛ teaspoon freshly ground black pepper

FOR DIPPING SAUCE #2

1 tablespoon olive oil

1 tablespoon balsamic vinegar

1 teaspoon Dijon mustard

1 very small garlic clove, pressed or mashed

⅛ teaspoon dried marjoram or oregano

The first thing I ever cooked in a pressure cooker was an artichoke. I was living in San Francisco, just north of the center of artichoke cultivation, and I had a source for really fresh, beautiful artichokes. For one glorious season, I ate them three or four times a week—and I never tired of them.

To make the artichokes

1. Trim the artichokes: Cut off about 1 inch from the top, and cut the stem so it sits flat. Using scissors, trim the tops of the outer leaves.

2. To a stove-top or electric pressure cooker, add the water and insert the steamer basket or trivet. Place the artichokes, top-side up, on the steamer insert.

3. Lock the lid in place, and bring the pot to high pressure (15 psi for stove top or 9 to 11 psi for electric).

STOVE TOP: Maintain pressure for 15 minutes, adjusting the burner as necessary.
ELECTRIC: Cook at high pressure for 15 minutes.

4. After cooking, use the *quick method* to release pressure.

5. Unlock and remove the lid. Remove the artichokes and let them cool while you make the sauces (or you can make them while the artichokes cook, but the artichokes still need to cool).

To make dipping sauce #1

In a small bowl, whisk together the mayonnaise, lemon juice, garlic, and pepper.

To make dipping sauce #2

To a small jar with a tight-fitting lid, add the olive oil, balsamic vinegar, mustard, garlic, and marjoram and shake vigorously until the sauce emulsifies.

Serve the artichokes with the sauce of your choice or with both.

TIP *Although artichokes are delicious served warm, they're equally good cool (but not ice cold). If you like, cool the cooked artichokes for 10 minutes at room temperature, and then refrigerate 1 hour before serving.*

PER SERVING (WITH DIPPING SAUCE 1): CALORIES: 193; FAT: 5G; SODIUM: 372MG; CARBOHYDRATES: 34G; FIBER: 15G; PROTEIN: 10G

PER SERVING (WITH DIPPING SAUCE 2): CALORIES: 199; FAT: 8G; SODIUM: 296MG; CARBOHYDRATES: 31G; FIBER: 15G; PROTEIN: 10G

Ratatouille

SERVES 4

PRESSURE: High
TIME UNDER PRESSURE: 4 minutes
RELEASE: Quick

PALEO, VEGAN

Kosher salt, for salting
   and seasoning

1 small eggplant, peeled and
   sliced ½ inch thick

1 medium zucchini, sliced
   ½ inch thick

2 tablespoons olive oil

1 cup chopped onion

3 garlic cloves, minced
   or pressed

1 small green bell pepper,
   cut into ½-inch chunks
   (about 1 cup)

1 small red bell pepper,
   cut into ½-inch chunks
   (about 1 cup)

1 rib celery, sliced
   (about 1 cup)

1 (14.5-ounce) can diced
   tomatoes, undrained

¼ cup water

½ teaspoon dried oregano

¼ teaspoon freshly ground
   black pepper

2 tablespoons minced
   fresh basil

¼ cup pitted green or black
   olives (optional)

Long before the movie *Ratatouille* came out, I tried a recipe for the dish from one of Julia Child's cookbooks. All the vegetables were cooked separately, which, needless to say, took a long time. When I combined it all, I was very disappointed. It was tasty, but not worth the time and effort. This much-streamlined method results in a delicious dish in a fraction of the time. Don't skip salting the eggplant and zucchini; it draws out moisture and keeps the vegetables from collapsing and turning to mush. While the olives are not traditional, they add a nice tangy note to the finished dish.

1. Place a rack over a baking sheet. With kosher salt, very liberally salt one side of the eggplant and zucchini slices, and place them, salted-side down, on the rack. Salt the other side. Let the slices sit for 15 to 20 minutes, or until they start to exude water (you'll see it beading up on the surface of the slices and dripping into the sheet pan). Rinse the slices, and blot them dry. Cut the zucchini slices into quarters and the eggplant slices into eighths.

2. In a stove-top pressure cooker set over medium heat, or an electric cooker set to "brown," heat the olive oil until it shimmers and flows like water. Add the onion and garlic, and sprinkle with a pinch or two of kosher salt. Cook for about 3 minutes, stirring, until the onions just begin to brown. →

3. Add the eggplant, zucchini, green bell pepper, red bell pepper, celery, tomatoes with their juice, water, and oregano.

4. Lock the lid in place, and bring the pot to high pressure (15 psi for stove top or 9 to 11 psi for electric).

STOVE TOP: Maintain pressure for 4 minutes, adjusting the burner as necessary.
ELECTRIC: Cook at high pressure for 4 minutes.

5. After cooking, use the ***natural method*** to release pressure.

6. Unlock and remove the lid. Stir in the pepper, basil, and olives (if using). Taste, adjust the seasoning as needed, and serve.

TIP *While this vegetable dish is usually served on its own, it's great tossed with cooked pasta or served over polenta.*

PER SERVING: CALORIES: 149; FAT: 8G; SODIUM: 55MG; CARBOHYDRATES: 20G; FIBER: 8G; PROTEIN: 4G

Balsamic-Braised Brussels Sprouts

SERVES 2

PRESSURE: High
TIME UNDER PRESSURE: 1 minute
RELEASE: Quick

PALEO

1 bacon slice, diced

½ pound Brussels sprouts,
    root ends trimmed, halved

¼ teaspoon kosher salt

1 garlic clove, minced

¼ cup Chicken Stock (page 262)
    or low-sodium broth

1 tablespoon balsamic vinegar

People seem to either love or hate Brussels sprouts. If you're in the former camp, this recipe will be right up your alley. If you're in the latter camp, you probably won't try it, but you really should. You might be surprised. Because, well, you know: bacon.

1. To a stove-top pressure cooker set over medium heat, or an electric cooker set to "brown," add the bacon, and cook for 4 to 7 minutes, stirring, until the bacon is crisp and has rendered its fat. Using a slotted spoon, transfer the bacon to paper towels to drain. Set aside.

2. To the cooker, add the Brussels sprouts, and sprinkle with the kosher salt. Let sit for about 1 minute, undisturbed, or until they brown in spots. Stir and cook for 1 minute more so the other sides start to brown. Add the garlic, and cook for 1 minute; then pour in the chicken stock.

3. Lock the lid in place, and bring the pot to high pressure (15 psi for stove top or 9 to 11 psi for electric).

STOVE TOP: Maintain pressure for 1 minute, adjusting the burner as necessary.
ELECTRIC: Cook at high pressure for 1 minute.

4. After cooking, use the *quick method* to release pressure.

5. Unlock and remove the lid. Place the stove-top cooker over medium-high heat, or turn the electric cooker to "brown." Cook for 2 to 4 minutes, stirring, just until the liquid in the cooker evaporates. Drizzle the balsamic vinegar over, and stir to coat. Serve sprinkled with the reserved bacon.

PER SERVING: CALORIES: 5; FAT: 1G; SODIUM: 362MG; CARBOHYDRATES: 11G; FIBER: 4G; PROTEIN: 5G

Beets *and* Greens *with* Horseradish Sauce

SERVES 4

PRESSURE: High
TIME UNDER PRESSURE: 10 minutes
RELEASE: Natural

VEGETARIAN

2 large or 3 small beets with greens, scrubbed and root ends trimmed

1 cup water, for steaming (double-check the pressure cooker manual to confirm amount, and follow the manual if there is a discrepancy)

2 tablespoons sour cream

1 tablespoon whole milk

1 teaspoon prepared horseradish

¼ teaspoon lemon zest

⅛ teaspoon kosher salt, divided

2 teaspoons unsalted butter

1 tablespoon minced fresh chives

Earthy beets and pungent horseradish are a match made in heaven. In this dish, beets and their greens are complemented by a delicious sour cream–based dressing with a strong punch from the horseradish and the brightness of lemon zest. For a refreshing salad, toss cold cooked beets with the dressing.

1. Trim off the beet greens and set aside. If the beets are very large (3 inches or more in diameter), quarter them; otherwise, halve them.

2. To a stove-top or electric pressure cooker, add the water and insert the steamer basket or trivet. Place the beets on the steamer insert.

3. Lock the lid in place, and bring the pot to high pressure (15 psi for stove top or 9 to 11 psi for electric).

STOVE TOP: Maintain pressure for 10 minutes, adjusting the burner as necessary.
ELECTRIC: Cook at high pressure for 10 minutes. When the timer goes off, turn the cooker off. Do not let it switch to the "warm" setting.

4. After cooking, use the *natural method* to release pressure.

5. While the beets are cooking and the pressure is releasing, wash the greens and slice them into ½-inch-thick ribbons, removing any tough stems. In a small bowl, whisk together the sour cream, milk, horseradish, lemon zest, and ¹⁄₁₆ teaspoon of kosher salt.

6. When the pressure has released completely, unlock and remove the lid. Remove the beets and cool slightly; then use a paring knife or peeler to peel them. Slice them into large bite-size pieces and set aside.

7. Remove the steamer from the pressure cooker, and pour out the water. Place the stove-top cooker over medium heat, or turn the electric cooker to "brown." Add the butter to melt. When the butter stops foaming, add the beet greens and sprinkle with the remaining $\frac{1}{16}$ teaspoon of kosher salt. Cook for 3 to 4 minutes, stirring, until wilted. Return the beets to the pressure cooker and heat for 1 or 2 minutes, stirring. Transfer the beets and greens to a platter, and drizzle with the sour cream mixture. Sprinkle with the chives, and serve.

TIP *It may be tempting to cool the beets completely before you peel them, but that would be a mistake. Beets are easiest to peel when they're just cool enough to handle; if they get too cool, the skins tend to stick.*

PER SERVING: CALORIES: 70; FAT: 4G; SODIUM: 162MG; CARBOHYDRATES: 9G; FIBER: 2G; PROTEIN: 2G

Beet Salad *with* Mint *and* Feta Cheese

SERVES 2

PRESSURE: High
TIME UNDER PRESSURE: 12 minutes
RELEASE: Natural

GLUTEN FREE, VEGETARIAN

1 cup water, for steaming
   (double-check the pressure
   cooker manual to confirm
   amount, and follow
   the manual if there is
   a discrepancy)

2 small beets, scrubbed, root
   ends trimmed, and halved

2 teaspoons red wine vinegar

2 tablespoons olive oil

¼ teaspoon kosher salt

⅛ teaspoon ground allspice

3 tablespoons feta cheese

2 tablespoons coarsely
   chopped fresh mint

1 scallion, sliced thin

2 cups arugula or mixed baby
   salad greens (optional)

Salty feta cheese and bright mint combine so well with sweet, earthy beets that it's no wonder variations of this salad show up everywhere. I make other beet salads, but this is a great introduction to them if you're dubious. It's good enough to convert almost everyone who claims to hate beets.

1. To a stove-top or electric pressure cooker, add the water and insert the steamer basket or trivet. Place the beets on top of the steamer insert.

2. Lock the lid in place, and bring the pot to high pressure (15 psi for stove top or 9 to 11 psi for electric).

STOVE TOP: Maintain pressure for 12 minutes, adjusting the burner as necessary.
ELECTRIC: Cook at high pressure for 12 minutes. When the timer goes off, turn the cooker off. Do not let it switch to the "warm" setting.

3. After cooking, use the *natural method* to release pressure.

4. While the beets are cooking and the pressure is releasing, in a small bowl, whisk together the red wine vinegar, olive oil, kosher salt, and allspice, or put them in a jar with a tight-fitting lid and shake to combine.

5. When the pressure has released in the cooker, unlock and remove the lid. Remove the beets and cool slightly, then peel with a paring knife or peeler. Slice into large bite-size pieces, and place them in a medium bowl. Add the feta, mint, and scallion.

6. Pour the dressing over the salad, and toss gently to combine.

7. Spread the arugula (if using) on a serving platter or divide among individual plates. Top with the beet salad, and serve.

TIP *A few toasted walnuts or hazelnuts make a nice addition to this salad. During tangerine season, I also like to add the segments of a small tangerine. Just make sure you get one that's seedless!*

PER SERVING: CALORIES: 212; FAT: 17G; SODIUM: 533MG; CARBOHYDRATES: 12G; FIBER: 3G; PROTEIN: 5G

Braised Celery *and* Tomatoes

SERVES 4

PRESSURE: High
TIME UNDER PRESSURE: 12 minutes
RELEASE: Quick

GLUTEN FREE, PALEO

1 teaspoon olive oil

3 bacon slices, diced
(about ½ cup)

2 cups thinly sliced onion

½ teaspoon kosher salt, plus
additional for seasoning

1 (1-pound) celery bunch,
cut into 1-inch pieces
(about 4 cups)

⅓ cup dry white wine

1 (14.5-ounce) can diced
tomatoes, drained

Freshly ground black pepper

½ cup pale yellow celery
leaves, roughly chopped
(optional)

Poor celery; it's almost always in the background or relegated to the relish tray. But as the star of this savory braised side dish, it gets a chance to shine. I won't say that it will convert celery haters, but if you're used to thinking of this lowly vegetable only as an addition to onions and carrots in soups and sauces, you may be pleasantly surprised. The dish is based on one by the well-known Italian cookbook author Marcella Hazan.

1. In a stove-top pressure cooker set over medium heat, or an electric cooker set to "brown," add the olive oil and bacon. Cook for about 3 minutes, stirring, until the bacon has released most of its fat and just begun to brown. Add the onion, and sprinkle with ½ teaspoon of kosher salt. Cook for about 2 minutes, stirring, until the onions begin to soften; then add the celery. Stir to coat the celery with the bacon fat. Add the white wine and tomatoes.

2. Lock the lid in place, and bring the pot to high pressure (15 psi for stove top or 9 to 11 psi for electric).

STOVE TOP: Maintain pressure for 12 minutes, adjusting the burner as necessary.
ELECTRIC: Cook at high pressure for 12 minutes.

3. After cooking, use the *quick method* to release pressure.

4. Unlock and remove the lid. If there is a lot of liquid in the pressure cooker, put the cooker over medium heat, or turn the electric cooker to "brown," and simmer until most of the liquid is gone. Season to taste with a few grinds of pepper and additional salt, if necessary. Garnish with the celery leaves (if using), and serve.

TIP *This dish works best with the larger, outer celery stalks. Reserve the small, pale inside stalks for another use. One large bunch of celery should provide the 4 cups called for in this recipe.*

PER SERVING: CALORIES: 114; FAT: 4G; SODIUM: 248MG; CARBOHYDRATES: 13G; FIBER: 4G; PROTEIN: 4G

Curried Cauliflower

SERVES 4

PRESSURE: High
TIME UNDER PRESSURE: 7 minutes
RELEASE: Quick

GLUTEN FREE, PALEO FRIENDLY

½ cup white wine

1 cup Chicken Stock (page 262)
or low-sodium broth

2 tablespoons unsalted butter
or olive oil

2 teaspoons curry powder

2 teaspoons kosher salt

1 whole head cauliflower,
base trimmed flat and any
leaves removed

Cauliflower florets are not an ideal match for a pressure cooker; they overcook too quickly. But a whole cauliflower head is a different story. Prep is a breeze, and once the head is cooked, it's really easy to separate the florets. A simple yet flavorful curry sauce is a good match for this vegetable.

1. Into a stove-top pressure cooker set over medium heat, or an electric cooker set to "brown," pour in the white wine and Chicken Stock. Add the butter, curry powder, and kosher salt. Simmer for about 1 minute, or until the butter just melts and is incorporated into the sauce. Add the cauliflower.

2. Lock the lid in place, and bring the pot to high pressure (15 psi for stove top or 9 to 11 psi for electric).

STOVE TOP: Maintain pressure for 7 minutes, adjusting the burner as necessary.
ELECTRIC: Cook at high pressure for 7 minutes.

3. After cooking, use the *quick method* to release pressure.

4. Unlock and remove the lid. Using two large forks or slotted spatulas, transfer the cauliflower to a cutting board. →

5. Place the stove-top cooker over medium-high heat, or turn the electric cooker to "brown." Simmer the sauce for about 6 minutes, or until reduced by about two-thirds.

6. Meanwhile, break the cauliflower into florets. Discard the core. When the sauce has reduced to the desired consistency, add the cauliflower, toss to coat, and serve.

TIP *If you are a fan of mashed cauliflower, cook the whole cauliflower for 15 minutes on high pressure with a quick release for cauliflower so soft it will practically mash itself. Reduce the sauce by about half, and then mash the cauliflower into it, adding more broth or butter as desired.*

PER SERVING: CALORIES: 144; FAT: 7G; SODIUM: 373MG; CARBOHYDRATES: 13G; FIBER: 6G; PROTEIN: 5G

Braised Red Cabbage *and* Apples

SERVES 2

PRESSURE: High
TIME UNDER PRESSURE: 10 minutes
RELEASE: Quick

GLUTEN FREE, PALEO FRIENDLY, VEGETARIAN

2 tablespoons unsalted butter

½ cup sliced onion

1 teaspoon kosher salt, plus additional for seasoning

4 cups sliced red cabbage (about ½ small cabbage head)

½ small Granny Smith apple, peeled, cored, and chopped

⅛ teaspoon freshly ground black pepper, plus additional for seasoning

¼ teaspoon dried thyme

¼ cup low-sodium vegetable or chicken broth

1 tablespoon packed brown sugar, plus additional as needed

2 tablespoons cider vinegar, divided

Red cabbage takes on an unpleasant bluish-purple color when cooked, but a splash of acid keeps the color bright. Vinegar sets the color, and apples, sugar, or both balance the flavor. In the pressure cooker, the tang and flavor of the vinegar gets muted, so I reserve some of it to add to the dish after it's cooked. If you like a subtler taste, leave it out.

1. In a stove-top pressure cooker set over medium heat, or an electric cooker set to "brown," heat the butter until it stops foaming. Add the onion, and sprinkle with a pinch or two of kosher salt. Cook for about 3 minutes, stirring, until the onions just begin to brown. Add the cabbage and apple, and stir to coat them with the butter.

2. Add the pepper, thyme, vegetable broth, brown sugar, 1 tablespoon of cider vinegar, and 1 teaspoon of kosher salt. Stir to combine.

3. Lock the lid in place, and bring the pot to high pressure (15 psi for stove top or 9 to 11 psi for electric).

STOVE TOP: Maintain pressure for 10 minutes, adjusting the burner as necessary.
ELECTRIC: Cook at high pressure for 10 minutes.

4. After cooking, use the *quick method* to release pressure.

5. Unlock and remove the lid. Place the stove-top cooker over medium heat, or turn the electric cooker to "brown." Simmer the cabbage for 3 to 4 minutes, or until most of the liquid has evaporated, then stir in the remaining 1 tablespoon of cider vinegar, and season with several grinds of pepper. Cook for 1 minute, then taste, adding more brown sugar or salt as needed, and serve.

PER SERVING: CALORIES: 194; FAT: 12G; SODIUM: 197MG; CARBOHYDRATES: 22G; FIBER: 5G; PROTEIN: 3G

Glazed Onions

SERVES 4

PRESSURE: High
TIME UNDER PRESSURE: 6 minutes
RELEASE: Quick

PALEO FRIENDLY, VEGETARIAN

2 tablespoons unsalted butter

1 pound boiling onions (very
small white onions less
than 2 inches in diameter),
peeled, root ends trimmed
with most of the root left
intact so the onions don't
fall apart

Kosher salt

¼ cup dry white wine

3 tablespoons packed
brown sugar

1 tablespoon Dijon mustard

½ cup low-sodium vegetable or
chicken broth

1 teaspoon fresh thyme leaves
(optional)

Part of my family's Thanksgiving tradition always included creamed onions. While they were absolutely delicious, it seems like the last thing anyone needs on Thanksgiving is another creamy, rich side dish. This recipe yields an equally delicious, but much lighter, onion dish.

1. In a stove-top pressure cooker set over medium heat, or an electric cooker set to "brown," heat the butter until it stops foaming. Add the onions, and sprinkle with a pinch or two of kosher salt. Cook for 4 to 6 minutes, turning occasionally, until the onions turn golden brown in spots. Add the white wine, scraping the bottom of the pan to loosen any browned bits. Cook for 2 to 3 minutes, or until reduced by about half. Add the brown sugar, mustard, and vegetable broth. Stir to combine. Bring to a simmer for about 1 minute, or until the sugar dissolves.

2. Lock the lid in place, and bring the pot to high pressure (15 psi for stove top or 9 to 11 psi for electric).

STOVE TOP: Maintain pressure for 6 minutes, adjusting the burner as necessary.
ELECTRIC: Cook at high pressure for 6 minutes.

3. After cooking, use the *quick method* to release pressure.

4. Unlock and remove the lid. Place the stove-top cooker over medium heat, or turn the electric cooker to "brown." Simmer the onions for about 4 minutes, or until the liquid has evaporated enough to form a glaze. Sprinkle with the thyme (if using), and serve.

PER SERVING: CALORIES: 139; FAT: 6G; SODIUM: 140MG; CARBOHYDRATES: 18G; FIBER: 3G; PROTEIN: 2G

Carrots Escabeche

SERVES 4

PRESSURE: High
TIME UNDER PRESSURE: 2 or 3 minutes
RELEASE: Quick

PALEO, VEGAN

1 pound carrots, peeled and cut into ½-inch-thick slices

¼ cup white wine vinegar

⅓ cup olive oil

½ teaspoon kosher salt

3 tablespoons chopped fresh cilantro

2 tablespoons chopped fresh flat-leaf parsley

2 teaspoons chopped fresh mint

1 garlic clove, minced

Many Latin American cuisines feature vegetables prepared "escabeche" style, meaning they are blanched and marinated in a vinaigrette. Jalapeños are typically used alone or with other vegetables, but milder combinations are also popular. This beautiful, delicious version with bright orange carrots, based on a recipe by cookbook author Sandra Gutierrez, is great served with spicy meat dishes, like Chili Verde (page 64), or grilled fish.

1. In a stove-top or electric pressure cooker, place the carrots, and pour in enough water to cover them.

2. Lock the lid in place, and bring the pot to high pressure (15 psi for stove top or 9 to 11 psi for electric).

STOVE TOP: Maintain pressure for 3 minutes, adjusting the burner as necessary.
ELECTRIC: Cook at high pressure for 2 minutes.

3. After cooking, use the *quick method* to release pressure.

4. Drain the carrots, and transfer them to a medium bowl. In a small bowl, whisk together the white wine vinegar, olive oil, and kosher salt. Pour the mixture over the hot carrots, and stir gently. Cool the carrots to room temperature, then add the cilantro, parsley, mint, and garlic. Stir gently to combine. Serve slightly chilled or at room temperature.

PER SERVING: CALORIES: 232; FAT: 21G; SODIUM: 371MG; CARBOHYDRATES: 12G; FIBER: 3G; PROTEIN: 1G

Warm French Potato Salad

SERVES 2

PRESSURE: High
TIME UNDER PRESSURE: 6 minutes total
RELEASE: Quick

PALEO FRIENDLY, VEGAN

FOR THE DRESSING

2 tablespoons red wine vinegar

¼ cup olive oil

½ teaspoon Dijon mustard

½ teaspoon kosher salt

⅛ teaspoon freshly ground
     black pepper

FOR THE POTATOES AND
     GREEN BEANS

1 cup water, for steaming
     (double-check the pressure
     cooker manual to confirm
     amount, and follow
     the manual if there is
     a discrepancy)

8 ounces small red potatoes,
     quartered (1-inch chunks)

3 ounces green beans, trimmed

1 small shallot, chopped
     (about ¼ cup), or
     2 scallions, chopped
     (about ⅓ cup)

1 celery stalk, sliced thin

2 tablespoons chopped
     fresh parsley

Green beans make a good match for the potatoes in this warm salad, and the mustardy vinaigrette complements them both beautifully. In this recipe, I find it easiest to use a regular collapsible steamer basket, instead of the trivet that came with my pressure cooker, so I can lift it out after I open the pressure cooker. Then I can just dump out the water, rather than having to dump the vegetables into a colander and try to keep the trivet from coming out, too.

To make the dressing

To a small jar with a tight-fitting lid, add the red wine vinegar, oil, mustard, kosher salt, and pepper, and shake to combine. Set aside.

To make the potatoes and green beans

1. To a stove-top or electric pressure cooker, add the water and insert the steamer basket or trivet. Add the potatoes.

2. Lock the lid in place, and bring the pot to high pressure (15 psi for stove top or 9 to 11 psi for electric).

STOVE TOP: Maintain pressure for 4 minutes, adjusting the burner as necessary.
ELECTRIC: Cook at high pressure for 4 minutes.

3. After cooking, use the *quick method* to release pressure.

4. Unlock and remove the lid. Add the green beans on top of the potatoes, and replace the lid.

5. Lock the lid in place, and bring the pot to high pressure (15 psi for stove top or 9 to 11 psi for electric).

STOVE TOP: Maintain pressure for 2 minutes, adjusting the burner as necessary.
ELECTRIC: Cook at high pressure for 2 minutes.

6. After cooking, use the *quick method* to release pressure.

7. Unlock and remove the lid. Drain the potatoes and green beans in a colander. Transfer them to a large bowl, and pour the dressing over them. Cool for 5 minutes, and then add the shallot, celery, and parsley. Stir gently to combine, and serve.

PER SERVING: CALORIES: 319; FAT: 26G; SODIUM: 615MG; CARBOHYDRATES: 23G; FIBER: 4G; PROTEIN: 3G

Breakfast and Dessert

CHAPTER EIGHT

My approach to pressure-cooker breakfasts and desserts is different from that found in many recipes I've read in other books. Instead of large desserts that make four to six servings, almost all the recipes in this chapter make two individual servings. Working with larger volumes is tricky for a couple of reasons. First, you have to use large dishes, which are difficult to get into and—especially—out of the cooker. And maybe it's just me, but large desserts just don't seem to cook evenly. Finally, from a personal standpoint, I don't like having a huge dessert sitting around: It's too tempting!

Note: Most of the recipes in this chapter call for small, heatproof dishes. I use Pyrex custard cups, but you can also use small ramekins. Either can be purchased at any cookware store or most hardware stores. Whatever you use should have a capacity of about 1 cup.

"Softboiled" Eggs

SERVES 2

PRESSURE: High
TIME UNDER PRESSURE: 3 or 4 minutes
RELEASE: Quick

GLUTEN FREE, PALEO FRIENDLY, VEGETARIAN

2 teaspoons unsalted butter, at room temperature, divided

2 large eggs

¼ teaspoon kosher salt, divided

Freshly ground black pepper

1 cup water, for steaming (double-check the pressure cooker manual to confirm amount, and follow the manual if there is a discrepancy)

2 slices of toast (optional)

I like softboiled eggs, but I never used to make them. No matter how many ways I tried, too many variables would affect the cooking time: the size of the egg, how long it had been out of the refrigerator, the stove's heat level, the amount of water in the pan, and more, ad infinitum. And the only way to know whether the egg is cooked the way you want it is to crack it open. By then, it's too late. Technically, my way is cheating, but so what? It works every time because you can check how the egg is done by looking. Not done enough? Simply crimp the foil back on and set the cup back in the (still warm) cooker for 30 seconds more.

1. Using ½ teaspoon of butter each, coat the insides of 2 heatproof custard cups or small ramekins. Crack 1 egg into each cup, and sprinkle each with ⅛ teaspoon of kosher salt and some pepper. Divide the remaining 1 teaspoon of butter in half, and top each egg with one piece. (You can omit the butter on top of the egg, but it is delicious. Don't skip buttering the dish, though, or the egg won't come out.) Cover the cups with aluminum foil, crimping it down around the sides.

2. To a stove-top or electric pressure cooker, add the water and insert the steamer basket or trivet. Carefully transfer the cups to the steamer insert.

3. Lock the lid in place, and bring the pot to high pressure (15 psi for stove top or 9 to 11 psi for electric).

STOVE TOP: Maintain pressure for 4 minutes, adjusting the burner as necessary.
ELECTRIC: Cook at high pressure for 3 minutes.

4. After cooking, use the **quick method** to release pressure.

5. Unlock but *don't remove* the lid for another 30 seconds; this will help ensure that the whites are fully cooked. Using tongs, remove the cups from the cooker and peel off the foil. Scoop each egg out onto a slice of toast (if desired), and serve.

TIP *If you want two eggs per person, don't add two eggs to one cup; it throws off the cooking time. Instead, use four cups. If they won't fit in a single layer in your pressure cooker, it's okay to put three on the bottom and stack the fourth on top in the middle. The steam will circulate fine, and they should all cook evenly.*

PER SERVING: CALORIES: 105; FAT: 9G; SODIUM: 388MG; CARBOHYDRATES: 0G; FIBER: 0G; PROTEIN: 3G

Egg *and* Cheese Breakfast Sandwiches

SERVES 2

PRESSURE: High
TIME UNDER PRESSURE: 4 or 5 minutes
RELEASE: Quick

VEGETARIAN

1 teaspoon unsalted butter, at room temperature, divided

2 large eggs

¼ teaspoon kosher salt, divided

Freshly ground black pepper

2 tablespoons grated aged Cheddar or Parmesan cheese, divided

1 cup water, for steaming (double-check the pressure cooker manual to confirm amount, and follow the manual if there is a discrepancy)

2 English muffins

In the time it takes to toast an English muffin, you can have a delicious breakfast sandwich. The eggs for these sandwiches are cooked just enough so the yolk doesn't leak all over and make a mess.

1. Using ½ teaspoon of butter each, coat the insides of 2 heatproof custard cups or small ramekins. Crack 1 egg into each cup, and carefully pierce the yolks in several places to make sure the yolk cooks through evenly. Sprinkle each with ⅛ teaspoon of kosher salt, some pepper, and 1 tablespoon of Cheddar cheese, covering the eggs. Cover the cups with aluminum foil, crimping it around the sides.

2. To a pressure cooker, add the water and insert the steamer basket or trivet. Place the cups on the insert.

3. Lock the lid in place, and bring the pot to high pressure (15 psi for stove top or 9 to 11 psi for electric).

STOVE TOP: Maintain pressure for 5 minutes, adjusting the burner as necessary.
ELECTRIC: Cook at high pressure for 4 minutes.

4. After cooking, use the *quick method* to release pressure.

5. Toast the English muffins while the eggs cook.

6. Unlock but *don't remove* the lid for another 30 seconds; this helps ensure that the whites are fully cooked. Using tongs, remove the cups from the cooker and peel off the foil.

7. Using a small offset spatula or knife, loosen the eggs, then tip each one out onto the bottom half of one of the English muffins. Top with the other half, and enjoy.

PER SERVING: CALORIES: 241; FAT: 9G; SODIUM: 682MG; CARBOHYDRATES: 26G; FIBER: 2G; PROTEIN: 14G

Breakfast Grits *with* Cranberries *and* Almonds

SERVES 4

PRESSURE: High
TIME UNDER PRESSURE: 10 minutes
RELEASE: Quick

ONE POT, VEGETARIAN

¾ cup grits or polenta
    (not quick cook or instant)

3 cups water

⅛ teaspoon kosher salt

½ cup dried cranberries

1 tablespoon unsalted butter

1 tablespoon heavy
    (whipping) cream

2 tablespoons honey

½ cup slivered almonds,
    toasted (see Tip, page 89)

I, like many people not raised in the South, did not grow up eating grits—and even now I don't eat them for breakfast. Truth be told, I just don't think of them as breakfast food, but they actually make a delicious alternative to oatmeal or farina. This recipe pairs them with cranberries and almonds, with a touch of honey for sweetness.

1. In a stove-top or electric pressure cooker, combine the grits, water, kosher salt, and dried cranberries.

2. Lock the lid in place, and bring the pot to high pressure (15 psi for stove top or 9 to 11 psi for electric).

STOVE TOP: Maintain pressure for 10 minutes, adjusting the burner as necessary.
ELECTRIC: Cook at high pressure for 10 minutes. If using an electric cooker, turn the cooker off; do not let it switch to the "warm" setting.

3. After cooking, use the *quick method* to release pressure.

4. Unlock and remove the lid. Quickly add the butter, heavy cream, and honey, and stir vigorously with a wooden spoon or paddle until smooth and creamy. Spoon into bowls, top with the toasted almonds, and serve.

PER SERVING: CALORIES: 251; FAT: 11G; SODIUM: 62MG; CARBOHYDRATES: 35G; FIBER: 3G; PROTEIN: 5G

Steel-Cut Oatmeal *with* Apples *and* Cinnamon

SERVES 4

PRESSURE: High
TIME UNDER PRESSURE: 12 minutes
RELEASE: Natural

ONE POT, VEGETARIAN

3 cups water

2 tablespoons packed
brown sugar

½ teaspoon ground cinnamon

¼ teaspoon kosher salt

¾ cup steel-cut oats

1 small apple, peeled, cored,
and diced

1 teaspoon unsalted butter

1 tablespoon heavy
(whipping) cream

Everyone cooks steel-cut oats in a slow cooker. Why not be the first on your block to cook them in a pressure cooker? While they're a little time consuming if you're rushing off to work in the morning, they make a great weekend breakfast.

1. In a stove-top or electric pressure cooker, stir together the water, brown sugar, cinnamon, and kosher salt, dissolving the salt and sugar. Pour in the oats, add the apple, and stir again.

2. Lock the lid in place, and bring the pot to high pressure (15 psi for stove top or 9 to 11 psi for electric).

STOVE TOP: Maintain pressure for 12 minutes, adjusting the burner as necessary.
ELECTRIC: Cook at high pressure for 12 minutes. When the timer goes off, turn the cooker off. Do not let it switch to the "warm" setting.

3. After cooking, use the **natural method** to release pressure.

4. Unlock and remove the lid. Stir the oats, and taste; if you like them softer, place the lid on the cooker, but *don't lock* it. Let the oats sit for 5 to 10 minutes more. When they are ready to serve, stir in the butter and heavy cream.

TIP *If you want a sweeter apple that will soften a lot, use a Gala or McIntosh. For a tart apple that will hold its shape better, Granny Smith is a good choice.*

PER SERVING: CALORIES: 181; FAT: 4G; SODIUM: 157MG; CARBOHYDRATES: 31G; FIBER: 4G; PROTEIN: 5G

Crustless Quiche Cups *with* Bacon *and* Onions

SERVES 2

PRESSURE: High
TIME UNDER PRESSURE: 7 or 8 minutes
RELEASE: Quick

GLUTEN FREE, ONE POT

Butter, at room temperature,
    for coating

2 bacon slices, diced

¼ cup thinly sliced onion

¼ teaspoon kosher salt, plus
    additional for seasoning

2 large eggs

2 tablespoons whole milk

2 tablespoons heavy
    (whipping) cream

Freshly ground black or
    white pepper

1 cup water, for steaming
    (double-check the pressure
    cooker manual to confirm
    amount, and follow
    the manual if there is
    a discrepancy)

I love quiche, but it takes a long time to make, and when you factor in the crust, it's full of calories (delicious calories, but calories nonetheless). It's a special-occasion dish for me, but I've always wished there was a way to have it more often. These little savory custard cups are the next best thing, delivering the flavor and texture of quiche filling in a fraction of the time. Don't skip the cream and milk; they add a bit of fat but keep the filling creamy rather than rubbery, and no one wants rubbery quiche.

1. Using a small amount of butter, coat the insides of 2 heatproof custard cups or small ramekins.

2. To a stove-top pressure cooker set over medium heat, or an electric cooker set to "brown," add the bacon. Cook for 2 to 3 minutes, stirring occasionally, until the bacon renders most of its fat and is mostly crisp. Add the onion, and sprinkle with a pinch or two of kosher salt. Cook for about 3 minutes, stirring, until the onions just begin to brown. Transfer the bacon and onions to paper towels to drain briefly. Wipe out the inside of the pressure cooker. If you prefer, sauté the bacon and onions in a small skillet, and you won't have to clean out the pressure cooker.

3. Into a small bowl, crack the eggs. Add the milk, heavy cream, and ¼ teaspoon of kosher salt, and season with the pepper. Whisk until the mixture is homogeneous; no streaks of egg white should remain. Pour one-quarter of the egg mixture into each cup or ramekin. Sprinkle half of the bacon and onions over each, and evenly divide the remaining egg over the bacon and onions.

4. To a stove-top or electric pressure cooker, add the water and insert the steamer basket or trivet. Carefully transfer the custard cups to the steamer insert. Place a sheet of aluminum foil over the cups. You don't have to crimp it down; it's just to keep steam from condensing on top of the custard.

5. Lock the lid in place, and bring the pot to high pressure (15 psi for stove top or 9 to 11 psi for electric).

STOVE TOP: Maintain pressure for 8 minutes, adjusting the burner as necessary.
ELECTRIC: Cook at high pressure for 7 minutes.

6. After cooking, use the *quick method* to release pressure.

7. Unlock and remove the lid. Using tongs, carefully remove the custard cups from the pressure cooker. Cool for 1 to 2 minutes before serving. If you want to unmold the quiches, run the tip of a thin knife around the inside edge of the cups. One at a time, place a small plate over the top of the cups, and invert the quiches onto the plate.

TIP *Once you have this cooking technique down, add any fillings you like. Aim for 1 to 2 tablespoons total of vegetables, cheese, or meat. Any vegetables should be cooked before being added; raw vegetables will exude water and ruin the texture of the quiche.*

PER SERVING: CALORIES: 144; FAT: 12G; SODIUM: 392MG; CARBOHYDRATES: 3G; FIBER: 0G; PROTEIN: 8G

Individual Spinach *and* Feta Stratas

SERVES 2

PRESSURE: High
TIME UNDER PRESSURE: 10 minutes
RELEASE: Quick

VEGETARIAN

1 teaspoon unsalted butter, melted, divided

2 large eggs

½ cup whole milk

⅛ teaspoon kosher salt

⅛ teaspoon granulated garlic

⅛ teaspoon freshly ground black pepper

2 cups ¾-inch bread cubes

4 tablespoons chopped frozen spinach, thawed and thoroughly drained, divided

4 tablespoons crumbled feta cheese, divided

1 cup water, for steaming (double-check the pressure cooker manual to confirm amount, and follow the manual if there is a discrepancy)

3 teaspoons grated Parmigiano-Reggiano or similar cheese, divided

Oven-baked stratas require assembly the night before cooking and serving, which is significantly more planning that I usually exert for breakfast. Cooking stratas in the pressure cooker lets you skip that step, and making individual servings means they cook even faster. This version gets a Greek twist with spinach and feta cheese.

1. Using ½ teaspoon of melted butter each, brush the insides (bottom and sides) of 2 heatproof custard cups or small ramekins.

2. Into a medium bowl, crack the eggs. Add the milk, kosher salt, granulated garlic, and pepper, and whisk until the mixture is homogeneous; no streaks of egg white should remain. Add the bread cubes, and toss to coat. Soak the bread in the egg mixture for 2 to 3 minutes, gently tossing several times so the mixture is evenly distributed and completely absorbed.

3. Scoop ⅓ cup of the bread mixture into each of the two cups, and top each with 1 tablespoon of spinach and 1 tablespoon of feta cheese. Cover each with another ⅓ cup of the bread mixture, and add another 1 tablespoon of spinach and 1 tablespoon of feta cheese to each. Finish with the remaining bread mixture. Cover each cup with a small square of aluminum foil.

4. To a stove-top or electric pressure cooker, add the water and insert the steamer basket or trivet. Carefully transfer the custard cups to the steamer insert.

5. Lock the lid in place, and bring the pot to high pressure (15 psi for stove top or 9 to 11 psi for electric).

STOVE TOP: Maintain pressure for 10 minutes, adjusting the burner as necessary.
ELECTRIC: Cook at high pressure for 10 minutes.

6. After cooking, use the *quick method* to release pressure.

7. Preheat the broiler while the stratas cook, and position an oven rack in the second-highest position.

8. When the pressure cooking time has elapsed, unlock and remove the lid. Let the cups sit in the cooker for about 3 minutes, then carefully transfer them to a small baking sheet. Remove the foil.

9. Sprinkle 1½ teaspoons of Parmigiano-Reggiano evenly over the top of each strata. Place the baking sheet in the oven, and broil the stratas for about 5 minutes, or until the cheese starts to brown, and serve.

TIP *If you prefer more distinct bread chunks in your strata, lightly toast the bread cubes before tossing with the egg mixture.*

PER SERVING: CALORIES: 223; FAT: 14G; SODIUM: 533MG; CARBOHYDRATES: 11G; FIBER: 0G; PROTEIN: 13G

Cinnamon French Toast Bread Pudding

SERVES 2

PRESSURE: High
TIME UNDER PRESSURE: 10 minutes
RELEASE: Quick

VEGETARIAN

3 teaspoons unsalted butter, melted, divided

2½ teaspoons granulated sugar

¼ teaspoon plus ⅛ teaspoon ground cinnamon, divided

1 large egg

⅔ cup whole milk

¼ teaspoon vanilla extract

Pinch kosher salt

1 teaspoon maple syrup

2 cups ¾-inch bread cubes

1 cup water, for steaming (double-check the pressure cooker manual to confirm amount, and follow the manual if there is a discrepancy)

No, you can't make French toast in the pressure cooker. But you can make this bread pudding, which tastes like the eggy interior of French toast topped with crunchy cinnamon sugar. With no frying necessary, there's very little mess.

1. Using ½ teaspoon of butter each, brush the insides (bottom and sides) of 2 heatproof custard cups or small ramekins.

2. In a small bowl, stir together the sugar with ¼ teaspoon of cinnamon. Sprinkle ½ teaspoon of the cinnamon sugar in the bottom of each custard cup. Set the remaining cinnamon sugar aside.

3. Into a small bowl, crack the egg. Add the milk, vanilla, kosher salt, maple syrup, and remaining ⅛ teaspoon of cinnamon, and whisk until the mixture is homogeneous; no streaks of egg white should remain. Add the bread cubes, and toss to coat. Soak the bread in the egg mixture for 2 to 3 minutes, gently tossing several times so the mixture is evenly distributed and completely absorbed.

4. Evenly divide the mixture between the 2 cups, and cover each with a small square of aluminum foil.

5. To a stove-top or electric pressure cooker, add the water and insert the steamer basket or trivet. Carefully transfer the custard cups to the steamer insert.

6. Lock the lid in place, and bring the pot to high pressure (15 psi for stove top or 9 to 11 psi for electric).

STOVE TOP: Maintain pressure for 10 minutes, adjusting the burner as necessary.
ELECTRIC: Cook at high pressure for 10 minutes.

7. After cooking, use the *quick method* to release pressure.

8. Preheat the broiler while the puddings cook, and position an oven rack in the second-highest position.

9. When the pressure cooking time has elapsed, unlock and remove the lid. Let the cups sit in the cooker for about 3 minutes, then carefully transfer them to a small baking sheet. Remove the foil.

10. Drizzle the remaining 2 teaspoons of melted butter evenly over the tops of the two puddings; then sprinkle the reserved cinnamon sugar over them in equal amounts.

11. Place the baking sheet in the oven, and broil the puddings for about 5 minutes, or until the cinnamon sugar is bubbling and the tops start to brown, and serve.

TIP *This recipe is doubled easily, and the extras can be refrigerated and finished later in the week if you want an even easier weekday breakfast. Let them cool after pressure cooking (leaving the foil on), then refrigerate. To finish, remove from the refrigerator and bake at 400°F for 10 minutes, and then finish as directed in steps 10 and 11.*

PER SERVING: CALORIES: 206; FAT: 12G; SODIUM: 282MG; CARBOHYDRATES: 19G; FIBER: 0G; PROTEIN: 7G

Blueberry *and* Peach Compote

MAKES 8 (⅓-CUP) SERVINGS

PRESSURE: High
TIME UNDER PRESSURE: 2 minutes
RELEASE: Quick

GLUTEN FREE, VEGAN

3 cups fresh blueberries, divided
1 small peach or nectarine,
     peeled and cut into chunks
1 tablespoon cornstarch
1 tablespoon water
¼ cup granulated sugar
1 teaspoon freshly squeezed
     lemon juice
¼ teaspoon lemon zest
Pinch kosher salt

I've heard it said that blueberries are a superfood. I don't know whether that's true, but I liked them long before I heard that. This recipe brings out the best of the berries—cooking part of them with peach purée makes a delicious sauce, while adding half of them at the end keeps their texture and flavor fresh. This compote is fabulous over yogurt or, for a more decadent breakfast, spooned over pancakes or French toast.

1. Sort through the blueberries to remove any bits of stem. Measure 1 cup of the berries, including any that are particularly soft.

2. Using a blender, immersion blender, or small food processor, purée the peach. Pass the purée through a medium-coarse strainer to remove any stringy or chunky bits. You should have about ⅓ cup; if not, add enough water to make ⅓ cup.

3. In a stove-top pressure cooker set over medium heat, or an electric cooker turned to "brown," add the peach purée and the measured 1 cup of blueberries. Cook for 1 to 2 minutes, or until the liquid starts to boil. In a small bowl, whisk together the cornstarch and water, and add this mixture, along with the sugar, lemon juice, zest, and kosher salt, to the berries in the pressure cooker. Stir to distribute the cornstarch mixture. →

4. Lock the lid in place, and bring the pot to high pressure (15 psi for stove top or 9 to 11 psi for electric).

STOVE TOP: Maintain pressure for 2 minutes, adjusting the burner as necessary.
ELECTRIC: Cook at high pressure for 2 minutes.

5. After cooking, use the *quick method* to release pressure.

6. Unlock and remove the lid. Stir in the remaining 2 cups of blueberries, stirring until coated with the cooked mixture. Cool, then serve over pancakes, French toast, or yogurt. Leftovers will keep up to 1 week in the refrigerator.

TIP *It's not just for breakfast! Top ice cream or Lemon Custard (page 246) with this compote for a quick, delicious dessert.*

PER SERVING: CALORIES: 66; FAT: 0G; SODIUM: 20MG; CARBOHYDRATES: 17G; FIBER: 2G; PROTEIN: 1G

Coconut Rice Pudding *with* Dates

SERVES 4

PRESSURE: High
TIME UNDER PRESSURE: 12 minutes
RELEASE: Natural

VEGETARIAN

1 (14-ounce) can coconut milk, divided
1 tablespoon unsalted butter
¾ cup arborio or similar medium-grain rice
½ cup water
¼ cup whole milk
⅓ cup granulated sugar
⅓ cup chopped pitted dates

Coconut milk makes this rice pudding extra creamy without the common addition of egg and heavy cream, and the dates add a complex sweetness. If your coconut milk doesn't have a layer of "cream" on top, don't worry. Just add 1 cup of the coconut milk during cooking and as much as you need afterward to get the consistency you like.

1. Without shaking the can, open the coconut milk. Into a small bowl, skim off as much of the heavy coconut cream as possible from the top. Set aside. Measure 1 cup of the watery liquid that remains.

2. In a stove-top pressure cooker set over medium heat, or an electric cooker set to "brown," melt the butter, and add the rice. Cook for 1 minute, stirring. Add the water, milk, the measured 1 cup of coconut liquid, and the sugar, and bring to a simmer. Cook for about 2 minutes, stirring to dissolve the sugar. Make sure no rice is sticking to the bottom of the cooker.

3. Lock the lid in place, and bring the pot to high pressure (15 psi for stove top or 9 to 11 psi for electric).

STOVE TOP: Maintain pressure for 12 minutes, adjusting the burner as necessary.
ELECTRIC: Cook at high pressure for 12 minutes. When the timer goes off, turn the cooker off. Do not let it switch to the "warm" setting.

4. After cooking, use the ***natural method*** to release pressure.

5. Unlock and remove the lid. Stir in the reserved coconut cream and the dates, adding the remaining coconut liquid if you want a looser texture, and serve.

PER SERVING: CALORIES: 521; FAT: 27G; SODIUM: 456MG; CARBOHYDRATES: 69G; FIBER: 5G; PROTEIN: 6G

Vanilla-Ginger Custard

SERVES 2

PRESSURE: High
TIME UNDER PRESSURE: 6 or 8 minutes
RELEASE: Natural

GLUTEN FREE, VEGETARIAN

⅓ cup whole milk

⅓ cup heavy (whipping) cream

½ teaspoon vanilla extract

¼ teaspoon ground ginger

2 large egg yolks

⅓ cup granulated sugar

1 cup water, for steaming
(double-check the pressure
cooker manual to confirm
amount, and follow
the manual if there is
a discrepancy)

2 teaspoons chopped
crystalized ginger (optional)

This simple custard gets a burst of flavor from ginger in two forms. Ground ginger is added to the custard mix, and crystalized ginger tops the finished dessert. While the recipe calls for thoroughly chilling the custards so they firmly set, you can also let them cool for 20 to 30 minutes, then stir in the ginger for a softer, more pudding-like dessert.

1. In a small saucepan set over medium heat, combine the milk, heavy cream, vanilla, and ground ginger, and bring the mixture just to a simmer. Take it off the heat and cool slightly.

2. In a small bowl, whisk together the egg yolks and sugar until the sugar is dissolved and the mixture is pale yellow. Working slowly, whisk a few tablespoons of the milk mixture into the egg mixture, then repeat with a little more. Once the egg mixture is warmed, whisk in the remainder of the milk mixture.

3. Pour the custard into 2 heatproof custard cups or small ramekins. Cover with aluminum foil, and crimp to seal around the edges.

4. To a stove-top or electric pressure cooker, add the water and insert the steamer basket or trivet. Place the custard cups on the steamer insert.

5. Lock the lid in place, and bring the pot to high pressure (15 psi for stove top or 9 to 11 psi for electric).

STOVE TOP: Maintain pressure for 8 minutes, adjusting the burner as necessary.

ELECTRIC: Cook at high pressure for 6 minutes. When the timer goes off, turn the cooker off. Do not let it switch to the "warm" setting.

6. After cooking, use the *natural method* to release pressure.

7. Unlock and remove the lid. Using tongs, carefully remove the custards from the cooker and remove the foil. The custards should be set but still a bit soft in the middle; they'll firm as they cool. Cool for 20 to 30 minutes, then refrigerate for several hours to chill completely. When ready to serve, top with the crystalized ginger (if using).

PER SERVING: CALORIES: 375; FAT: 23G; SODIUM: 43MG; CARBOHYDRATES: 40G; FIBER: 0G; PROTEIN: 5G

Lemon Custard

SERVES 2

PRESSURE: High
TIME UNDER PRESSURE: 6 or 8 minutes
RELEASE: Natural

GLUTEN FREE, VEGETARIAN

1 lemon

⅓ cup whole milk

⅓ cup heavy (whipping) cream

2 large egg yolks

⅓ cup granulated sugar

1 tablespoon freshly squeezed lemon juice

1 cup water, for steaming (double-check the pressure cooker manual to confirm amount, and follow the manual if there is a discrepancy)

I love lemon in desserts and use every chance I have to try a new lemon recipe. This rich custard is sweet and tart at the same time—the perfect balance. While it both goes together and cooks quickly, it does need time to set, so make it early in the day or the day before you plan to serve it.

1. Using a vegetable peeler, remove the peel from from the lemon in strips.

2. In a small saucepan set over medium heat, stir to combine the milk, heavy cream, and lemon peel, and bring the mixture just to a simmer. As soon as it reaches a simmer, remove it from the heat and cool slightly. Remove and discard the lemon peel.

3. In a small bowl, whisk together the egg yolks and sugar until the sugar dissolves and the mixture is pale yellow. Whisk in the lemon juice. Working slowly, whisk a few tablespoons of the milk mixture into the egg mixture, then repeat with a little more. Once the egg mixture is warmed, whisk in the remainder of the milk mixture.

4. Pour the custard into 2 heatproof ramekins or custard cups. Cover with aluminum foil, and crimp to seal around the edges.

5. To a stove-top or electric pressure cooker, add the water and insert the steamer basket or trivet. Place the custard cups on the steamer insert.

6. Lock the lid in place, and bring the pot to high pressure (15 psi for stove top or 9 to 11 psi for electric).

STOVE TOP: Maintain pressure for 8 minutes, adjusting the burner as necessary.

ELECTRIC: Cook at high pressure for 6 minutes. When the timer goes off, turn the cooker off. Do not let it switch to the "warm" setting.

7. After cooking, use the *natural method* to release pressure.

8. Unlock and remove the lid. Using tongs, carefully remove the custards from the cooker and remove the foil. The custards should be set but still a bit soft in the middle; they'll firm as they cool. Cool for 20 to 30 minutes, refrigerate for several hours to chill completely, and serve.

TIP *These are delicious on their own, but they're especially good topped with a small scoop of Blueberry and Peach Compote (page 241).*

PER SERVING: CALORIES: 381; FAT: 23G; SODIUM: 45MG; CARBOHYDRATES: 43G; FIBER: 1G; PROTEIN: 6G

Poached Pears *in* Port

SERVES 2

PRESSURE: High
TIME UNDER PRESSURE: 4 minutes
RELEASE: Quick

VEGAN

1 cup medium-sweet
   Moscato, Riesling, or
   Gewürztraminer wine
½ cup ruby port
⅓ cup granulated sugar
1 lemon peel strip
1 cinnamon stick
2 large, firm pears, peeled,
   halved, and cored

I have a love-hate relationship with pears. I love them, but I hate the inconsistent results when picking them out. One will be perfectly juicy and sweet; the next will be dry and mealy. The beauty of poaching pears is that it can save less-than-perfect fruit but doesn't mask the flavor and texture of the good ones.

1. To a stove-top pressure cooker set over medium heat, or an electric cooker set to "brown," add the wine, port, sugar, lemon peel, and cinnamon stick, and bring to a simmer. Cook for 1 to 2 minutes, stirring, until the sugar dissolves. Add the pears, and stir to coat.

2. Lock the lid in place, and bring the pot to high pressure (15 psi for stove top or 9 to 11 psi for electric).

STOVE TOP: Maintain pressure for 4 minutes, adjusting the burner as necessary.
ELECTRIC: Cook at high pressure for 4 minutes.

3. After cooking, use the *quick method* to release pressure.

4. Unlock and remove the lid. Using tongs or a large slotted spoon, transfer the pears to a serving bowl.

5. Place the stove-top pressure cooker over medium heat, or turn the electric cooker to "brown," and bring the cooking liquid to a boil. Cook for about 4 minutes, or until reduced to a thin syrup. Remove and discard the lemon peel and cinnamon stick. Pour the warm syrup over the pears, and serve.

TIP *This recipe can be doubled easily and the leftover pears refrigerated with their sauce. Just warm the pears in the sauce, and serve, adding a little water if necessary to thin the sauce.*

PER SERVING: CALORIES: 433; FAT: 0G; SODIUM: 5MG;
CARBOHYDRATES: 80G; FIBER: 7G; PROTEIN: 1G

Brandy-Spiced Apples

SERVES 2

PRESSURE: High
TIME UNDER PRESSURE: 4 minutes
RELEASE: Quick

VEGAN

1 cup medium-dry white
    wine, such as Riesling or
    Gewürztraminer

½ cup brandy or cognac

⅓ cup packed brown sugar

1 orange peel strip

1 cinnamon stick

2 or 3 cardamom pods (optional)

2 large Granny Smith apples,
    peeled, halved, and cored

Like poached pears, poached apples make an elegant dessert that's not too filling. They're perfect for the end of a heavier meal—but don't stop there. They're great for breakfast, too; poach them as directed, then cut the poached halves into chunks and serve with their sauce over waffles or oatmeal.

1. To a stove-top pressure cooker set over medium heat, or an electric cooker set to "brown," add the wine, brandy, brown sugar, orange peel, cinnamon stick, and cardamom (if using), and bring to a simmer. Cook for 1 to 2 minutes, stirring, until the sugar dissolves. Add the apples.

2. Lock the lid in place, and bring the pot to high pressure (15 psi for stove top or 9 to 11 psi for electric).

STOVE TOP: Maintain pressure for 4 minutes, adjusting the burner as necessary.
ELECTRIC: Cook at high pressure for 4 minutes.

3. After cooking, use the *quick method* to release pressure.

4. Unlock and remove the lid. Using tongs or a slotted spoon, transfer the apples to a serving bowl.

5. Place the stove-top pressure cooker over medium heat, or turn the electric cooker to "brown," and bring the cooking liquid to a boil. Cook for about 4 minutes, or until reduced to a thin syrup. Remove and discard the orange peel, cinnamon stick, and cardamom pods (if using). Pour the warm syrup over the apples, and serve.

PER SERVING: CALORIES: 351; FAT: 0G; SODIUM: 15MG; CARBOHYDRATES: 55G; FIBER: 4G; PROTEIN: 1G

Chocolate Brownie Cake

SERVES 2

PRESSURE: High
TIME UNDER PRESSURE: 15 minutes
RELEASE: Quick

VEGETARIAN

2 tablespoons unsalted butter

1 tablespoon dark
   chocolate chips

⅓ cup granulated sugar

1 egg

⅛ teaspoon vanilla extract

¼ cup all-purpose flour

2 tablespoons cocoa powder

1 cup water, for steaming
   (double-check the pressure
   cooker manual to confirm
   amount, and follow the
   manual if there is a
   discrepancy)

1 tablespoon confectioners'
   sugar or powdered sugar

Part brownie, part cake, this dessert is incredibly moist. If you can manage not to eat the whole thing at once, it will keep, covered, for two or three days.

1. In a small microwave-safe bowl, microwave the butter and chocolate chips for 30 seconds on high to melt. Into a small mixing bowl, scrape the chocolate mixture, and add the sugar. Beat for about 2 minutes. Add the egg and vanilla, and beat for about 1 minute more, until smooth. Sift the flour and cocoa powder over the wet ingredients, and beat until just combined.

2. Spoon the batter into a nonstick mini springform pan (4½ inches) or a mini loaf pan (3-by-5-inch), and smooth the top.

3. To a stove-top or electric pressure cooker, add the water and insert the steamer basket or trivet. Place the loaf pan on the steamer insert. Place a square of aluminum foil over the pan, but don't crimp it down; it's just to keep steam from condensing on the surface of the cake.

4. Lock the lid in place, and bring the pot to high pressure (15 psi for stove top or 9 to 11 psi for electric).

STOVE TOP: Maintain pressure for 15 minutes, adjusting the burner as necessary.
ELECTRIC: Cook at high pressure for 15 minutes.

5. After cooking, use the *quick method* to release pressure.

6. Unlock and remove the lid. Using tongs, remove the sheet of foil. Transfer the pan to a cutting board or rack to cool. Dust the cake with the confectioners' sugar, slice, and serve.

PER SERVING: CALORIES: 370; FAT: 16G; SODIUM: 114MG; CARBOHYDRATES: 58G; FIBER: 2G; PROTEIN: 6G

Bourbon-Maple Bread Pudding

SERVES 2

PRESSURE: High
TIME UNDER PRESSURE: 10 minutes
RELEASE: Quick

VEGETARIAN

3 teaspoons unsalted butter, melted, divided

3 teaspoons packed brown sugar, plus 1 tablespoon

1 large egg

⅔ cup whole milk

¼ teaspoon vanilla extract

Pinch kosher salt

2 teaspoons bourbon, divided

3 tablespoons maple syrup, divided

2 cups ¾-inch bread cubes

1 cup water, for steaming (double-check the pressure cooker manual to confirm amount, and follow the manual if there is a discrepancy)

Sweeter than the breakfast Cinnamon French Toast Bread Pudding (page 238), this dish is meant to be served for dessert— as if the bourbon in the ingredient list weren't a clue. If you don't have bourbon on hand, substitute brandy, or omit it altogether.

1. Using ½ teaspoon of melted butter each, brush the insides (bottom and sides) of 2 heatproof custard cups or small ramekins. Sprinkle ½ teaspoon of brown sugar on the bottom of each cup.

2. Into a small bowl, crack the egg. Add the milk, vanilla, kosher salt, 1 teaspoon of bourbon, 2 tablespoons of maple syrup, and 2 teaspoons of brown sugar. Whisk until the mixture is homogeneous; no streaks of egg white should remain. Add the bread cubes, and toss to coat. Soak the bread in the egg mixture for 2 to 3 minutes, gently tossing several times so the mixture is evenly distributed and completely absorbed.

3. Equally divide the mixture between the 2 cups. Cover each cup with a small square of aluminum foil.

4. To a stove-top or electric pressure cooker, add the water and insert the steamer basket or trivet. Place the cups on the steamer insert.

5. Lock the lid in place, and bring the pot to high pressure (15 psi for stove top or 9 to 11 psi for electric).

STOVE TOP: Maintain pressure for 10 minutes, adjusting the burner as necessary.
ELECTRIC: Cook at high pressure for 10 minutes.

6. After cooking, use the *quick method* to release pressure.

7. Preheat the broiler while the puddings cook. Position an oven rack in the second-highest position. In a small bowl, stir together the remaining 2 teaspoons of butter, remaining 1 teaspoon of bourbon, and remaining 1 tablespoon of maple syrup. Place the bowl in the microwave, and cook for 15 seconds on high power. Set aside.

8. When the pressure cooking time has elapsed, unlock and remove the lid. Let the cups sit in the pressure cooker for about 3 minutes, then carefully transfer them to a small baking sheet. Remove the foil.

9. Drizzle the maple syrup mixture evenly over the tops of the 2 puddings, then sprinkle the remaining 1 tablespoon of brown sugar over them.

10. Place the baking sheet in the oven, and broil the puddings for 3 to 5 minutes, or until the brown sugar is bubbling and the tops start to brown, and serve.

PER SERVING: CALORIES: 301; FAT: 12G; SODIUM: 287MG; CARBOHYDRATES: 40G; FIBER: 0G; PROTEIN: 7G

Blueberry Clafouti

SERVES 2

PRESSURE: High
TIME UNDER PRESSURE: 11 or
14 minutes
RELEASE: Quick

VEGETARIAN

1 teaspoon unsalted butter, at
   room temperature, divided
½ cup fresh blueberries, divided
⅓ cup whole milk
3 tablespoons heavy
   (whipping) cream
3 tablespoons sugar
¼ cup all-purpose flour
1 large egg
¼ teaspoon vanilla extract
¼ teaspoon lemon zest
⅛ teaspoon ground cinnamon
Pinch fine salt
1 cup water, for steaming
   (double-check the pressure
   cooker manual to confirm
   amount, and follow
   the manual if there is
   a discrepancy)
2 teaspoons confectioners'
   sugar or powdered sugar

Clafouti (traditionally, *clafoutis*) is a French dessert traditionally made with fresh cherries when they're in season. Being too lazy to pit cherries, I've never made the dish with them but instead use berries; blueberries are one of my favorites. Part custard, part soufflé, part cake, clafouti is a delicious, easy way to showcase any fresh fruit. My version is not very sweet, making it as good for breakfast as it is for dessert.

1. Using ½ teaspoon of butter each, coat the insides of each of 2 custard cups or small ramekins. Put ¼ cup of blueberries in each cup.

2. In a medium bowl, combine the milk, heavy cream, sugar, flour, egg, vanilla, lemon zest, cinnamon, and fine salt. Using a hand mixer, beat the ingredients for about 2 minutes on medium speed, or until the batter is smooth. Evenly divide the batter between the 2 cups, filling them about three-fourths full with batter.

3. To a stove-top or electric pressure cooker, add the water and insert the steamer basket or trivet. Place the custard cups on the steamer insert. Place a square of aluminum foil over the pan, but don't crimp it down; it's just to keep steam from condensing on the surface of the clafouti.

4. Lock the lid in place, and bring the pot to high pressure (15 psi for stove top or 9 to 11 psi for electric).

STOVE TOP: Maintain pressure for 14 minutes, adjusting the burner as necessary.
ELECTRIC: Cook at high pressure for 11 minutes.

5. After cooking, use the *quick method* to release pressure.

6. Unlock and remove the lid. Using tongs, remove the foil. Transfer the cups to a small baking sheet. Preheat the broiler, and position a rack close to the broiler element. Place the baking sheet under the broiler for 3 to 4 minutes, or until the tops brown slightly. Cool for at least 10 minutes. Sift the confectioners' sugar over the clafouti, and serve warm.

PER SERVING: CALORIES: 314; FAT: 15G; SODIUM: 153MG; CARBOHYDRATES: 41G; FIBER: 1G; PROTEIN: 7G

Molten Gingerbread Cake

SERVES 2

PRESSURE: High
TIME UNDER PRESSURE: 15 minutes
RELEASE: Combination

VEGETARIAN

3 tablespoons very hot water
¼ cup vegetable oil
¼ cup packed brown sugar
¼ cup molasses
1 large egg
⅔ cup all-purpose flour
¾ teaspoon ground ginger
½ teaspoon ground cinnamon
¼ teaspoon kosher salt
¼ teaspoon baking powder
¼ teaspoon baking soda
1 cup water, for steaming
(double-check the pressure
cooker manual to confirm
amount, and follow the
manual if there is a
discrepancy)

Like the famous molten chocolate cakes on restaurant menus, this spicy cake makes its own sauce—a gooey pudding-like center in a moist, dense cake. It's even a breeze to make. What's not to like? Don't worry if the top looks a little lopsided; cooking it under pressure can cause uneven rising. It still tastes delicious.

1. In a small bowl, using a hand mixer, mix together the hot water, vegetable oil, brown sugar, molasses, and egg. In another small bowl, sift together the flour, ground ginger, cinnamon, kosher salt, baking powder, and baking soda. Add the dry ingredients to the liquid mixture. Mix on medium speed until the ingredients are thoroughly combined, with no lumps. Pour the batter into a nonstick mini (3-by-5-inch) loaf pan. Cover the pan with aluminum foil, making a dome over the pan.

2. To a stove-top or electric pressure cooker, add the water and insert the steamer basket or trivet. Carefully place the loaf pan on the steamer insert.

3. Lock the lid in place, and bring the pot to high pressure (15 psi for stove top or 9 to 11 psi for electric).

STOVE TOP: Maintain pressure for 15 minutes, adjusting the burner as necessary.
ELECTRIC: Cook at high pressure for 15 minutes. When the timer goes off, turn the cooker off. Do not let it switch to the "warm" setting.

4. After cooking, use the *natural method* to release pressure for 5 minutes, then the **quick method** to release the remaining pressure.

5. Unlock and remove the lid. Using tongs, carefully remove the pan from the pressure cooker. Let the cake rest for 2 to 3 minutes, remove the foil, slice, and serve.

TIP *To sift the dry ingredients, place a medium-coarse sieve over a small bowl or on a sheet of wax paper or parchment paper. Measure the dry ingredients into the sieve. Tap the side of the sieve to move the contents through the sieve to the bowl or parchment paper; then transfer the sifted ingredients to the wet ingredients.*

PER SERVING: CALORIES: 639; FAT: 30G; SODIUM: 506MG; CARBOHYDRATES: 87G; FIBER: 2G; PROTEIN: 8G

Creamy Orange Cheesecakes

SERVES 4

PRESSURE: High
TIME UNDER PRESSURE: 6 or 7 minutes
RELEASE: Combination

VEGETARIAN

FOR THE CRUST

- ⅔ cup vanilla wafer cookie crumbs or graham cracker crumbs
- 3 tablespoons unsalted butter, melted, plus additional butter at room temperature for greasing

FOR THE FILLING

- 2 tablespoons sour cream
- 6 ounces cream cheese, at room temperature
- ¼ cup granulated sugar
- 1 large egg
- 2 teaspoons orange juice concentrate
- 2 teaspoons orange liqueur
- ½ teaspoon vanilla extract
- ½ teaspoon orange zest
- 1 cup water, for steaming (double-check the pressure cooker manual to confirm amount, and follow the manual if there is a discrepancy)

These little cheesecakes are reminiscent of Creamsicles but are a more sophisticated version of that childhood treat. Subtly flavored with orange and vanilla, they're a delicious way to enjoy cheesecake without all the fuss. Vanilla cookies will make a sweeter crust; substitute graham crackers for a more traditional base.

To make the crust

In medium bowl, mix together the cookie crumbs with the melted butter. Brush the sides of 4 ramekins or custard cups with room-temperature butter. Scoop about 3 tablespoons of the crumb mixture into each of the ramekins. If you like, for a crisper crust, place the ramekins into a 350°F oven and bake for 5 to 8 minutes, or until lightly browned and fragrant. Let the ramekins cool.

To make the filling

1. In a small bowl, using a hand mixer, beat the sour cream and cream cheese until smooth. Gradually add the sugar, continuing to beat until the mixture is smooth again. Beat in the egg until fully incorporated. Mix in the orange juice concentrate, orange liqueur, vanilla, and orange zest.

2. Evenly divide the batter among the ramekins (a generous ¼ cup is about the right amount).

3. To a stove-top or electric pressure cooker, add the water and insert the steamer basket or trivet. Place the ramekins on the steamer insert. If they won't fit in one layer, it's fine to layer them—three on the bottom and one on top in the middle. Cover with foil, but don't crimp it down; it's just to keep steam from condensing on top of the cheesecakes.

4. Lock the lid in place, and bring the pot to high pressure (15 psi for stove top or 9 to 11 psi for electric).

STOVE TOP: Maintain pressure for 7 minutes.
ELECTRIC: Cook at high pressure for 6 minutes. When the timer goes off, turn the cooker off. Do not let it switch to the "warm" setting.

5. After cooking, use the ***natural method*** to release pressure for 8 minutes. After 8 minutes, if the pressure hasn't released entirely, use the ***quick method*** to release the rest of the pressure.

6. Using tongs, remove the foil from the ramekins. Remove the ramekins from the cooker. Place the ramekins on a small sheet pan or plate, and refrigerate to chill thoroughly (4 hours to overnight) before serving.

PER SERVING: CALORIES: 382; FAT: 28G; SODIUM: 348MG; CARBOHYDRATES: 29G; FIBER: 1G; PROTEIN: 6G

Stocks and Sauces

CHAPTER NINE

It's said that stock or broth is the backbone of the kitchen, and nowhere is that more evident than in pressure cooking, where the cooking liquid is one of the keys to success. This chapter includes three not-very-traditional versions of three traditional stocks: Chicken Stock, Beef Stock, and vegetable stock (Mushroom Stock). If you've never made homemade stock, I urge you to try at least one of them. You'll also find a more traditional recipe for a "new" discovery: "Bone" Broth. To finish, there are recipes for classic sauces like Quick Marinara Sauce and a few unusual ones, like Onion Jam, with suggestions for using them in other recipes or dishes.

Chicken Stock

MAKES 1 QUART

PRESSURE: High
TIME UNDER PRESSURE: 1 hour,
30 minutes
RELEASE: Natural

PALEO

2 pounds meaty chicken
  bones (backs, wing tips,
  leg quarters)
¼ teaspoon kosher salt, plus
  additional as needed
1 quart water, plus additional
  as needed

There are few things that make me feel more secure, culinarily, than having a few quarts of chicken stock in the freezer. Cutting the time down from the 8 (or more) hours it takes in a stockpot to a mere 90 minutes means I have virtually constant security in my kitchen. If you're used to stock recipes that call for the addition of vegetables and herbs, you may find this formula strange. Having made stock both ways, I've come to prefer it without the addition of vegetables, which can become bitter if overcooked and tend to mask the chicken flavor. If you like a more intense flavor, you can roast the bones as in the recipe for Beef Stock (see page 264).

1. To a stove-top or electric pressure cooker, add the chicken parts, and sprinkle with ¼ teaspoon of kosher salt. Add the water, plus additional as needed to cover the bones by about 1 inch.

2. Lock the lid in place, and bring the pot to high pressure (15 psi for stove top or 9 to 11 psi for electric).

STOVE TOP: Maintain pressure for 1 hour, 30 minutes, adjusting the burner as necessary.
ELECTRIC: Cook at high pressure for 1 hour, 30 minutes. When the timer goes off, turn the cooker off. Do not let it switch to the "warm" setting.

3. After cooking, use the *natural method* to release pressure.

4. Unlock and remove the lid.

5. Over a large bowl, place a colander lined with cheesecloth or a clean kitchen towel (you'll never get the towel completely clean, so don't use a nice one). Pour the chicken parts and stock into the colander to strain out the chicken and bones. Cool the stock, and refrigerate for several hours or overnight so the fat hardens on top.

6. Using a large spoon, peel the layer of fat off the stock. Measure the amount of stock. If you have more than 1 quart (you probably will), pour the stock into a pot set over high heat, and bring to a boil. Continue to boil for 15 to 30 minutes or more, until it is reduced to 1 quart. The reduction time will depend on how much water you start with. If you like, add ½ teaspoon of the remaining kosher salt per quart to approximate the salt level of commercial low-sodium broths. The stock can be refrigerated for several days or frozen for several months.

TIP *To cool the stock more quickly, plug your sink and fill it with ice water. Place the bowl of stock in the ice water, and stir occasionally for about 20 minutes.*

PER SERVING (1 CUP): CALORIES: 54; FAT: 3G; SODIUM: 213MG; CARBOHYDRATES: 8G; FIBER: 0G; PROTEIN: 6G

Beef Stock

MAKES 1 QUART

PRESSURE: High
TIME UNDER PRESSURE: 2 hours
RELEASE: Natural

PALEO

1 tablespoon olive oil

2 pounds meaty beef bones
(back ribs, beef shanks,
short ribs, oxtails)

¼ teaspoon kosher salt, plus
additional as needed

1 quart water, plus additional
as needed

Unlike what I recommend for making Chicken Stock (page 262), here I recommend roasting or searing the bones for beef stock before they go in the water—especially if you have bones without much meat, as they can taste a bit harsh when cooked raw. As in the chicken recipe, I don't add vegetables to my beef stock. I prefer the simpler taste of just the beef. If what you're looking for is a beef broth with vegetables, you'll want to check out the recipe for "Bone" Broth (page 266).

1. In a stove-top pressure cooker set over medium heat, or an electric cooker set to "brown," heat the olive oil until it shimmers and flows like water. Add the beef bones in a single layer, and sear on at least two sides. Work in batches if necessary so as not to crowd the pot. If you prefer, place the bones on a baking sheet, and broil them for 5 to 10 minutes, or until browned.

2. Sprinkle the bones with the ¼ teaspoon of kosher salt. Add the water, plus additional as needed to cover the bones by 1 inch.

3. Lock the lid in place, and bring the pot to high pressure (15 psi for stove top or 9 to 11 psi for electric).

STOVE TOP: Maintain pressure for 2 hours, adjusting the burner as necessary.
ELECTRIC: Cook at high pressure for 2 hours. When the timer goes off, turn the cooker off. Do not let it switch to the "warm" setting.

4. After cooking, use the *natural method* to release pressure.

5. Unlock and remove the lid.

6. Over a large bowl, place a colander lined with cheesecloth or a clean kitchen towel (you'll never get the towel completely clean, so don't use a nice one). Pour the beef bones and stock into the colander to strain. Cool the stock, and refrigerate for several hours or overnight so the fat hardens on top.

7. Using a large spoon, peel the layer of fat off the stock. Measure the amount of stock. If you have more than 1 quart (you probably will), pour the stock into a pot set over high heat, and bring to a boil. Boil for 15 to 30 minutes or more, until it's reduced to 1 quart. The reduction time will depend on how much water you start with. If you like, add ½ teaspoon of the remaining kosher salt per quart to approximate the salt level of commercial low-sodium broths. The stock can be refrigerated for several days or frozen for several months.

TIP *Before freezing stock, divide it into 1-cup portions, and pour it into small, resealable freezer bags or containers. Then you can pull out just the amount you need and thaw it in no time.*

PER SERVING (1 CUP): CALORIES: 52; FAT: 1G; SODIUM: 134MG; CARBOHYDRATES: 0G; FIBER. 0G, PROTEIN: 4G

Bone Broth

MAKES 1½ QUARTS

PRESSURE: High
TIME UNDER PRESSURE: 2 hours
RELEASE: Natural

PALEO

1 tablespoon olive oil

2 pounds meaty beef or veal bones (back ribs, beef shanks, short ribs, oxtails) or a mix of beef and chicken parts

½ teaspoon kosher salt

1 tablespoon tomato paste

2 medium onions, peeled and halved

1 large carrot, peeled and cut into 3 or 4 pieces

1 large celery stalk, cut into 3 or 4 pieces

1 or 2 fresh thyme or parsley sprigs or both

So-called "bone broth" is the perfect example of the adage "What's old is new again." Classically trained chefs (that is, chefs trained in the French/European tradition) know bone broth by its old name: stock. In the French kitchen, most savory dishes started with veal or beef stock, which also included tomato paste, vegetables, and herbs. The main difference between today's bone broth and yesterday's stock is the way it's used. Then, it was an ingredient; now, it's a dish on its own. Whichever way you want to use it, this recipe will give you a delicious version in a fraction of the time it used to take in the classical kitchen.

1. In a stove-top pressure cooker set over medium heat, or an electric cooker set to "brown," heat the olive oil until it shimmers and flows like water. Add the beef bones in a single layer, and sear on at least two sides. Work in batches if necessary so as not to crowd the pot. If you prefer, place the bones on a baking sheet, and broil them for 5 to 10 minutes, or until browned.

2. Sprinkle the bones with the kosher salt, and add the tomato paste to the pressure cooker. Stir to coat the bones with the tomato paste, and cook for 1 to 2 minutes, or until the paste darkens slightly. Add the onions, carrot, celery, and thyme. Add enough water to the pot to cover the contents by 1 inch.

3. Lock the lid in place, and bring the pot to high pressure (15 psi for stove top or 9 to 11 psi for electric).

STOVE TOP: Maintain pressure for 2 hours, adjusting the burner as necessary.

ELECTRIC: Cook at high pressure for 2 hours. When the timer goes off, turn the cooker off. Do not let it switch to the "warm" setting.

4. After cooking, use the *natural method* to release pressure.

5. Unlock and remove the lid.

6. Over a large bowl, place a colander lined with cheese-cloth or a clean kitchen towel (you'll never get the towel completely clean, so don't use a nice one). Pour the beef bones, vegetables, and stock into the colander to strain. Cool the stock, and refrigerate for several hours or overnight so that the fat hardens on top.

7. Using a large spoon, peel the layer of fat off the stock. Measure the amount of stock. If you have more than 1½ quarts (you probably will), pour the stock into a pot set over high heat, and bring to a boil. Boil for 15 to 30 minutes or more, until reduced to 1½ quarts. The reduction time will depend on how much water you start with. The stock can be refrigerated for several days or frozen for several months.

PER SERVING (1 CUP): CALORIES: 66; FAT: 3G; SODIUM: 287MG; CARBOHYDRATES: 1G; FIBER: 0G; PROTEIN: 4G

Mushroom Stock

MAKES 1 QUART

PRESSURE: High
TIME UNDER PRESSURE: 45 or
55 minutes
RELEASE: Natural

PALEO, VEGAN

1 tablespoon olive oil

4 ounces (about 4 medium)
   shallots, sliced thin

1 pound cremini mushrooms,
   sliced thin

3½ cups water

In terms of culinary magic, it doesn't get better than this recipe. I first read about this method in Nathan Myhrvold's *Modernist Cuisine* and thought it couldn't be as good as everyone said it was—and was I ever wrong. It still amazes me that nothing but mushrooms and browned shallots can produce this much flavor in under an hour.

1. In a stove-top pressure cooker set over medium heat, or an electric cooker set to "brown," heat the olive oil until it shimmers and flows like water. Add the shallots, and cook for about 6 minutes, stirring, until the shallots are quite brown. Add the mushrooms and water.

2. Lock the lid in place, and bring the pot to high pressure (15 psi for stove top or 9 to 11 psi for electric).

STOVE TOP: Maintain pressure for 45 minutes, adjusting the burner as necessary.
ELECTRIC: Cook at high pressure for 55 minutes. When the timer goes off, turn the cooker off. Do not let it switch to the "warm" setting.

3. After cooking, use the *natural method* to release pressure.

4. Unlock and remove the lid. Pour the contents through a fine strainer into a bowl, and use.

PER SERVING (1 CUP): CALORIES: 81; FAT: 4G; SODIUM: 10MG; CARBOHYDRATES: 9G; FIBER: 1G; PROTEIN: 4G

Onion Jam

MAKES 5 TO 6
(2-TABLESPOON) SERVINGS

PRESSURE: High
TIME UNDER PRESSURE: 35 or
40 minutes
RELEASE: Quick

**GLUTEN FREE, PALEO FRIENDLY,
VEGETARIAN**

2 tablespoons unsalted butter

5 cups sliced onions

1 teaspoon kosher salt, plus
additional as needed

1½ teaspoons balsamic
vinegar, plus additional
as needed

Similar to what many people call "caramelized onions," Onion Jam is simply onions with a bit of butter cooked slowly until the onions become soft and sweet. While these onions don't turn as dark as those cooked by conventional methods, the cooking time is cut substantially—and the flavor is still as delicious. Use Onion Jam on sandwiches, stir it into Tangy Garlic Mashed Potatoes (page 202), or use it as a base for French Onion Soup (page 130). The onions will keep for 1 week in the refrigerator or several months in the freezer.

1. In a stove-top pressure cooker set over medium heat, or an electric cooker set to "brown," heat the butter until it melts. Add the onions and kosher salt, and stir just to distribute the salt and coat the onions with the butter.

2. Lock the lid in place, and bring the pot to high pressure (15 psi for stove top or 9 to 11 psi for electric).

STOVE TOP: Maintain pressure for 35 minutes, adjusting the burner as necessary.
ELECTRIC: Cook at high pressure for 40 minutes.

3. After cooking, use the *quick method* to release pressure.

4. Unlock and remove the lid. The onions should be very soft and light tan, and there will be a lot of liquid in the pressure cooker. Place the stove-top cooker over medium-high heat, or turn the electric cooker to "brown." Boil off the liquid for about 15 minutes, or until the onions hold together and darken slightly. Stir in the balsamic vinegar, and taste, adding more kosher salt or vinegar, if necessary.

PER SERVING: CALORIES: 73; FAT: 4G; SODIUM: 419MG; CARBOHYDRATES: 9G; FIBER: 2G; PROTEIN: 1G

Quick Marinara Sauce

MAKES ABOUT 4 CUPS (8 SERVINGS)

PRESSURE: High
TIME UNDER PRESSURE: 8 minutes
RELEASE: Quick

PALEO, VEGAN

1 (28- to 32-ounce) can whole tomatoes

3 tablespoons olive oil

2 tablespoons very coarsely chopped garlic

2 large jalapeños, seeded and chopped

1 to 2 fresh oregano sprigs, or ½ teaspoon dried oregano

1 teaspoon kosher salt, plus additional for seasoning

Say good-bye to the jar. Marinara sauce is so easy to make that once you try this recipe, you'll never buy the jarred stuff again. Start with good-quality tomatoes; San Marzano tomatoes are classic for marinara recipes. Jalapeños add heat and flavor, but they're not exactly traditional. If you prefer, swap them out for ⅛ teaspoon of red pepper flakes.

1. In a large bowl, use your hands, a large fork, or a potato masher to break up the tomatoes. You can use an immersion blender, but go easy if you do; you want chunks of tomatoes, not a purée.

2. In a stove-top pressure cooker set over medium heat, or an electric cooker set to "brown," heat the olive oil until it shimmers and flows like water. Add the garlic and jalapeños, and cook for about 2 minutes, stirring, until the garlic pieces begin to brown. Add the tomatoes, oregano, and kosher salt, and stir to combine.

3. Lock the lid in place, and bring the pot to high pressure (15 psi for stove top or 9 to 11 psi for electric).

STOVE TOP: Maintain pressure for 8 minutes, adjusting the burner as necessary.
ELECTRIC: Cook at high pressure for 8 minutes.

4. After cooking, use the *quick method* to release pressure.

5. Unlock and remove the lid. The sauce should be fairly thick; if there is a lot of liquid left in the cooker, place the stove-top cooker over medium heat, or turn the electric cooker to "brown," and simmer until the excess liquid evaporates. Taste and adjust the seasoning, if needed.

PER SERVING: CALORIES: 72; FAT: 5G; SODIUM: 465MG; CARBOHYDRATES: 6G; FIBER: 1G; PROTEIN: 1G

Red Table Salsa

MAKES ABOUT 2½ CUPS

PRESSURE: High
TIME UNDER PRESSURE: 3 minutes
RELEASE: Quick

PALEO, VEGAN

1 (14-ounce) can fire-roasted
   tomatoes, undrained

1 large red bell pepper, roasted

1 or 2 chipotle peppers
   (reconstituted in boiling
   water for 10 minutes,
   if dried)

1 very small onion,
   cut into chunks

2 tablespoons olive oil

1 tablespoon cider vinegar

2 teaspoons ground cumin

1 teaspoon kosher salt

This is one of those recipes that seem too simple to taste so good. I tried dozens of combinations of chiles and tomatoes, both roasted and raw, before I settled on this version, which always gets rave reviews. Once I served it at a cooking class, and one of the students asked whether he could buy the leftovers to take home. It's that good.

1. In a blender or food processor, purée the tomatoes with their juice and the roasted red bell pepper, chipotle pepper, and onion until mostly smooth.

2. In a stove-top pressure cooker set over medium heat, or an electric cooker set to "brown," heat the olive oil until it shimmers and flows like water. Add the tomato mixture.

3. Lock the lid in place, and bring the pot to high pressure (15 psi for stove top or 9 to 11 psi for electric).

STOVE TOP: Maintain pressure for 3 minutes, adjusting the burner as necessary.
ELECTRIC: Cook at high pressure for 3 minutes.

4. After cooking, use the *quick method* to release pressure.

5. Unlock and remove the lid. Stir in the cider vinegar, cumin, and kosher salt. Let cool, taste, and adjust the seasoning if necessary. The salsa will last refrigerated for 10 days to 2 weeks; it can be frozen for several months.

PER SERVING (½ CUP): CALORIES: 63; FAT: 4G; SODIUM: 483MG;
CARBOHYDRATES: 6G; FIBER: 1G; PROTEIN: 1G

Applesauce

PRESSURE: High
TIME UNDER PRESSURE: 4 minutes
RELEASE: Natural

GLUTEN FREE, VEGAN

2½ to 3 pounds McIntosh, Gala, or Jonathan apples, peeled, halved, and cored

¾ cup unsweetened apple juice or apple cider

2 tablespoons packed brown sugar, plus additional as needed

1 tablespoon freshly squeezed lemon juice

1 small cinnamon stick

2 or 3 whole cloves or allspice berries (optional)

Pinch kosher salt

Pressure-cooker applesauce is so fast and easy, you won't believe you've never made it before. While a mixture of apples produces a more complex flavor, you can use just one variety; I generally get whatever is on sale. The cinnamon is traditional, but if you want a truer apple flavor, then leave it out.

1. Cut each apple into 8 wedges, and cut each wedge in half widthwise.

2. To a stove-top or electric pressure cooker, add the apples, apple juice, brown sugar, lemon juice, cinnamon stick, whole cloves (if using), and kosher salt, and stir to combine.

3. Lock the lid in place, and bring the pot to high pressure (15 psi for stove top or 9 to 11 psi for electric).

STOVE TOP: Maintain pressure for 4 minutes, adjusting the burner as necessary.
ELECTRIC: Cook at high pressure for 4 minutes. When the timer goes off, turn the cooker off. Do not let it switch to the "warm" setting.

4. After cooking, use the *natural method* to release pressure.

5. Unlock and remove the lid. Remove and discard the cinnamon stick and whole cloves (if used). For a chunky applesauce, use the back of a large spoon to break up the apples. For a smooth applesauce, use an immersion blender to purée. A potato masher will produce applesauce with a texture between the two.

PER SERVING (½ CUP): CALORIES: 108; FAT: 0G; SODIUM: 23MG; CARBOHYDRATES: 29G; FIBER: 4G; PROTEIN: 1G

Cranberry-Apple Chutney

MAKES 2 CUPS

PRESSURE: High
TIME UNDER PRESSURE: 6 minutes
RELEASE: Quick

GLUTEN FREE, VEGAN

1 cup chopped dried apples
1 cup dried cranberries
½ cup cider vinegar
3 tablespoons packed
   brown sugar
2 tablespoons minced or grated
   fresh ginger
2 garlic cloves, finely minced
1 teaspoon red pepper flakes
2 teaspoons orange zest
2 tablespoons water

Think of this as a more complex cranberry sauce for Thanksgiving dinner, but don't think you have to wait for that holiday to enjoy it. The zesty chutney is also a delicious accompaniment to pork chops or roast. It will keep in the refrigerator for a couple of weeks.

1. Into a pressure cooker, add the apples, cranberries, cider vinegar, brown sugar, ginger, garlic, red pepper flakes, orange zest, and water.

2. Lock the lid in place, and bring the pot to high pressure (15 psi for stove top or 9 to 11 psi for electric).

STOVE TOP: Maintain pressure for 6 minutes, adjusting the burner as necessary.
ELECTRIC: Cook at high pressure for 6 minutes.

3. After cooking, use the *quick method* to release pressure.

4. Unlock and remove the lid. If there is liquid sitting on the bottom of the pressure cooker, place the stove-top cooker over medium heat, or turn the electric cooker to "brown," and simmer until the liquid evaporates.

5. Cool, and serve at room temperature.

PER SERVING (¼ CUP): CALORIES: 38; FAT: 0G; SODIUM: 2MG; CARBOHYDRATES: 8G; FIBER: 1G; PROTEIN: 0G

Tomato Relish

MAKES ABOUT 1¼ CUPS

PRESSURE: High
TIME UNDER PRESSURE: 8 minutes
RELEASE: Quick

GLUTEN FREE, VEGAN

1 tablespoon olive oil
½ cup chopped onion
1 garlic clove, finely chopped
1½ teaspoons granulated sugar
½ teaspoon curry powder
1 tablespoon sherry vinegar
1 tablespoon whole yellow
  mustard seeds
1 (14.5-ounce) can diced
  tomatoes
½ teaspoon dried oregano
1 teaspoon kosher salt
⅛ teaspoon freshly ground
  black pepper
2 tablespoons chopped
  fresh parsley

TIP *Use the relish on burgers, or roast beef sandwiches. It's also a delicious topper to scrambled eggs.*

I'm a big sandwich aficionado, so when I spied a copy of Tom Colicchio's sandwich book, 'Wichcraft, I couldn't resist. The first recipe I tried was for meatloaf sandwiches with tomato relish and cheddar; and the whole thing took close to half a day to make. It was, however, out of this world. I've streamlined it here, and cooking it in the pressure cooker makes it even faster, with no loss of quality.

1. In a stove-top pressure cooker set over medium heat, or an electric cooker set to "brown," heat the olive oil until it shimmers and flows like water. Add the onion and garlic. Cook for about 6 minutes, stirring, until the onions are golden brown. Add the sugar and curry powder, and stir. Cook for 2 to 3 minutes, or until the sugar melts and the curry powder is fragrant. Stir in the sherry vinegar, mustard seeds, tomatoes, oregano, kosher salt, and pepper. Bring to a simmer.

2. Lock the lid in place, and bring the pot to high pressure (15 psi for stove top or 9 to 11 psi for electric).

STOVE TOP: Maintain pressure for 8 minutes, adjusting the burner as necessary.
ELECTRIC: Cook at high pressure for 8 minutes.

3. After cooking, use the *quick method* to release pressure.

4. Unlock and remove the lid. Using a potato masher or large fork, break up the tomatoes to form a more homogeneous mixture. If the relish is very watery, drain it through a coarse sieve to remove some of the liquid. Cool for 5 to 10 minutes, and stir in the parsley. The relish will keep, refrigerated, for up to 1 week.

PER SERVING (¼ CUP): CALORIES: 60; FAT: 3G; SODIUM: 471MG; CARBOHYDRATES: 7G; FIBER: 2G; PROTEIN: 2G

PRESSURE COOKING TIME CHARTS

The following charts provide approximate times for a variety of foods. Because cookers and stoves vary, actual cooking times may be different. To begin, you may want to cook for a minute or two less than the times listed; you can always simmer foods at natural pressure to finish cooking. Keep in mind that these times are for the foods cooked in water (or broth) or steamed, and for the foods cooked alone. The cooking times for the ingredients when they are part of a recipe may differ because of additional ingredients or cooking liquids, or a different release method than the one listed here.

MEAT

Except as noted, these times are for braised meats; that is, meats that are partially submerged in liquid.

	MINUTES UNDER PRESSURE:		PRESSURE	RELEASE
	STOVE TOP	ELECTRIC		
Beef, shoulder (chuck) roast (2 pounds)	60	60	High	Natural
Beef, shoulder (chuck), 2-inch chunks	25	25	High	Natural
Beef, bone-in short ribs	40	40	High	Natural
Beef, flatiron steak, cut into ½-inch strips	10	10	High	Quick
Lamb, shoulder, 2-inch chunks	35	35	High	Natural
Lamb, shanks	40	40	High	Natural
Lamb, leg roast (2 pounds), boneless	40	40	High	Natural
Pork shoulder roast (2 pounds)	25	25	High	Natural
Pork, shoulder, 2-inch chunks	25	25	High	Natural
Pork tenderloin	5	5	High	Natural
Pork back ribs (steamed)	30	30	High	Quick
Pork spareribs (steamed)	20	20	High	Quick
Smoked pork sausage, ½-inch slices	20	20	High	Quick

POULTRY

Except as noted, these times are for braised poultry; that is, poultry that is partially submerged in liquid.

| | MINUTES UNDER PRESSURE: | | PRESSURE | RELEASE |
	STOVE TOP	ELECTRIC		
Chicken thigh, bone-in	25	25	High	Natural
Chicken thigh, boneless, whole	8	8	High	Natural
Chicken thigh, 1-inch to 2-inch pieces	5	5	High	Quick
Duck quarters, bone-in	35	35	High	Quick
Turkey breast, boneless, 12 ounces (tenderloin)	10 (steamed)	10 (steamed)	High	Quick
Turkey thigh, bone-in	30	30	High	Natural

FISH AND SEAFOOD

All times are for steamed fish and shellfish.

| | MINUTES UNDER PRESSURE: | | PRESSURE | RELEASE |
	STOVE TOP	ELECTRIC		
Halibut (1 inch thick)	3	3	High	Quick
Mussels	1	1	High	Quick
Salmon (1 inch thick)	4	4	High	Quick
Tilapia or cod	1	1	High	Natural for 4 minutes, then quick

BEANS AND LEGUMES

The chart below assumes that beans have been soaked for 8 to 24 hours in salted water, unless otherwise noted.

When cooking beans, if you have a pound or more, it's best to use low pressure and increase the cooking time by one minute or two (with larger amounts, there's more chance for foaming at high pressure). If you have less than a pound, high pressure is fine. A little oil in the cooking liquid will reduce foaming. Where two times are listed, the shorter time is for high pressure and the longer time is for low pressure.

	MINUTES UNDER PRESSURE:		PRESSURE	RELEASE
	STOVE TOP	ELECTRIC		
Black-eyed peas	5	5	High	Natural for 8 minutes, then quick
Cannellini beans	5 to 7	5 to 7	Low or high	Natural
Chickpeas (garbanzo beans)	3 to 4	3 to 4	Low or high	Natural for 3 minutes, then quick
Kidney beans	5 to 7	5 to 7	Low or high	Natural
Lentils (unsoaked)	10	10	High	Quick
Lima beans	4 to 5	4 to 5	Low or high	Natural for 5 minutes, then quick
Navy beans	8 to 10	8 to 10	Low or high	Natural
Pinto beans	8 to 10	8 to 10	Low or high	Natural
Soybeans, dried	12 to 14	12 to 14	Low or high	Natural
Soybeans, fresh, unsoaked	1 to 2	1 to 2	High	Quick
Split peas (unsoaked)	5 to 8	5 to 8	High	Natural

GRAINS

To prevent foaming, it's best to include a very small amount of butter or oil with the cooking liquid for these grains or to rinse them thoroughly before cooking.

	LIQUID PER 1 CUP OF GRAINS	MINUTES UNDER PRESSURE:		PRESSURE	RELEASE
		STOVE TOP	ELECTRIC		
Barley, pearled	2½	10	10	High	Natural
Buckwheat	1¾ cups	2 to 4	2 to 4	High	Natural
Medium-grain brown rice	1½ cups	6 to 8	6 to 8	High	Natural
Long-grain brown rice	1½ cups	13	13	High	Natural for 10 minutes, then quick
Farro, whole grain	3 cups	15 to 18	22 to 24	High	Natural
Farro, pearled	2 cups	6 to 8	6 to 8	High	Natural
Long-grain white rice	1½ cups	3	3	High	Quick
Oats, rolled	3 cups	3 to 4	3 to 4	High	Quick
Oats, steel-cut	4 cups	12	12	High	Natural
Quinoa	2 cups	2	2	High	Quick
Wheat berries	2 cups	30	30	High	Natural for 10 minutes, then quick
Wild rice	2½ cups	18 to 20	18 to 20	High	Natural

VEGETABLES

The cooking method for all the following vegetables is steaming; if the vegetables are cooked in liquid, the times may vary.

	PREPARATION	MINUTES UNDER PRESSURE: STOVE TOP	ELECTRIC	PRESSURE	RELEASE
Artichokes, large	Whole	15	15	High	Quick
Beets	Quartered if large; halved if small	9	9	High	Natural
Brussels sprouts	Halved	2	2	High	Quick
Butternut squash	Peeled, cut into ½-inch chunks	12	12	High	Quick
Cabbage	Cut into wedges	15	15	High	Quick
Carrots	½-inch to 1-inch slices	3	2	High	Quick
Cauliflower	Whole	7	7	High	Quick
Green beans	Cut in half or thirds	2	2	High	Quick
Potatoes, large russet	Quartered; for mashing	8	8	High	Natural for 8 minutes, then quick
Potatoes, red	Whole if 1½ inches across or smaller; halved if larger	8	8	High	Quick
Sweet potatoes	Halved lengthwise	8	8	High	Natural

MEASUREMENT CONVERSION CHARTS

Volume Equivalents (Liquid)

US STANDARD	US STANDARD (OUNCES)	METRIC (APPROXIMATE)
2 tablespoons	1 fl. oz.	30 mL
¼ cup	2 fl. oz.	60 mL
½ cup	4 fl. oz.	120 mL
1 cup	8 fl. oz.	240 mL
1½ cups	12 fl. oz.	355 mL
2 cups or 1 pint	16 fl. oz.	475 mL
4 cups or 1 quart	32 fl. oz.	1 L
1 gallon	128 fl. oz.	4 L

Oven Temperatures

FAHRENHEIT (F)	CELSIUS (C) (APPROXIMATE)
250°	120°
300°	150°
325°	165°
350°	180°
375°	190°
400°	200°
425°	220°
450°	230°

Volume Equivalents (Dry)

US STANDARD	METRIC (APPROXIMATE)
⅛ teaspoon	0.5 mL
¼ teaspoon	1 mL
½ teaspoon	2 mL
¾ teaspoon	4 mL
1 teaspoon	5 mL
1 tablespoon	15 mL
¼ cup	59 mL
⅓ cup	79 mL
½ cup	118 mL
⅔ cup	156 mL
¾ cup	177 mL
1 cup	235 mL
2 cups or 1 pint	475 mL
3 cups	700 mL
4 cups or 1 quart	1 L

Weight Equivalents

US STANDARD	METRIC (APPROXIMATE)
½ ounce	15 g
1 ounce	30 g
2 ounces	60 g
4 ounces	115 g
8 ounces	225 g
12 ounces	340 g
16 ounces or 1 pound	455 g

THE DIRTY DOZEN & THE CLEAN FIFTEEN

A nonprofit and environmental watchdog organization called Environmental Working Group (EWG) looks at data supplied by the US Department of Agriculture (USDA) and the Food and Drug Administration (FDA) about pesticide residues. Each year it compiles a list of the best and worst pesticide loads found in commercial crops. You can use these lists to decide which fruits and vegetables to buy organic to minimize your exposure to pesticides and which produce is considered safe enough to buy conventionally. This does not mean they are pesticide-free, though, so wash these fruits and vegetables thoroughly.

These lists change every year, so make sure you look up the most recent one before you fill your shopping cart. You'll find the most recent lists as well as a guide to pesticides in produce at EWG.org/FoodNews.

2015 DIRTY DOZEN

Apples	Peaches	*In addition to the dirty dozen, the EWG added two kinds of produce contaminated with highly toxic organo-phosphate insecticides:*
Celery	Potatoes	
Cherry tomatoes	Snap peas (imported)	
Cucumbers	Spinach	
Grapes	Strawberries	Kale/Collard greens
Nectarines (imported)	Sweet bell peppers	Hot peppers

2015 CLEAN FIFTEEN

Asparagus	Eggplants	Papayas
Avocados	Grapefruits	Pineapples
Cabbage	Kiwis	Sweet corn
Cantaloupes (domestic)	Mangoes	Sweet peas (frozen)
Cauliflower	Onions	Sweet potatoes

ABOUT THE AUTHOR

Janet A. Zimmerman has been teaching culinary classes and writing about food for more than 15 years. She's written for *Martha Stewart Living*, NPR's Kitchen Window blog, and About.com. A recipient of the Bert Greene Journalism Award from the International Association of Culinary Professionals, she is also the author of *All About Cooking for Two: A Very Quick Guide*. Janet and her partner Dave live in Atlanta, Georgia.

ACKNOWLEDGMENTS

The author wishes to thank Matt South, Robyne Fullager, and the rest of the staff at The Cook's Warehouse for answering questions and allowing her to check out equipment.

RECIPE INDEX

INDEX OF RECIPES BY LABEL

INDEX